GET BACK
into WHACK

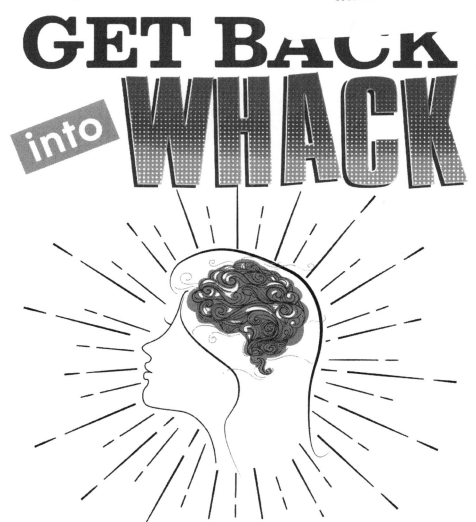

How to Easily **REWIRE YOUR BRAIN** to
Outsmart Stress, Overcome Self-Sabotage,
and *Optimize Healing* from
Fibromyalgia and *Chronic Illness*

Susan E. Ingebretson

ISBN: 978-0-9843118-3-5

Library of Congress Control Number: 2019910831

Printed in the United States of America
Ordering information https://www.RebuildingWellness.com

Cover Design by 100Covers.com
Interior Design by FormattedBooks.com

NorseHorse Press
PO Box 6722
Orange, CA 92863-6722

How healthy is your brain?

Do you wonder if you have an *Out of Whack* brain challenge?

Find out right away.

Download your **Brain Quiz & Mini Workbook** now by visiting:

https://rebuildingwellness.com/brain-quiz

Advance Praise for *Get Back into Whack*

"Although addressing fibromyalgia's biochemistry with the SHINE Protocol can result in marked improvement, it is also critical to reset the brain, limbic system, and autonomic nervous system. This results in dramatic improvement in many people, especially those with severe sensitivities, trauma history, or anxiety as part of their condition. Sue Ingebretson offers incredible help and techniques for helping the fibromyalgia and chronic illness community. I highly recommend using these integrated mind, body, and spirit approaches found in *Get Back into Whack!*"

Jacob Teitelbaum, MD, Founder of EndFatigue.com,
Bestselling Author of *From Fatigued to Fantastic!*

"Sue's new book, *Get Back into Whack*, is a masterpiece and a must-read for those who want to delve deeper. You may have been told, 'stop and smell the roses,' but Sue digs into the why's of noses and roses. This is a 'curl up in bed each night until you're done, then start it again' kind of book. Many will benefit!"

Doug Kaufmann, Author, Medical Researcher,
TV Host of *Know the Cause!*

"Brilliant! This book skillfully connects BOTH mind and body approaches to healing. It provides readers with a wealth of knowledge and fun strategies on how to use the mind to create their best selves."

Jessie Jones, Ph.D., Co-author,
***In Full Bloom: Brain Education for Successful Aging*,**
and Former Director, Center for Fibromyalgia and
Chronic Pain, California State University, Fullerton

"Sue writes of the inner landscape of chronic illness, filled with plenty of practical exercises and personal experiences to help you along. Read it and let her help you *Get Back into Whack.*"

Martin C. Hart, DC Senior Doctor at Biologix Center for Optimum Health

"*Get Back into Whack* offers a natural, and comprehensive approach to optimizing health—especially suited to those struggling with chronic illness and pain conditions such as Fibromyalgia. Highly recommended!"

Sandip Sekhon, Pain Researcher and Expert, Founder of Pathways Pain Relief App

"Sue Ingebretson's *Get Back into Whack* is a refreshingly light and easy to read guidebook, which explores the psychological aspects of brain function and the powerful impact the mind has on our health and wellbeing. Sue's personal journey healing from fibromyalgia was the driving force behind acquiring this knowledge, and she shares her wisdom of how to reevaluate and consciously shift thoughts, perceptions, belief systems and habits, making this a compelling read for anyone wishing to do the same."

Kristen Willeumier, Ph.D., Neuroscientist Author of *Rewind Your Brain*

"The overwhelming truth is that when faced with chronic illness, there's no one-size-fits-all response. In *Get Back into Whack,* Sue provides a whole host of tools that allow you to change the way you think and feel, which leads to healing and transformation. The best part is how easy the tools are to understand and to start using right away."

Gene Monterastelli, Author, Founder and Editor of TappingQandA.com

"*Get Back into Whack* is a leading-edge book that compiles the best of brain science as it relates to pain. Sue Ingebretson has done an incredible job of explaining the mind-body connection and also revealing simple techniques to help end suffering now. This book is a powerful resource for anyone looking to ease the pain of Fibromyalgia and also understand the brain's role in the healing process. Valuable information and an interesting read!"

Dana Wilde, the bestselling author of *Train Your Brain* and the host of *The Mind Aware Show*

"Sue writes with much detail and offers not only concise and accurate knowledge but practicality to get back to the driver's seat as we journey through the Fibromyalgia alley. A must-read!"

Maribel Aviles, M.D., Practicing Physician, fibromyalgia overcomer, and host of the International Conquering Fibromyalgia Summit

"Get Back into Whack is a humorous and clever book offering simple tools to re-wire the nervous system and help you to re-engage in a life you create. All done while honoring the stage of health you're in. This book is a must for those healing from chronic illness and pain."

Nikki Alstedter and Lora Pavilack, Authors of *Pain-Free Posture Handbook*

"Get Back into Whack does an excellent job of explaining how our everyday thoughts and actions play a role in how we feel physically. Sue provides actionable steps to help you determine the thoughts and actions that may be contributing to your health challenges, and help you change your focus to finally begin feeling better. Even after years of following similar principles, I found this book full of great tips and reminders to help me stay on track."

Julie Ryan, Fibromyalgia Blogger and Health Activist at CountingMySpoons.com

"Sue Ingebretson hits it out of the park again! Her practical advice, coupled with a generous and loving spirit, of how to live with and move beyond the limitations of chronic illness are a gift to every reader. I encourage every person living with pain of any kind to *Get Back into Whack!*"

Cindy Leyland, PAINS-KC Coordinator
at the Center for Practical Bioethics

"Get Back into Whack provides powerful recommendations and tools needed to 'change the brain's channel' from negative to positive. Medical science is clear—the immune system follows thoughts. I remind patients that their bodies listen to their words; the body responds in healthy ways to positive reinforcements. Sue's book provides numerous suggestions to make this much-needed shift."

Timothy Noble, DC, DACBSP, CSCS

"Wow, what a breath of fresh air! *Get Back into Whack* by Sue Ingebretson provides the missing piece of the puzzle to creating a new health experience. In her original chronic illness best seller, *FibroWHYalgia*, Sue shared many of the physical and functional needs in regard to turning your health around. And with her newest release, Sue provides the deeper mental, emotional, and energetic expression truly needed to heal at the deepest level. If your goals and intentions are to escape your symptoms and pain, this is the book that needs to be on your shelf and more importantly, utilized in your life."

Glen Depke, Traditional Naturopath, Depke Wellness

"In *Get Back into Whack*, Sue Ingebretson provides inspiring tools that will benefit many who are suffering from various chronic symptoms. Her writing style is easy to follow, and she wonderfully explains how and why she offers each pathway. She lays out step-by-step homework, and for those who are taking the first step, this book can lead them to a happier life."

Shoosh Lettick Crotzer,
Author of *Yoga for Fibromyalgia*

"As someone who suffered from fibromyalgia and related illnesses myself, I believe *Get Back into Whack* is a must-read for anyone touched by fibromyalgia. Sue Ingebretson combines scientific evidence on the mindset needed to heal chronic illness with a light-hearted tone that is very non-technical and turns it into a compelling read. This book, based on the brain/body connection, is a narrative that will be your go-to-guide for many years to come."

Yvonne Keeny, Founder and Executive Director
Fibromyalgia Coalition International

"Get Back into Whack is a fascinating read! I enjoyed learning more about how the brain works and how to use that knowledge to my advantage in dealing with my chronic pain and fibromyalgia. Learning there's an easier and more effective way to adopt and stick with self-care practices than to rely on sheer willpower gives me hope that I can experience lasting improvements in how I feel. After reading Sue's book, I now reframe my thinking to prevent self-sabotage. I know how to bolster my motivation to ensure that it becomes a lifestyle. There's so much helpful material in this book that can benefit the ME/Fibromyalgia and Chronic Pain community."

Kaye Witte, Co-Organizer of the
Chronic Pain, Fatigue, and Fibromyalgia Support Group

To my personal posse: the beautiful women who know my deepest fears and flaws yet answer my calls anyway. I'm so very grateful that you're available for consoling, confiding, gabbing, or blabbing.

Sage Susanne, Generous Patty,
Tai chi Queen Melissa, Kindhearted Julie,
Candid Fran, Caring Karen, & Gracious Fawn

TABLE OF CONTENTS

Directory of Key Topics and Strategies

INTRODUCTION

If you've met me through family, friends, my chronic illness bestselling book, *FibroWHYalgia*, magazine articles, my Rebuilding Wellness blog, or my social media posts, you'll likely know that I'm all about the "why."

I want to know WHY things happen.

It's not to blame—or even less helpful—to assign guilt. It's to empower myself to make educated choices. If I know WHY something happens then I can choose a different path next time. My choice isn't based on some weird cosmic chance.

That's how I approached my healing journey. After dealing with fibromyalgia (and a smattering of additional diagnoses), I wanted a better understanding.

Here's the deal.

> ### *You have to know WHY you got sick before you can implement HOW to get better.*

In this book, I'll share the discovery of how. It's the journey that set me onto an unexpected path. It's my wish that you start your own healing journey this very moment.

Well, right after you read the following chapters.

For now, here's what's expected of you:

* *Relax and keep an open mind.*

  It's human nature to look for a magic wand solution; the ONE single answer that'll fix everything. We gravitate toward the notion of one fix rather than many.

* *Suspend your objections.*

  If at any time you hear yourself think, "I already know this," or "this is too simple," beware. These thoughts prevent learning. They keep you stuck and limit your options for creative solutions. They shut down the possibility and hope for change. Rather than search for the validity of these thoughts, simply permit yourself to suspend analysis for later.

* *You don't need to apply (or even remember) everything in this book.*

  I hope this book serves as a jumping-off point and a map of where to go once you jump. Don't feel that you have to do everything at once. Some things you might not even do at all.

- *Use support materials.*

   Additionally, you may find my *Get Back into Whack Workbook* useful for tracking your progress, ideas, and successes. Look for it on Amazon or wherever you purchased this book. Whether you choose to use the workbook or a simple pen, paper, and calendar is up to you. In any case, I encourage you to use a highlighter in this book or underline what's important to you. You have my permission (and encouragement) to dog-ear it too, to your heart's content.

- *What do you want to get from this book?*

   Make up your mind now to discover exactly what you're looking for. Do you want encouragement, support, guidance, and hope? Check. Do you want concrete ideas to try? Check. Do you want examples of how to apply these ideas? Check. Decide—right now—what you're looking for and move forward with that intention and a sense of purpose.

That's it! That's all you need to do. For now, kick back, grab a cuppa tea, a highlighter, and dig in.

So… what's expected from me?

I have high expectations for myself. In the following chapters, I plan to bring my A-game. I'm laying it all out and giving you the nitty-gritty. This is what you need to know to change your health *and* life.

Are you ready?

CHAPTER 1

What Drives You?

As you may have heard, I've experienced a transformational journey from chronic illness to chronic wellness. I healed from the inside out. Afterward, I wrote a book about it, began sharing health protocols and methods, and the rest, as they say, is history, right?

Everything clicked along tickety-boo.

I worked with delightful clients who followed my path. They effortlessly made the healthy nutritional improvements I suggested, became tuned into their body's needs, and they surrounded themselves with a loving and caring support system.

And, they all found amazingly profound results.

Well, *almost.*

Let's get real. While most followed the guidance offered, some did not. Some struggled, weirdly sabotaging their efforts at every turn. It defied logic and made little sense to me.

This only happened with a couple of clients in those first few years after my recovery. But two was too many. I viewed anything less than complete success as complete failure on my part. Their "short of the mark" results affected me deeply, and I felt stymied and discouraged.

I want *all* of my clients to experience the healing transformation that I've found. I want them all to feel in charge of their personal healing options. I want my clients to **conquer rather than cope with their limiting symptoms.**

If the path that worked for me works for most—but not all—I had to figure out why.

This was the catalyst for the second, and even more powerful, segment of my healing journey. I dove head-first into the study of behavioral psychology, neurophysiology, and neuroscience. For the past ten years, I've specifically studied the narrow field of habit formation, adaptation to change, and the brain's willingness and capacity to do so.

Habits and dagnabbits

What drives behavior when it comes to change? Most of us follow one of three behavioral choices.

> *We're either inactive,*
> *reactive, or proactive.*

When faced with unplanned change, we may choose to do nothing, struggle with the inevitability, or take charge of the situation with an optimistic view.

Personal characteristic traits come into play big-time.

What makes some people adapt to change with seemingly no effort at all? What makes them quickly adopt healthy habits while others drag their feet? And what about those who either take no action or reject the idea of taking action?

I have many favorite books on the subject, but these are the top three that pop into my mind at this writing. An all-time favorite is *The Power of Habit* by Charles Duhigg. In practical terms, he explains the exact steps needed to form successful habits.[1] As a nutritional habit resource, I still read and re-read *Mindless Eating* by Brian Wansink. Any book that tackles this weighty subject with levity is a hit with me. With humorous and fascinating examples, *Mindless Eating* details the myriad of influences that affect our food choices. I'm also a big fan of *Better Than Before* by happiness author, Gretchen Rubin. She outlines core personality types and how they differ in their adaptation to change.

In case you're wondering, there's no "correct" or perfect way to approach change. We are each independently and biochemically unique. I've researched tendencies, personality types, and how our brains affect our ability (and even desire) to make habit changes. The common thread found in all this research is that a productive response is singularly different for each individual. Finding a successful combination of helpful approaches—that works for YOU—gives you the key to crafting an individualized plan.

I've done this for myself and others. I love my job as it launches me on fact-finding expeditions. I spend gobs of time pitching myself down

---

1   http://charlesduhigg.com/wp-content/uploads/2012/02/A-guide-to-changing-habits.pdf

rabbit holes of research. Fascinating topics, including brain function, nonconscious behaviors, awareness, and perceptions, are often fodder for dinner table conversations in my home. (If invited, consider yourself forewarned.)

■ Brain function 101

You may have heard that the logical brain is defined as the cerebral cortex, where all thinking, reasoning, and rational thought happens. The functioning of the whole brain is far more complex. The two aspects we'll review most here are the prefrontal cortex and the limbic brain.

The prefrontal cortex is often referred to as the conscious mind. It's responsible for critical thinking, organization of complex behaviors, impulse control, prioritization, executive function, and more.[2]

The limbic system, often referred to as the nonconscious mind, is the emotion center of the brain. Its super-fast ability to process feelings and emotions is designed to keep us safe. It's responsible for the body's fight, flight, or freeze response and the storage and organization of memories.[3]

The nonconscious mind is also sometimes referred to as the subconscious, unconscious, or other-than-conscious mind. For the purposes of consistency, I'll use the term nonconscious as it reflects a diametrically opposed or different position in relation to the conscious mind.

But that's just me. If you feel so inclined, grab a pen and insert the term that resonates most with you.

---

2 http://www.goodtherapy.org/blog/psychpedia/prefrontal-cortex
3 https://www.health.harvard.edu/staying-healthy/understanding-the-stress-response

An estimated 100 billion neurons make 100 trillion connections in the brain.[4] These connections make us uniquely who we are. When it comes to how we operate as humans, the different (and many times opposing) operations of the brain help to illustrate why we're not getting the results we want. More importantly, it sheds light on what we can do differently. Four primary components form our healing behaviors.

Recognize that stuff happens. How we react to "stuff" is where we gain clarity over our choices in life. Here's the four-pathway model of how we process information and arrive at our outcomes.

Our potential for healing stems from—

1. The thoughts we think
2. The emotions that follow
3. The actions we take
4. The way we interpret our results

Notice that the development of healthy habits begins with *how* we think.

Our thoughts create a picture across the movie screen of our mind. Feelings are generated from those images, and much of what we feel comes from nonconscious imagery. By definition, we're not consciously aware of this process. If you believe you don't make mental pictures, that's okay. We'll address that later.

For now, recognize that there's a big difference between conscious and nonconscious thoughts.

---

4   http://nautil.us/issue/59/connections/why-is-the-human-brain-so-efficient

Do you know that conscious thoughts travel at speeds over 100 miles per hour?[5] The brain is the fastest known supercomputer in the universe. We filter through approximately 60,000 to 90,000 thoughts per day. Not surprisingly, negative thoughts are coupled with the lion's share of these notions. What may be surprising to you is…

> *96% of these thoughts are the SAME ones we had yesterday!*[6]

If that makes you say, "dagnabbit," look at the bright side. *Repetitive thoughts* have the most impact on our lives.

Good thing **we get to choose** what to repeat.

If we let our thoughts choose themselves, we attain what Dana Wilde from The Mind Aware calls, "The Cycle of Perpetual Sameness."[7] I love this phrase because it conjures up an immediate image of dysfunction. Whether it's a picture of plodding along a path to nowhere or one that's stuck in an endless loop, the feeling of futility is almost palpable.

That's why the study of the mind—and how we think—is so important. The brain's data processing capacity is astounding. The conscious mind processes approximately 2,000 bits of data or information per second. But here's the kicker—*the nonconscious mind has the ability to process approximately 400 billion bits per second!*[8]

---

5   https://earthsky.org/human-world/what-is-the-speed-of-thought
6   https://learnevolveandthrive.com/how-to-break-the-cycle-of-perpetual-sameness/
7   http://www.danawilde.com/cops
8   https://www.basicknowledge101.com/subjects/brain.html

This raises the next question. If we experience both conscious and nonconscious-mind thoughts, which do you think are more powerful?

Mull on that for a bit as we dig deeper.

If you're like me, you find the difference between the two processes quite intriguing. What's the purpose of this vast disparity? Why can the conscious mind only process a mere fraction of what's capable at the nonconscious level?

The answer may come to you instantly once you think about it. For just a second, consider what it would be like if your conscious mind could process 400 billion bits of information per second. If so, it would analyze absolutely every single thing that you see, hear, feel, smell, touch, or taste.

Every. Single. Thing.

Imagine being aware of *every* external stimulus as if it were new data. The sheer volume of mental information would be enough to drive you batty. You'd go throughout your day like a live wire—experiencing one shocking event after another.

To put this into perspective, think about driving a car. If you experienced every stimulus at a conscious level, you'd notice the traffic conditions, cloud patterns, positions of other vehicles, and every sign, light, home, building, pedestrian, animal, and insect along the way. You'd hear every single sound and feel every sensation right down to the squeak of your leather seats and the tightness of your canvas shoes.

A tad overwhelming, eh?

Fortunately, that's not the case. We don't have to suffer through input overload. The brilliant Divine design of our body has a solution in hand. Our built-in brain filtering system is so sophisticated that we aren't even aware of the process.

It's difficult to define, but I'll try anyway. Here goes....

■ The sifting brain

Our brain has an incredible capacity to sift through information. It uses a data filter to simplify the process. This filter is called the Reticular Activating System (RAS).[9]

Over time, your RAS is developed and fine-tuned by your unique life experiences. Everything you see, hear, feel, touch, taste, and think is filtered through your RAS without the bother of conscious thought. The RAS (part of the nonconscious mind) looks for patterns and matches situations to evaluate and assess objects, people, and experiences that are familiar.

For this reason, I refer to the RAS as your **Mind's Assessment of your Personal Patterns (MAPP)**. A Global Positioning System (GPS) helps to identify your physical position in this world. Your MAPP helps to identify your emotional position—who you are and how you react in this world. Your MAPP is truly the map of how you view, filter, and navigate the experiences around you. The term MAPP also emphasizes the personalized and distinctive nature of this vital brain function.

---

9   http://www.wisegeek.org/what-is-the-reticular-activating-system.htm

> ***Your MAPP is unique to you. No one else can experience life through your filters.***

The most common parameters of your MAPP are formed and finalized, for the most part, around the age of seven or so. It's as unique as your fingerprints. It's like a pair of glasses through which you view the world. The lens you use changes what you see based on your past experiences and beliefs. Your MAPP serves either as a blessing or a curse. Often, it's both.

Everything you encounter in life is filtered through your MAPP and compared to what you already know. The information is accepted as new or filed away as "been there, done that." Your decisions (reactions) are made based on how you process this actual information—*as filtered by your MAPP.*

Consider this core understanding.

> ***You don't make decisions based on what you literally see or experience. You make them based on your* perceptions *of what you see and experience.***

Recognize the difference?

This fact explains why three different people may see the same accident yet share three widely differing viewpoints. This variance applies to our everyday life, too. We hear things and interpret them based on our past perceptions. We taste things and like or dislike the flavors based on our filters of what we've tasted before.

Every phenomenon is filtered.

Your marvelous brain uses this system to make sense of all that it experiences. It filters everything through your MAPP and then makes internal representations of the situation. Your perceptual filters cause you to do one or a combination of these three things to all that you experience: delete, distort, and generalize.[10] We may delete information if it doesn't automatically fit or make sense to us. We often distort what we experience so that it can mold or match something we already understand or believe to be true. And, we also generalize material and situations to streamline our ability to process what we experience.

Your MAPP is designed to help you simplify the act of making sense of your environment. Of course, the devil is in the details. What's the tendency of your MAPP? Negative associations and unhelpful conclusions? Or, positive expectations and constructive beliefs? The world around you lines up according to your MAPP.

It also allows you to easily and effortlessly fall back into familiar and well-worn patterns. Your MAPP essentially creates a simplified guide for you to follow through life. It serves as a tap on the shoulder to remind you to take action or behave in a certain way. The surprising truth is that we can add to and subtract from the filters that make up our MAPP to fine-tune (with intention) our future success.

> *"The best way to predict your*
> *future is to create it."*
> —Stephen Covey

---

10   http://www.huffingtonpost.com/russell-bishop/generalizing-deleting-distorting_b_847217.html

■ Brain optimization

We can optimize our mental function by paying attention to how we use the gray matter between our ears.

Repeated thoughts and patterns create strong neural pathways in the brain. In this way, thoughts can become "hardwired." Until fairly recent history, these strengthened pathways were thought to be permanent. Fortunately (for you and me both), the discovery of neuroplasticity, the brain's ability to adapt and change,[11] reveals this permanence to be untrue.

Why is this important?

If your brain is hardwired for specific tendencies such as perpetual negativity, insecurity, or believing you're Murphy in the Murphy's Law scenarios, then it's time to rewire it for something else.

This "something else" can be as simple as switching subjects similar to the Monty Python phrase, "And, now for something completely different." In my book, *FibroWHYalgia*,[12] I mention changing the channel of your thoughts. We can intentionally apply different practices which then create new neural pathways in the brain. Doing so not only changes how we think, *it changes who we become.*

This introduces one of my favorite topics—emotional intelligence (or emotional quotient). The study of changing human behavior often brings up discussions on how to change thoughts, conduct, and patterns. Some refer to this as mindset. I believe using this term causes an unfortunate misdirect.

---

11   https://www.sciencedirect.com/topics/neuroscience/neuroplasticity
12   http://amzn.to/2bscprl (Affiliate Link to Amazon)

I've heard clients say that the term mindset makes them think of their ability (or lack of) to achieve their goals. Don't get me wrong. Goal-achievement is an important topic. But that's not all there is to mindset.

The way I see it, emotional intelligence is the larger umbrella under which mindset and other motivational practices find shelter. Emotional intelligence encompasses a trio of identifiable skills. It brings together the awareness of your emotions (and the emotions of others), the problem-solving ability that comes from applying this awareness, and the ability to regulate your own emotions as well as affect the emotions of others.[13]

From the get-go, put the skills implicit in your emotional intelligence to work *for* you. This provides the resources you need to generate successful behaviors and habits. For example, if you amplify the opportunity your emotional intelligence offers, you'll not only create the motivation to get what you want, you'll also discover how to boost your motivation in the first place.

> *Your emotions shape the operating system that runs your life.*

For the sake of simplicity in this book, I may refer to the brain or the mind interchangeably. While the literal definition of the brain is the organ inside of our skulls and how we use it is more in the realm of the mind, I don't want to belabor the distinction.

The positive suggestions outlined in this book contribute to a healthy brain *and* a healthy mind. Both are necessary.

---

13   https://www.psychologytoday.com/basics/emotional-intelligence

At the end of each chapter I've defined a few, simple key action steps for you to practice. Since they're geared to help you change your thinking patterns, I refer to them as Head Work rather than homework. Immersing yourself in these questions after each chapter dramatically increases your ability to absorb and retain what you've learned.

■ Chapter 1 – Head Work

1. Review how the limbic system of the brain differs from the cerebral cortex. How does this apply to you and your goals?

2. How does your MAPP make things easier for you day-to-day? How might it create limits that aren't so helpful?

3. Why is neuroplasticity important when it comes to adopting new habits? For example, if someone considers themselves to be a negative thinker and says, "that's just who I am," does the neuroplasticity principle prove this belief true or false?

Next up, we'll get into the specific characteristics that make *your* mind unique.

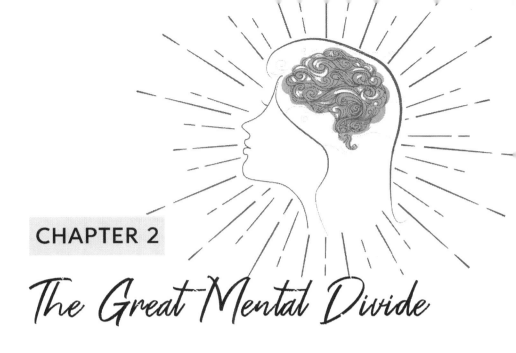

CHAPTER 2

The Great Mental Divide

Have you ever searched for an item in a messy drawer only to find it later, in plain view, in the very same drawer?

You may question your eyesight (or even your sanity), but there's more to it.

The brain tells us what we see through the filter of our MAPP. There's an interpreter between what we experience and our brain. This interpretation does funny things to our "seek and find" system. I once searched high and low for a blue folder that contained an important document, only to find that the folder was bright yellow. (Point of fact, it was never blue. My brain somehow filled in that erroneous information.)

In the early days of my health recovery, I had no clue about the different parts of the mind. To me, all of my actions and behaviors came from the same cesspool of disjointed thoughts. Without understanding the difference between the conscious and nonconscious mind, I thought that any success came from my ability to power through and persevere.

I now see the downfall of this fallacy.

You can guess what happened when my actions weren't so successful. I believed I was a complete failure. I was particularly confused when my thoughts were duplicitous. When they weren't clear (either positive or negative), it got muddy somewhere in the middle. I couldn't put my finger on exactly why I sometimes felt okay, but for the most part, I felt lousy. Despairing thoughts swarmed my mind like oversized Minnesota mosquitos.

My good and bad thought patterns repeated for years. Feelings of frustration, guilt, shame, and confusion spurred an overall sensation of hopelessness.

I could have spared myself a lot of angst had I known the following.

Characteristics of the conscious and nonconscious mind

Remember how your personal MAPP filters everything you experience? With this crucial understanding in mind, take a look at the differing roles and characteristics of the conscious and nonconscious mind. This list represents just a few key ways in which they operate.

- The **conscious mind** is analogous to the captain of a ship (the **nonconscious mind**, the crew). The conscious mind declares a destination, and the nonconscious mind says, "Aye, aye Captain!"

- The **conscious mind** is creative (we can think, plan, and formulate wishes and desires).

- The **conscious mind** creates narratives and stories to add meaning to what we see, hear, smell, feel, taste, and touch.

- The **conscious mind** allows us to accept or reject ideas as well as the ability to create new ones.

- The **conscious mind** is the goal-*setter,* the **nonconscious mind** the goal-*getter.*

- The **conscious mind** thinks; the **nonconscious mind** feels.

- The **conscious mind** uses critical thinking and logic. The **nonconscious mind** (once accessed) is open to ideas, suggestions, and direct orders.

- The **conscious mind** can be critical and judgmental. The **nonconscious mind** does not judge the intentions of the conscious mind. It only follows given directions.

For obvious reasons, photographs of giant icebergs are often used to depict the workings of the two separate parts of the mind. The relatively small portion of the iceberg that's visible above sea level represents the conscious mind. The massive submerged portion of the iceberg represents the powerful influence of the nonconscious mind.

There's always more going on than what's visible.

The nonconscious mind has an exponentially higher capacity to gather, process, implement, and store bits of information. By deliberately planting seeds of what we truly want into our nonconscious mind, we can tap into this potent resource.

My early studies of *how* the brain functions led me to the field of Neuro-Linguistic Programming (NLP). As a proven success philosophy, it teaches us to not only study the nonconscious mind, but also how to *change* the function of our nonconscious mind for peak, positive, and lasting results.

Here are more fascinating behaviors of the nonconscious mind, listing just some of the high spots.

- The **nonconscious mind** upholds instincts and general automatic behaviors.

- The **nonconscious mind** is habitual (it runs on automatic processes and programs).

- The **nonconscious mind** is non-linear, meaning it doesn't relate to time in the same way as does the conscious mind. To the nonconscious mind, a memory can feel as if it were yesterday, five years ago, or even a dream of five years from now.

- The **nonconscious mind** is highly symbolic and thinks in terms of pictures, words, images, sounds, and feelings.

- The **nonconscious mind** does *not* process negatives. (Say to yourself "I won't think of a neon blue sunflower" and what do you see in your mind's eye? This is why telling yourself you won't think of donuts only magnifies the desire.)

- The **nonconscious mind** is highly moral[14] and has a strong inner sense of right and wrong.

- The **nonconscious mind** is considered to be the "place" for our heart, soul, or our inner spirit.

- The **nonconscious mind** stores and organizes memories.

- The **nonconscious mind** manages basic body functions (heart rate, breathing, etc.) and perpetuates general homeostasis or wellbeing. The nonconscious mind is your body's autopilot feature.

- The **nonconscious mind** follows the path of least resistance and always chooses options that take the least effort.

- The **nonconscious mind** is where emotions are stored. Powerful emotions are often linked to images and words.

- The **nonconscious mind** values being of service and especially values clear, concise, and direct orders to follow. (It doesn't like what's unfamiliar and may perceive it as complicated or reject it.)

- The **nonconscious mind** houses an internal catalog of all unresolved emotions.

- The **nonconscious mind** doesn't evaluate thoughts for ration or reason. Because it's non-judgmental, it doesn't need information to be logical or even for it to make sense.

---

14   https://www.psychologytoday.com/us/blog/focus-forgiveness/201307/conscious-the-unconscious

- Two types of thoughts tend to become deeply embedded in the **nonconscious mind**—ones that repeat often and ones highly charged with emotion (either negative or positive).

- The **nonconscious mind** drives behavior that it believes is in your best interest (based on your repeated thoughts and beliefs).

In contrast, the **conscious mind** leans toward—

- Catastrophizing
- Paranoia
- Erroneous assumptions (jumping the gun)
- Over-generalizing
- Repetitive negative thoughts
- Fears stemming from shoulda-woulda-coulda syndrome
- Judgmental black and white thinking with no wiggle room for grace

Notice that the nonconscious mind does none of these.

■ Salient tasks of the nonconscious mind

As an archiving computer, the nonconscious mind governs our inner intelligence. It's our internal programming for all we experience. This is true for both real and vividly imagined experiences.

The part of the brain responsible for nonconscious thought represents 5/6 of our total brain mass and controls 96-98% of our perceptions and behaviors. It can average 400 billion operations per second![15] We experience 95% or more of our day running our nonconscious mind

---

15   http://unifiedfieldtechnology.blogspot.com/2015/09/12-amazing-facts-about-your-brain. html

programs. These "non-thought" programs allow us to deal with everything that comes our way.

Besides the processing duties of the brain, it's vital to grasp how the nonconscious mind stores our thoughts. Have you ever noticed that memories come to mind in pictures? These pictures may be still (like a snapshot) or moving (like video memes or snippets of a movie). The images, combined with thoughts and emotions, create our internal representations of a situation or circumstance. Some call it **our story**.

Every day we live and re-live events, making our own internal home movies. We recreate the past with mental movies of what we've experienced. Often, the mental movies we make of our past fuel sadness, depression, frustration, and anger. We also create mental images of the future we're afraid of experiencing or that we think we should experience but won't for some reason. Mental movies of our perceived future can generate fears and anxiety (increasing perceptions of pain).

The only time we're not making mental movies is when we're deliberately super-focused on the present moment. Which, as you may have noticed, is very difficult to do. Even more challenging is holding that present-minded focus for very long.

That's why sustained, deep, active meditation is an art. It takes practice and devotion to achieve a non-thinking state.

Why even try?

Deep meditation is one of many ways to feel "in the moment." Feeling present allows us to bat away our unhelpful thoughts. It gives us a method to overcome the mental habits of living either in the past (sadness/depression) or the future (worry/anxiety). It allows discovery and adaptation to powerful changes necessary for self-growth. *Making a focused connection to the nonconscious mind is the key to this process.*

> ## "The past is heavy. Put it down."
> —Unknown

My next quest

Once I realized the importance of establishing a direct connection to my nonconscious mind, I had to figure out *how*. I looked for the one, singular pathway—the absolute shortcut. I wanted to skip past my conscious mind's logical guard at the gate so I could tell my nonconscious mind a thing or two.

Easy, right?

I researched and read. As it turns out, access to the nonconscious mind isn't very direct at all. At least not from a conscious standpoint. I found various methods and protocols. I experimented and practiced ways that worked. It was extra challenging for me due to my highly logical, practical (and often self-judgmental) mind.

Some methods I researched were quite sophisticated. They featured technical aspects such as brainwave states and levels of awareness. Most referenced meditative relaxation processes.

I was both intrigued and put off.

Many of these protocols also mentioned *hypnosis* which, I'll admit, freaked me out. It sounded too Viva Las Vegas-ish to me. So, I kept on practicing familiar methods with a modicum of success.

Fortunately, I figured it out. With repetition, I discovered how to access the astonishing workings of my nonconscious mind.

In my continued research, I discovered that some brainwave states similar to hypnosis happen naturally. Color me intrigued. I was excited to learn that I could experience the benefits of hypnosis with none of the "you're getting veeerrry sleepy" hype.

Even better, I read that these naturally-occurring circumstances also invite a sense of relaxation, single-minded focus, and openness to new ideas.

Sign me up.

I've since learned a lot about healing tools and have accepted various comfort levels using them. One discovery wasn't so much about the tool as it was about the user. I heard a colleague once say, *"A hammer isn't innately evil. Yet, it's sometimes used for evil purposes. Any tool is just that. It's the intention of the user that counts."*

I finally realized that hypnosis is just a tool. It's neither right nor wrong. In simple broad terms, it's a generalized state of relaxation where the mind can let go just a smidge.

Here are a few examples of naturally occurring hypnotic states:

- The state between being fully awake and fully asleep (happens to us all at least twice a day)

- A runner's high or being "in the zone"

- Prayer and meditation

- Daydreaming

- Getting lost in thought from repetitive movements such as needlework, crafting, gardening, or working with our hands

- Zen-like state that occurs when gazing at a fireplace, fire pit flames, or when watching fish in an aquarium

- Driver's trance—finding that you've driven some distance or perhaps to your location with no memory of the drive (sometimes called highway hypnosis)

- Getting consciously lost (losing a sense of time) in a good book, a movie, or while listening to music, etc.

- That peaceful non-thinking state that exists (even if momentarily) when experiencing pleasant sensory situations such as getting/giving a hug or a massage, cuddling your pet, or even getting your hair washed

It takes a lot of practice for me (I am a stoic Midwesterner after all), but I've learned to be non-judgmental when it comes to terms. Whether it's hypnosis, relaxation, meditation, or open-mind states, what matters most is the intention behind the term. I pay close attention to how someone is using it or the written context. From there, I decide whether or not it fits within the parameters of my beliefs. In other words, I give new ideas a bit of breathing room first.

These open-mind states—whatever you want to call them—create an opportunity to access a valuable (and widely unknown and underused) shortcut. Within these conditions, we can hop over the gate of the conscious mind and spoon-feed favorable information straight into the nonconscious mind.

Dr. Bruce Lipton[16] at Stanford University Medical Center explains it this way, *"The major problem is that most people are aware of their conscious beliefs and patterns, but not of nonconscious beliefs and behaviors. Most people don't even acknowledge that their nonconscious mind is at play, when the fact is, it's a million times more powerful than the conscious mind, and that we operate **95 to 99 percent of our lives from nonconscious programs.**"*

He goes on to say, *"Your nonconscious beliefs are either working for you or against you."*

Are alarm bells going off? I hope so!

Open and shut cases of the mind

Do any of these phrases sound familiar?

"I never stick with diet changes."
"I'm always late."
"I don't eat anything green."
"I'm a procrastinator—it's just who I am."

I refer to statements such as these as closed-door thoughts. They slam the door to possibilities and define the situation in black or white terms. No wiggle room. They define things as always or never. They usually begin with "I am," followed by a negative or limiting statement of identity.

If there's anything we do know, life isn't that simple.

Here's a good example. I once worked with a client to help her change jobs. She was desperate for a new career and disliked her current employment situation with a passion. We worked through some aptitude

---

16   https://www.brucelipton.com/resource/article/epigenetics

assessments and fine-tuned her likes and dislikes. I came up with a list of potential opportunities, and with the first idea barely out of my mouth, she cried, *"Oh no! I can't do that. That's illegal in my state."*

I knew that she literally meant the state of Nebraska. But I couldn't help but think of the other state in which she lived. She lived in the closed state of no options, no hope, and no potential. She wasn't open—or ready—to hear about the world of possibilities that surrounded her. (And, of course, the job I'd mentioned wasn't illegal. She simply wanted to be emphatic about believing it wasn't an option for her.)

Open-mind states hold different potential than closed-mind states. Thoughts viewed through a closed mind shuts the door to options, solutions, and opportunities.

Here's a quick tip you can put into practice right this instant. Mary Morrissey,[17] author of the book (turned into a PBS special) *Build Your Field of Dreams,* has a simple workaround for the problem of closed-door thoughts. As a transformation and mindset researcher focusing on positivity, she mentions that you can open your closed mental door—even just a crack—with a simple but miraculous phrase. When you find yourself thinking a closed-door thought, follow it up with these three words: **up until now**.

As an example, imagine saying to yourself, "I can't make the changes mentioned in this book. I never follow through with anything." Then apply this simple follow-up phrase, "up until now."

Did you feel the difference?

With practice, you'll find you can not only crack open the door, but you may even throw it wide open with possibilities and potential.

---

17   http://www.marymorrissey.com/

■ Chapter 2 – Head Work

1. List at least three different circumstances where you've ex-
    perienced natural brainwave states similar to the state of
    hypnosis.

2. What moments allow you to zone out—even if it's just for a
    bit? Try them out and make them more effective by creat-
    ing positive intentions while in these states. For example, the
    last thing before you fall asleep, and the first thing when you
    wake is a perfect time to implement gratitude and apprecia-
    tion practices. It's also a great time to set intentions and plans
    for the success of your day.

3. Practice paying attention to when and how closed-door
    thoughts pop into your mind. When this happens, follow up
    the thought with the three-word phrase shared in this chap-
    ter. See how your sense of potential shifts.

For faster results, learn to maneuver around pitfalls. In Chapter 3,
you'll learn powerful methods to work around or through more mental roadblocks.

Sabotage, Surprises, & Self-Chatter

Now that you know so much more about how the mind works, are you ready to kick it into gear? To apply that successful edge, let's take a quick look at what doesn't work. What holds us back? What leaves us wearing cement suede shoes at the precipice of success?

Uncovering these sometimes-startling truths gives us the insight to nudge (or shove) us in the right direction.

Do you flub-up at follow-up?

Do you ever feel completely motivated to do something, yet you just can't muster the oomph to start? Maybe you lose steam or get lost in the middle of the task. Or perhaps you power through most obstacles only to become derailed by a seemingly insurmountable one… right before the finish line.

What's going on?

You might think there is something wrong with you. Maybe you believe you're plagued by a gross character flaw that prevents you from reaching your goals—some nebulous thing outside of your jurisdiction.

To this, I'd say, "Bunk." Everything listed in the previous paragraph is false. There's no intrinsic flaw. You haven't failed. And you're far from helpless. Self-sabotage is at the heart of this challenge, and learning its sneaky ways prepares you for the bumpy road ahead. **Self-sabotage crams a nasty wedge between you and your desired outcome.** Its covert behaviors allow procrastination, avoidance, and distraction to bloom like black mold under a leaky sink.

Disappointing results mask one leading underlying cause of sabotage—one of which you're possibly not aware. It lurks unnoticed beneath your conscious (thinking) awareness. I'm referring to *nonconscious conflicting beliefs*.

Inconsistent follow-through doesn't stem from a lack of stick-to-itiveness. It's one sign that unresolved conflicts are getting in the way. This conflict is typically not something that comes to mind. These obscured motivational behaviors delay or prevent you from reaching your desired outcome.

Have you ever heard someone say, "I'm of two minds?" This exemplifies a conscious conflict. They may say, "On the one hand, I truly want A, but on the other, I have to do B."

This common type of conflict lies within our awareness. We know it and recognize it. We see that it interferes with our ability to make a quick decision. To find a workaround, look at it from within (our internal dialogue) and from without (by asking others).

But what about the conflicts that are not within your awareness? For obvious reasons, conflicts at the nonconscious level have an exponentially greater capacity to sabotage behavior. Their very nature is obscure. This is where things can go hinky. Nonconscious conflicting beliefs (commonly called limiting beliefs) wreak havoc for most of us.

It's time to sharpen the acuity on this fuzzy topic.

The study of limiting beliefs is another one of my falling-down-a-rabbit-hole topics. I've researched it in great depth in an exhaustive effort to uncover my own. When I began, I wanted the answer to this simple question—*why did I find it nearly effortless to adopt some healthy habits but not others?*

I learned that our goals must align with our core life values. Before you say "duh," I'd like to point out that the misalignments may not be obvious. In fact, they're usually at the nonconscious level. And while they can leave you feeling in the dark, once you figure out how, it doesn't take mad spelunking skills to illuminate them.

Fear as a flashlight

Nonconscious fears can lurk behind our opposition to change. We may not be able to put a finger on the specifics, but generalized fears can keep us frozen in our tracks. There is a part of us that wants to move forward, but another part feels apathy, hesitation, or even deep, heels-dug-in resistance.

This stop and go phenomenon has a name. When we feel that we take three steps forward and one back, cognitive dissonance[18] may be at play. Franz Fanon describes it this way, *"Sometimes people hold a core belief that is very strong. When they are presented with evidence that works against that belief, the new evidence cannot be accepted. It would create a feeling that's extremely uncomfortable, called cognitive dissonance. And because it is so important to protect the core belief, they will rationalize, ignore, and even deny anything that doesn't fit in with the core belief."*

With cognitive dissonance in place—two equal and opposing beliefs—forward motion is near impossible. At best, forward motion is sluggish and unproductive.

The nonconscious mind craves safety and security. You may not think that your goals are a threat to these fundamental needs, but you'll soon see how conflicts in this area are quite common.

If sabotaging behaviors show up in your life, take a deeper look. When there are two opposing ideas in motion, the mind deletes the one that is newer, harder to implement, or uncertain. In other words, *change.* Your nonconscious mind will always take the path of least resistance. If your new desired behavior pattern creates any sort of dissonance, your mind will look for every way possible to remove it and go back to what's familiar.

Are more alarm bells going off? I'm sure at some point you've been frustrated with your behavior (I certainly have with mine). Perhaps you've been blindsided by your uncanny knack for getting in your own way. This is how goal hijacking happens.

How do you know if you have hijacked goals?

---

18   https://www.verywell.com/what-is-cognitive-dissonance-2795012

This is more than a "duh, Barbie" question. Of course, failure to meet your goal is the most obvious clue. But look past the obvious. Have you ever thought about your new goal and felt fatigued, frustrated by perceived "mistakes," annoyed at your lack of progress, or filled with a sense of being overwhelmed? Does thinking of your goal make you want to take a nap? Does taking action feel pointless?

Your nonconscious mind may be telling you that you'll probably fail anyway… just as you did last time. So, why even try?

If you've experienced any of these roadblocks to your success, you're in good company. Just thinking about it may leave you feeling depleted because **brain chaos is exhausting**.

Negative thoughts about your progress create a pattern in the circuitry of your brain. Negative patterns create unproductive results. On the good side, positive patterns create brain circuitry shown to improve blood flow and improved brain health. Positive patterns can be developed through exercise, learning new things, and experiencing positive emotions.[19]

> ### *Our thoughts are either constructive or destructive.*

Neuroplasticity discoveries reveal that habit circuitry can change as new and positive habits are adopted. (It can also have a negative impact[20] depending on circumstances, but for the purposes here, we're focusing on positive thoughts and their beneficial impact on the brain.) One super effective method to address cognitive dissonance is to intentionally redirect your self-talk in positive directions. This

19   https://steptohealth.com/discover-5-ways-increase-blood-flow-brain/
20   https://www.youtube.com/watch?v=VI-QRgBwIb8 The Brain That Changes Itself

accelerates the benefits of neuroplasticity and can spark a needed breakthrough to overcome unwanted patterns of behavior.

Dr. Joe Dispenza, a neuroscience researcher, and professor says it this way. *"When you understand how neural pathways are created in the brain, you get a front-row seat for truly comprehending how to let go of habits. Neural pathways are like superhighways of nerve cells that transmit messages. You travel over the superhighway many times, and the pathway becomes more and more solid. The hopeful fact, however, is that the brain is always changing and you can forge new pathways and create new habits. That's called the neuroplasticity of the brain."*

There's no way around this fact. Changing familiar (and unhealthy) behavior patterns takes intentional effort. It might be uncomfortable at first or feel foreign, but don't give up.

> ## No radical, bolt of lightning ah-ha moment ever happens within your comfort zone.

Complacency hides inside the boundaries of comfort. Agitation is needed to stir things up. This is where what I call *gateway topics* can be helpful. External goals in the areas of nutrition, stress, fitness, relationships, finances, etc. can serve as an open door to deeper level issues that await resolution.

For example, you may decide that your mealtime choices and habits could use improvement. As you work on this broad subject, deeper-level ones will likely surface. Gateway topics act as a permission slip to address something that obviously needs improvement. It's the not-so-obvious topics that definitely need focused attention. They're often conflicting and in opposition to the conscious desire.

Here's a practical illustration.

Let's say Mary Beth feels out of shape. She decides that signing up to run a marathon will provide the motivation she needs to get healthy again. She strategizes her workout activities, buys new gear, and marks each step of her plan on her calendar. But as each day passes, she chooses the couch rather than the track. She steps into her spongy slippers rather than her spiffy new running shoes. What's going on?

She berates herself because she achieved a similar fitness goal before. She was once out of shape and then motivated herself to create a healthy exercise program by training for a marathon.

Mary Beth amps up her inspiration by listening to successful athlete podcasts. She reads motivational books and watches encouraging documentaries. She feels some motivation, but not enough. More often than not, she still chooses channel surfing over outdoor workouts.

She finally confides her frustration to a trusted friend. Her confession prompts her friend to reply, *"Isn't it weird that the last time you did this and got into shape, your life fell apart? Remember when Kevin dumped you? You two were pretty serious. Do you think you're worried about ruining your new relationship?"*

Mary Beth's first reaction is anger. She folds her arms across her chest and says, *"This isn't the same thing at all! He didn't dump me. Kevin and I decided to break up because he was jealous and immature, and it was just a coincidence that it happened when I got healthy. This time, my boyfriend IS supportive. He wants what's best for me."*

Later, this annoying conversation sticks with Mary Beth like a dull toothache. The thought niggles her brain in quiet moments. She wonders if there could be a link. At the conscious level, there doesn't seem to be. Things are different now. Yet, she knows enough about the nonconscious mind to realize that it views things from a safety angle.

She considers the possibility that her nonconscious mind connects a healthy and fit body with the pain of a disintegrating relationship.

Once she addresses this unconscious conflict, she's relieved to see her health plans get back on track. Here's a simplified view of what was going on.

Because Mary Beth's nonconscious mind believed that SUCCESS = PAIN, it produced every disrupting thought imaginable to derail her health plans. (Notice that it took an outside influence to uncover the possible conflict.) At a conscious level, Mary Beth rejected her friend's observations; however, her thoughts over the subsequent days gave her enough evidence to give her pause. She then sought a remedy.

At face value, it's perplexing. She was in pain over not achieving her goals, and yet her nonconscious mind believed that pain would worsen if she did. There's the rub.

I know the following to be true from my own experience.

> ### *Never underestimate the power of pain over your actions and behaviors.*

This illustration shows how easy it is to experience limiting beliefs that aren't immediately apparent. They lie outside our conscious awareness. It's very common to experience conflicts between what we want and the behaviors that would help us get there.

Just the facts, Jack

Don't let this simple point get lost in the shuffle—a belief is not the same thing as a fact. Facts are universally held and agreed upon understandings. Beliefs are the stories, conclusions, or definitions we create to make logical sense of a problem or circumstance.

Our MAPP creates stories for us. Stories are not bad or negative, per se; they're just our way of coping and adapting. Our stories are the internal representations we make of the information we've gathered from the world around us.

Here's a simple comparison.

Facts are about universal reality.

- *This pan of water is boiling because the temperature of its contents is over 212°F/100°C.*
- *I can see the sunrise from my bedroom window because it faces East.*
- *More people live in New York City, New York than Chandler, Oklahoma.*
- *A regulation bowling ball weighs between 10 and 16 pounds.*

Beliefs are about our interpretations or perceptions of reality.

- *I'll always be overweight because it's in my genes.*
- *Blue cars are the best ones to own because they're safer.*
- *Loyalty is the best measure of a good employee because they're committed to the work.*
- *People with high IQs are happier because they have better employment opportunities.*

Beliefs are subjective. Their veracity lies in the eye of the beholder (believer). A person may fervently feel that a belief is universally true… but that doesn't make it so.

One of the greatest ways to allow healing is to begin questioning your beliefs. Are they universally true? Are you labeling them as facts? This isn't about being right or wrong. It's a simple shift between thinking something is a fact (therefore unchangeable), or a belief (which is changeable).

Do persistent underlying beliefs hold you back?

To find out, do a quick inventory of your life. Do you have everything you desire? Are you able to set goals in any area and stick to them? Do you get what you want easily or do you stumble a bit here or there? Or perhaps stumble… a lot?

If so, welcome to the human race. Unhelpful beliefs afflict even those who've climbed to levels of elevated consciousness.

Consider that uncovering, working with and resolving nonconscious limiting beliefs is easiest with an objective outside source. Another person (a professional coach, therapist, holistic health practitioner, etc.) has the advantage of detached curiosity and objectivity.

It's hard, if not impossible, to see your own stuff. I love this wee bit of wit.

> **"You can't read the label when you're sitting inside the jar."**
> —Southern folk wisdom

That's not to say that self-growth work can't help. Practices detailed in Chapter 16 can definitely pave the way for future success. It's amazing what comes to mind when we give ourselves permission and breathing space to explore. Becoming aware of limiting thoughts can be the impetus for great change.

Cutting off the limiting belief at the roots starts with exploration and non-judgmental curiosity.

Take an objective look at any belief and question its validity (even if you firmly believe it to be true). If it doesn't positively serve you, follow a simple "remove and improve" method of self-growth. Remove the limiting belief and insert a better one.

Once you challenge a limiting belief (ask if it's true in all circumstances), it can shift into a "sometimes true" or even a "never true" category. Decide right now what it is that you'd rather believe. Meditate and pray on this new belief.

■ Chapter 3 – Head Work

1. Increase your awareness of internal conflicts. What makes you think "on the one hand…," or "part of me feels…." Notice these conflicts and consider any potential misalignments.

2. Increase your awareness of behaviors that don't match your plans. Are they sabotaging behaviors? What would you have to believe as true for you to stop the sabotage?

3. Jot down a list of "facts" you believe about your health and your ability to heal. Look for clues that indicate where they may limit you. Can you shift your understanding of these "facts" and instead see them as beliefs?

*

In Chapter 5, we'll take a look at a simple remedy for negative thoughts—a negativity antidote. You'll discover what it does for the brain and how to apply it for maximum impact.

But first, we'll reveal some surprising truths about your brain, your thoughts, and how they all relate to the actual pain and symptoms in your physical body.

The Pain Brain & Chronic Symptoms

Understanding the mind/body connection is more than just a platitude. The body works in a specific action-reaction sequence from signals it receives from the brain. *There's no dam at the neck.* Meaning, what happens in the brain happens in the body (and vice versa).

Surprising truths about our brain and our health

The programming that runs in our nonconscious minds (our MAPP) creates thoughts, emotions, and beliefs. These beliefs, developed over time, are powerful drivers that govern our behaviors and even our physiology.

Scientific studies have proven that our thoughts and beliefs have a direct impact on our physical health. **Our thoughts have the power to tell our bodies at the molecular level how to function.** Our genes turn on and off (genetic expression) based on several factors, including our beliefs and emotions.[21] A British study published as far back as 1988 states that personality types (and how they deal with stress) *"were much more predictive of death from cancer, cardiovascular disease, and smoking."*[22]

Surprised?

Here's a phrase I want you to write on a sticky note. Repeat it often:

> ### *My body feels and experiences*
> ### *every thought I think.*

You'll soon see why. For now, just let it sink in. This is the very basis of *why* it's essential to change how we think in order to heal.

The nonconscious mind has more surprising characteristics in addition to those mentioned in Chapter 2. This next one's a real corker.

The nonconscious mind can't tell the difference between fact and fiction.

Honestly! When it comes to thoughts, the nonconscious mind cannot differentiate between something that actually happened and something vividly imagined.

21   http://blog.mindvalleyacademy.com/alternative-healing/
scientist-show-subconscious-thoughts-can-cause-specific-molecular-changes-genes
22   http://onlinelibrary.wiley.com/doi/10.1111/j.2044-8341.1988.tb02765.x/abstract

Do you see the brilliant influence of your imagination?

> ***Imagining positive scenarios***
> ***creates positive physical reactions.***
> ***Imagining negative scenarios creates***
> ***negative physical reactions.***

Your body's responses are simply along for the ride. Thoughts impact your heart rate, hormonal shifts, digestion, and other basic body functions. Our thoughts and beliefs program our cells on how to react. Can you see the harm in repeated negative thoughts?

On this, I'm a pro. In my teens, I was in a terrifying multi-vehicle accident. Afterward, without conscious intention, I relived every aspect of the collision over and over in my head. In vivid slow motion, no less. Each time I closed my eyes, the same internal movie began to play. Unbidden. (We now consider this as a catalyst of Post Traumatic Stress Disorder—PTSD.)

I didn't know what to do.

My naïve solution was to avoid closing my eyes. It seemed logical at the time. After weeks of sleep deprivation, I added more problems to the list of injuries I'd already sustained. You can probably guess that this didn't play out well.

If you tend to disaster-cize (mentally role-play disasters), your body acts and reacts accordingly. All. The. Time. Does your imagination run rampant? If you internally rehearse worst-case scenarios and become hypervigilant, your body participates in the rehearsals too.

Let me clarify something.

There's a critical difference between being prepared for a disaster and the *expectation* of one.

Preparation is helpful. It's okay to think ahead and plan for whatever might arrive in your future. But when that preparation slides into expectation, there lies the problem. Shining a focused light on what we don't want out of life actually makes it expand, grow, and become more of a presence. Anything we push away or try to bury flourishes with a vengeance.

> *Whatever reality we choose—*
> *either positive or negative—*
> *is what we'll experience.*

It's also meaningful at this point to introduce the subject known as confirmation bias. This is the very human tendency to believe what we *want* to believe.[23] We actually influence our experiences by our beliefs of what will happen. Charlie Brown knows in advance that his kite will end up in a tree. Is the illustration in the last frame of the comic strip any surprise? No matter what's depicted in the frames in the middle, Charlie knows where his kite is headed… and so do we.

We'll talk more about how to overcome this trait by becoming a neutral observer in Chapter 5, but for now, experiment with the notion of candidly questioning your beliefs.

For example, seeing a Negative Nellie neighbor walk into your favorite support group may lead you to think, "Now everyone will catch her pessimistic comments and start complaining." In this state, would

---

23   https://www.psychologytoday.com/us/blog/science-choice/201504/
what-is-confirmation-bias

you be more or less likely to view her input as negative? Your anticipation of hearing things with a negative slant clouds your perception.

People share more than words. There's body language, tone, inflection, volume, and even facial expressions that accompany conversations. All of these are open to interpretation. Pay attention to your assumptions and question your thoughts. What if in this environment Nellie isn't negative? What if she has helpful and supportive things to contribute to the group?

The pain brain

Do you have chronic pain?

If so, it's likely that you also have persistent negative thought patterns. Who wouldn't? It's a normal part of the pain experience, so don't misinterpret the following information. This is key.

Chronic pain is not an isolated result of negative thoughts. Pain is a real, physical, and physiological experience. Strangely, we're often given only half the picture. We're told to view it as either a physical thing or a mental thing. Only by viewing it as a symphony of both can we grasp the complex harmony at play.

Accidents, injuries, traumas (both physical and emotional), etc. can trigger chronic pain. Later, negative thoughts can be a natural outcropping of prolonged suffering. At some point, the thoughts themselves add to existing circumstances and compound the problem of chronic pain.

Chronic pain is a physical issue directed by brain function.

The two can occur at the same time, but it doesn't happen in reverse for no reason. Meaning you wouldn't construct a scenario of chronic pain in your head without cause. Therefore, if anyone says "it's all in your head," you have my permission to roll your eyes. We know better. *The problem isn't psychological; it's neurological.*[24]

So, how do we address this issue?

We first need to become aware of and identify our negative thoughts and patterns.

You may not even be aware that negative thoughts are part of your daily mind banter. Thoughts are not the only trigger for chronic pain, but weeding the garden of negativity between your ears can bring significant pain relief. Even little weeds can have a big impact.

Digging into the roots can clear your way toward recovery. That's what happened to me.

One way to dig into the roots of your mental garden is through mindfulness. There are a variety of approaches to consider. When mindful, we direct our attention away from the extraneous and into the present moment. Being mindful can be as simple as noticing the stiffness of the chair you're sitting on or sensing the warmth from your lap dog. Mindfulness is anything that directs you to the present moment or your awareness of choice.

Visualization is a simple option, and one I used recently at my chiropractor's office. I mentioned to him that I employ intentional thoughts to augment my benefits. I use vivid imagery to visualize improved muscle tone, better cellular communication, less pain, etc. while I undergo cold laser therapy. He added this tidbit—

---

24   https://www.ncbi.nlm.nih.gov/pmc/articles/PMC3281476/

> **"That's called 'driving in the neurology.'
> Our thoughts can work synergistically
> with physical treatments. They work
> even better together."**
> —Dr. Timothy Noble, DC

The many forms of mindfulness have a wide variety of health benefits.

Mindfulness invites a sense of comfort and provides an open space for calm, peace, and relaxation to settle in. Newer explorations of mindfulness have entered the self-growth platform including the concepts of kindfulness (Ajahn Brahm, author of the book *Kindfulness*), heartfulness (from John Prendergast, founder of The Enough Project[25]), loving-kindness, and one of my favorite references, Vitamin K (Kindness). Notice the theme here. Being kind, particularly to yourself, helps to induce a sense of calm acceptance.

Mindfulness provides a primary step toward recovery. It's time to evaluate how to put this simple tool to use.

I'm of two minds (pssst... you are too)

Conscious and nonconscious thoughts have different attributes, as outlined in Chapter 2. But I bet you've never thought about how information passes from one part of your mind to the other.

It's necessary to discover *how* to share data with the nonconscious mind so that you can begin to reshape your MAPP for positive benefits.

---

25   https://enoughproject.org/about/john-prendergast

Conscious, repetitive thoughts can worm their way into the nonconscious mind. What thoughts do you ruminate on most? Which ones follow predictable patterns and form familiar loops? Paying attention to your thoughts takes practice. This act of noticing is called *awareness*.

Are you aware of your conscious self-talk?

Other terms may be more familiar to you—terms such as inner chatter, monkey mind, internal dialogue, mind banter, your conscience, your Jiminy Cricket voice, mind noise, or even mental chaos. I use various terms for inner self-talk in this work, but they all refer to the same notion.

My favorite depiction of inner thoughts comes from viewing old Hollywood classic movies. These films usually feature a heroine's descent into madness narrated by a silky resonant voice (George Sanders[26] to a T). Joan Crawford was a seasoned pro at the silent portrayal of inner dialogue. She'd wring her hands, cling to a bedpost (or a man), while sweaty beads of desperation formed on her brows. All done in high heels and form-fitting designer suits, of course. Obviously, Crawford's brows (not to mention shoulders) were built to bear the weight of all that angst.

I hope you're not too shocked to learn that Joan's movie world didn't have much to do with reality (but that's a different book). In daily living, our thoughts are much less direct. They drift in and out of our conscious minds like gauzy clouds or maybe pesky gnats. They may be annoying but not all that threatening. At least not all of the time.

Becoming aware of inner chit chat takes practice. Awareness of your self-talk may range from a little to not any. It's common to believe that you have none. That's how it was for me.

---

26   http://www.imdb.com/name/nm0001695/

Ignorance was both my companion and catalyst. I first learned about internal dialogue when reading a book on effective goal-setting. It pointed out that negative self-talk fosters stagnation and backsliding.

"That's weird," I thought. "Why would someone make a goal and then sabotage their plans with negative self-talk? Good thing I don't do that."

Oh, the absurdity! I truly believed I had no self-talk. Mine was so subversive; it scooted under the radar. It burbled beneath the surface of my awareness, unnoticed.

FYI, everyone has self-talk. We often experience looping scripts that run in our heads and feelings that reside in our bodies. Awareness varies widely. If you're not sure about yours, don't worry. Shedding light on self-talk takes practice and focused attention. We'll do that as we go, chapter by chapter.

■ Where ALL change begins

The first step to any change is awareness.

I found this part of the process annoying and confusing at first. I wasn't aware of my thoughts at all. So, my conclusion was that I must be different from everyone else. (Oh, you do that too?) I believed that if I had any inner self-talk at all, it must be stealth chatter. I knew I had feelings about things, but not a real dialogue.

Then something funny happened. Even though I still couldn't put a finger on my inner voice, I started to notice my reactions to things. I put hindsight into use and reverse-engineered the steps toward awareness. Instead of trying to discover my thoughts, I set my intention on noticing my unhealthy or unhelpful behaviors and reactions. When

I noticed something negative, I backtracked and pinpointed what I was feeling right before. That process pointed the finger at what I was thinking.

For me, noticing my reactions came first. Awareness of my mental chatter came second.

I began to notice how I reacted to what people said, what I read, and what I experienced in general. Sometimes I'd recall fragments of thought that prompted a behavior. Other times I remembered a sensation or an emotion. There wasn't always a clear memory or mental picture.

Inner thoughts aren't only words and sentences. They may also include vague or fuzzy feelings and ideas. I tripped over this experience once when looking at a magazine. I noticed a general feeling of sadness after reading a few fitness articles. I felt dissatisfied and at odds with myself. I soon realized the error of my logic. I believed I read these magazines for the abundance of healthy recipes. But I didn't think about the impact of the photos and images.

The illustrations featured women several decades younger than me, with impossibly (not to mention digitally-enhanced) lean bodies. Their unreal long torsos, pencil-thin legs, and gaunt faces stood in stark contrast to my self-perceptions. Next to them, I imagined myself looking like a sweater-clad, scarf-wearing stump.

Of course, this is an exaggerated (not to mention, unhelpful) self-perception.

As a result of this simple process, I discovered my inner chatter. I realized that the magazines I chose didn't support my health plans (which is akin to the wolf not supporting Little Red Riding Hood's travel plans). Subsequently, I started noticing the frequency of my self-deprecating thoughts and remarks.

Self-abnegation was my middle name, and I was proficient at negative personal quips.

Honestly, I still am. At the time, I considered this tendency to be the hallmark of humility. I believed that by taking myself down a notch or two with a slam or a compliment rebuff, I kept myself on an even keel. Of course, I was wrong. Now, if I slip up and verbally torch myself in front of others, I recognize it as an old familiar pattern and move on.

And if I don't happen to catch it, I have a son-in-law who does. (Thanks, Chris!)

What surprised me most as I bettered my skill at detection was the frequency. I talked smack about myself all the time. My negative body image self-talk was relentless, harsh, and downright mean. Maybe yours is too? This is sometimes referred to as the conditioned mind, and mine was conditioned to be ruthless.

I eventually connected the dots between my negative self-talk and the destructive mental pictures that tagged along. My derogatory inner language created vivid mental representations that kept me feeling as if I never measured up.

Here's a silly, but simple, example.

I often use humor to get my point across in lectures. I used to make fun of my short stature by stating that I couldn't wear basic t-shirts. I'd lament that a t-shirt transformed me from one unflattering shape to another—from pear to rectangle. *Not* an improvement.

While it may have been a teensy bit funny, there was a hidden problem. In my mind's eye, I saw an inflated picture of myself as a disproportionate pear and then a wide, blocky rectangle. My conscious mind may have recognized this as unfair, but I was painting vivid pictures for my powerful nonconscious mind that were both unhelpful and unsupportive of my goals.

It was silly to think that my self-jabbing humor kept me "real." What I thought was reality was just plain hurtful. *Negative images and feelings follow negative chatter*. Negative emotions and images keep us stuck. They cripple goals. They stifle progress.

I knew it had to stop. And I want it to stop for you too. This was part of my very long journey fine-tuning my awareness. If you put any of what you've learned in this book into practice, your journey will be much shorter. You now know what to look for and from what to steer clear.

Awareness of negative images that followed my negative thoughts was enlightening. On the grand scale, it was perhaps just one hop, skip, and a jump—one tiny step toward figuring things out. But it had a profound ripple effect for me. I noticed the negative thoughts and images that I allowed to take up space in the attic of my mind.

Then, I decided it was time for a clean sweep.

> **"It's not the load that breaks you down;**
> **it's how you carry it."**
> —attributed to Lena Horne

■ Chapter 4 – Head Work

1. Have you ever considered the connection between negative thoughts and chronic pain? Explore and list three examples of how your thoughts may transfer to physical consequences.

2. Awareness begins by paying attention to it. Merely notice your thoughts. (If you feel you don't have self-talk, take a look at your results. Are they what you want? Pay attention to your patterns of behavior, and you'll soon recognize the thoughts that drive them.) *Notice without judgment.* Make a mental note of your thoughts, feelings, patterns, and reactions to your surroundings. Do you often have knee-jerk reactions? Do you simmer? Do you ignore? Begin to notice and monitor them. Let this awareness percolate a few days and then jot down your discoveries into a journal or personal notebook.

3. Do you use self-deprecating humor? Do you deflect comments that make you feel uncomfortable with snarky remarks or put-downs at your own expense? Consider how your reactions are either supportive of your overall goals or how they have the potential to keep you stuck. Brainstorm at least three ways to shift this behavior. Create a personal script for how you'd rather react or respond.

This next chapter offers some exciting and practical steps to apply your newfound skill of awareness. Add these protocols to your healing toolbox and use them daily.

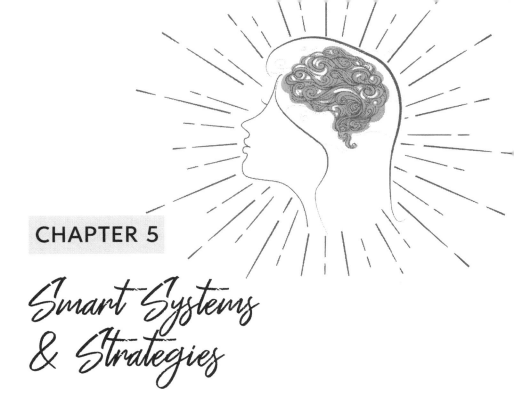

CHAPTER 5

Smart Systems & Strategies

Awareness of self-talk is the first step. Next, we'll bolster these awareness skills by breaking down the process into actionable steps.

Anatomy of self-talk

Self-talk comes in pictures, feelings, emotions, and words. It may be brief phrases or sentence fragments. Unlike what you see in TV commercials, there isn't a good angel sitting on one shoulder having an articulate exchange with a bad one on the other.

Self-talk is often called chatter for a reason. It can be like rowdy myna bird prattle.

Sometimes simple words or thoughts pop into mind with or without mental images. They can summon powerful emotions. I remember once losing a plastic food container. It wasn't all that significant. But because I couldn't put my hands on it, I magnified its importance in my thoughts. Nearly manic, I obsessed over it and bawled myself out in the process. How could I misplace it? I just saw it!

One overarching emotion descended over me like a cloud. It felt like the word "bad." I couldn't put my thumb on where this feeling came from, but it was very strong. I had a vague feeling of being scolded but no actual mental picture or memory. I just felt awful. The negative emotion swept over my entire body, and I felt like a failure.

Notice that the feeling was utterly disproportionate to the circumstance. We can thank our MAPP and cellular memory for that. Our brain remembers how we react to specific feelings, so we act or behave on autopilot. We often *amplify* negative emotions in a nonconscious attempt to keep ourselves in check somehow. This is a basic pattern we run intending to keep ourselves safe.

■ Lean toward negativity much?

You may have heard of the brain's phenomenon known as negativity bias.[27] Your brain naturally gives more credence to and increases your focus on negative emotions rather than on ones that are positive. Neuropsychologist Rick Hanson makes it easy to visualize with this apt description, *"The brain is like Velcro for negative experiences, but like Teflon for positive ones."*[28]

---

27   https://www.psychologytoday.com/articles/200306/our-brains-negative-bias
28   https://www.rickhanson.net/take-in-the-good/

Your memory is also hard-wired toward negativity. A deeper dive here helps to explain why. There are two types of memory—implicit and explicit.

Implicit memories are not easily brought to the conscious mind. Some may also refer to this type of memory as "muscle memory." Your body remembers how to do or experience something without conscious recall. For example, you may have an implicit memory of riding a bike, without having a conscious memory of how to make your body balance on two wheels. Implicit memories are non-verbal. They help us to remember safe and unsafe activities or circumstances.

Explicit memories can easily be brought to the conscious mind. You can remember a specific incident, for example, of riding your bike downhill lickety-split.

Because implicit memories are tied to safety, they're linked to our primal sense of survival. They're stored in the amygdala, the primitive part of the brain known for instinctual responses. Stronger ties are connected to memories of anything frightening, upsetting, or dangerous.

With this in mind, it makes sense that I can easily remember vivid details of surviving a tornado while spending the night at a friend's home, yet have little-to-no memory of other, perhaps fun but uneventful, sleepovers.

Another critical distinction between these different memory types is that explicit memories can be considered "plastic," meaning they can change. They're not necessarily the same each time the memory is accessed.

For the most part, implicit memories don't change. What they do, however, is impact everything that happens after them. Our negative experiences color our view of the world.

More on this as we continue to compare and contrast the conscious and nonconscious mind.

■ Our MAPP and negativity

As this relates to your MAPP, circumstances, or memories with a negative charge are more likely to imprint to your nonconscious mind. This allows shortcuts to form creating specific default patterns. This means that at the drop of a hat, you can go from slightly concerned to anxiety-ridden because of your default mental patterns.

In my popular article entitled, The Negativity Connection,[29] I share several factors that contribute to negativity—especially in the chronic illness community. (You can find an excerpt conveniently located in the Appendix.) Survival bias is one factor I refer to often. We each have an innate and compelling desire to keep ourselves safe. We are hard-wired to look for and react to anything threatening.

This means that we invite (unintentionally perhaps) sadness, frustration, and loss of hope when reflecting on negative experiences in life. Dr. Joe Dispenza shares this startling statement.

> *"We start each morning living in the past."*
> —Dr. Joe Dispenza

---

29   http://www.prohealth.com/fibromyalgia/library/showarticle.cfm?libid=21431

His definition of a habit makes it crystal clear. He says, *"A habit is when you've done something so many times that your body now knows how to do it better than your mind."* More information, including his description of PTSD (repeated thoughts of a past experience), can be found in his short YouTube video, Learn How to Control Your Mind.[30]

Emotional or traumatic events imprint negative factors into our MAPP. When it comes to getting information to pass through your critical faculty (the division between conscious awareness and the nonconscious mind), there's no better way than through drama or trauma. When we're in a state of shock or awe, our critical faculty goes on hiatus. In those moments, we're vulnerable to direct commands—especially ones from authorities.

But did you catch the exciting truth about this negative bias?

You now know how this mechanism works. Apply this understanding, and **you** can replicate it. Apply it *intentionally* for positive circumstances rather than unintentionally for negative ones. Positive events—especially awe, wonder, bliss, and joy—provide us with an opportune time to plant seeds of what we *want* to believe. For example, intentionally choose to immerse yourself in something beautiful and at the same time, repeat a favorite positive mantra (an affirmation that stirs up emotion).[31]

Negative self-talk impacts our present actions as well as our plans for the future. Negative chatter keeps us from trying new things. Thoughts such as, "I made a royal mess of it last time..." keep us stuck and stagnant.

---

30   https://youtu.be/v7KQsS2kLM4
31   http://www.danawilde.com/HowToRant

> ***Negative self-talk allows sandpaper
> words to rub you raw in tender places.***

Be kind to yourself.

Becoming aware of negative chatter takes patience and practice. Allow the space to recognize any form your thoughts may take—words, feelings, emotions, mental pictures, etc. Practice the art of silence and listen to what arrives in the moments of stillness. View these thoughts as a casual or neutral observer. That means being aware without judgment or analysis.

This is key.

Why no judgment? When we begin to hear our inner voice and recognize unhelpful patterns, it's common to feel we're doing something wrong. Paradoxically, this "wrong" feeling keeps us trapped in a loop of negativity.

Instead, simply observe. Pay attention to the words, ideas, and even the pictures you see in your head. Document what you learn and if anything at all, say to yourself, "Isn't this interesting?"

Who's in my head, anyway?

Once you've become more aware of your inner dialogue, notice a few characteristics of that voice. Is your voice sassy, snarky, and snippy? Or is it nagging, negative, and nasty? Maybe it swings from one to the other.

The personality of the voice you hear in your head was most likely formed before you turned six or seven years old. That voice is a representation of the most dominant person—or an amalgam of persons—in authority over you at the time. This is particularly true when the voice is negative, corrective, or rebuking.

The identity of your inner voice is *not* that specific person(s), but rather your representation of what you heard from that person(s) at a formative age. The main take-home here is that this voice **is not you**. It is not *your* voice trying to shame you into one thing or another. Once you can make this distinction, progress is at hand.

Your inner voice may be your greatest cheerleader, a sadistic dictator, or many shades in between. If it spurs you on like a guiding light… then, great. If not, it's time for a change.

It's also important to understand that our personalities are made up of internal parts. Here's an example. Imagine as an early teen, going to a theme park or fair with friends. Your peers goad you into trying a ride that wouldn't have been your idea. Part of you probably wants to show them you're not afraid. It's also likely that another part of you wants to run away and go home.

Both parts are valid. It's normal to fear the unknown. It's also normal to want to avoid feeling embarrassed in front of your friends.

Neither part is wrong.

You probably haven't thought about it before, but it makes sense to explore the different parts of your internal landscape. Some refer to these as sub-personalities.[32] You'll know you're dealing with a parts issue when you find yourself thinking, "On one hand," or "Part of me wants…."

---

32   https://www.goodtherapy.org/learn-about-therapy/types/internal-family-systems-therapy

I encourage you to mine for the gold here. This understanding can shift how you view your life—both past and future. If you chastise yourself for procrastinating, for example, think back to a time when you didn't procrastinate, or you overcame that tendency and got a specific task done. There's a big difference between labeling yourself as a procrastinator and noticing that *part of you* wants to procrastinate and *part of you* wants to finish the task at hand. Refrain from defining one facet as a fully-formed identity and the other as a transient circumstance. Both characteristics serve a purpose.

> ## *You are a multi-faceted gem.*

Each facet is part of who you are. As a whole, your brilliance reflects the world around you. Awareness of this aspect leads to acceptance.

Awareness is an art that blooms with practice. As you get better at it, apply the powerful strategies uncovered in this chapter. This helps to keep your negative nonsense from nipping at your heels.

■ Positivity clarification

This book isn't a simple endorsement of switching off your negative mindset and adopting an all-positive one. I'd never advocate that anyone should strive to the perfection this implies.

In fact, you may be surprised to hear me say this—***positivity is not the be-all and end-all.***

A life of happiness and joy does not come from the absence of negativity. Making it your lifelong aim to always feel positive is not only unrealistic; it's dangerous. It's a set-up for a lifelong struggle.

So, can striving for positivity be harmful?

It can if it makes you feel there's something wrong with you.

Life is full of many co-existing aspects. An abundant life will always have times of bright sun and dark shadows (no, not the Barnabas Collins type). Eliminating all shadows doesn't enhance the beauty of the sun. Even when both are present, the sun's rays filter through. And, sometimes...

> *Shadows can make the sun seem even more radiant.*

The purpose of this chapter is two-fold. I want you to be able to address, process, and repair your personal negativity bias. Second, through methods and systems found in this chapter as well as Chapter 10, I want you to learn to ADAPT and GROW into and through negative situations or thoughts as they arrive.

Negative thoughts are most dangerous when ignored.

Here, you'll find tools you need to make this process work. The following tips can transform you into a negative thought-busting pro in no time.

> *Make a deliberate decision to expect progress rather than perfection in your life.*

■ Strategies for dealing with negative self-talk

- **Become a neutral observer of your thoughts**. Just notice them with a general sense of curiosity. Is there something of value or importance to learn? Yes or no. If not, decide to let it go. No judgments.

- **Say a simple "thank you" out loud**. Do this when you notice a less-than-helpful comment in your head. (I still work on this one!) Snarky comebacks may come easily but instead, practice gratitude and appreciation. Even if it's dysfunctional at times, your thoughts are trying to protect you. Simply say, thanks for the good intentions. Or come up with your own supportive statement.

- **Refrain from comparisons**. Have you ever heard of the phrase compare and despair? Or maybe you've heard that comparison is the thief of contentment? Measuring up to worldly images, people, or ideals is pointless. Learn to question anything (especially in your thinking) that implies there's a set standard for appearance or accomplishments. Become especially attuned to the feeling of not measuring up in some way. This is SO common! *Comparisons extinguish joy.*

- **Laugh at yourself**. A sense of humor is a balm to the gritty impact of negativity. It lowers stress hormones.[33] It's a great way to handle difficulties in life, but remember that it doesn't include self-inflicted trash talk. When you learn to laugh at yourself with graciousness, you can laugh with others, too.

---

33   https://www.verywellmind.com/the-stress-management-and-health-benefits-of-laughter-3145084

- **Develop curiosity about your thoughts**. Do you give others the benefit of the doubt for what they say? Offer yourself the same courtesy. If your thoughts are negative, become curious about why. What is your mind trying to share with you? Is it trying to keep you safe? And if there's no positive value to a thought… simply let it go.

- **DO NOT claim that inner voice as *who* you are**. While that voice is familiar, we know the words, feelings, emotions, and memories are compiled from a variety of sources. That voice is NOT you. It's a false self. It doesn't define you, and it's not all that accurate when it comes to the truth. Who you were, who you are, and who you will be are three different versions of yourself. We're always in the process of reinventing ourselves, so don't be fooled by the misleading notion that the voice you hear in your head is your voice. It is not the soul of who you are.

- **Identify with your internal parts**. Notice situations where you feel conflicted, indecisive, or feel the need to procrastinate. We all have parts that feel one way and parts that feel another. That's just typical human behavior. Embrace the feeling of not being 100% sure of everything. It's okay. Decide to the best of your ability and move on.

- **Accept that negative emotions aren't the enemy**. Negative emotions happen just as positive ones. The key is understanding, processing, and changing them if need be. Here's a shocker—not all negative emotions need to be changed. Sometimes, it's important to feel sad, to grieve, or experience anger. Ideally, we mature to the level where we can choose when to feel these emotions and when to allow them to move on.

> **When you accept an emotion perceived as negative, you give it permission to have a voice and then pass through you.**

Sticks, stones, and brain science

The old children's rhyme "words can never hurt me" should be followed by another, "liar, liar pants on fire." It's simply not true. Words (emotional traumas) can be equally, if not more damaging than physical traumas—especially in the long-term. Every thought we feel has physical energy and emotion attached. Emotion actually means *energy in motion*.[34] These emotions translate into physical effects such as pain, fatigue, and general dysfunction.

Emotions create a cascade of chemicals that consistently bathe our brains.[35] Our brain chemistry (neurotransmitters) communicates with every cell in the body. These chemicals create feelings which become the basis of our behaviors, and we take action based on how we *feel* about something.

Most of us believe this process happens the other way around.

So, how do you *want* to feel? Nope, not a trick question. Do you think that you're a victim of whatever thoughts float your way? Not so, Tonto. You can choose to redirect your thoughts in a helpful direction.

---

34 https://www.psychologytoday.com/us/blog/in-flux/201106/emotions-change-energy-in-motion

35 http://www.humanillnesses.com/Behavioral-Health-A-Br/Brain-Chemistry-Neurochemistry.html

Through practices we'll discuss in depth later in this book, we can change our thoughts and behaviors. They are mutable. Thoughts can be morphed, manipulated, coaxed, arranged, and rearranged.

Changing our thoughts and behaviors benefits our mind, soul, and body.

Get committed... now

It takes practice to redirect negative inner chatter. While in the process—*always be kind to yourself.* Be patient. You're creating new and different patterns which feel foreign. That's okay. Your unhealthy patterns took a lifetime (so far) to create. It's time for a change. From this day forward, you have the opportunity to reshape your patterns into ones that support your dreams.

Change—when repeated and reinforced—becomes effortless. The next time a negative thought or image pops into your awareness, simply say, "Thanks. I appreciate the input and I choose to focus on something else right now."

Then shift gears. Transfer your attention to something constructive and invigorating. What makes you feel joy, love, peace, or gratitude? Awareness techniques allow you to cut the negative ties that anchor you to past behaviors.

Don't forget. Once you dismiss a negative thought, there's vacancy for a new one. Make it good. What would you rather experience? Replace negative thoughts with something exciting or interesting. Remove and improve. The nonconscious mind naturally fills up empty spaces. Make it your focus to replace unintentional negative thoughts with intentional positive ones.

> ## *Focus is the most powerful*
> ## *healing tool you have.*

Here's a basic method of dealing with negative thoughts. With a few added tweaks, it's based on a fundamental cognitive behavioral therapy (CBT) model of stress management.

The FIVE 180 Reset method

To shift your negative self-talk into a positive gear, follow this simple paint-by-number approach. There are five easy steps. This method pivots your perspective 180 degrees; from harmful to helpful. This is a powerful pattern interrupt[36] practice.

When a negative thought drifts into your awareness—

1. Imagine a STOP sign or a PAUSE button in your mind. Allow yourself space to think. You may wish to say, "stop" or "pause" either aloud or to yourself.

2. IDENTIFY and label the dominant emotion you feel (anger, sadness, fear, frustration, anxiety, etc.) and state it (out loud if practical). It's necessary to do this with NO resistance or judgment about this emotion. Just identify it as "this anger" or "this sadness," etc. You may also wish to identify where, in your body, you feel this emotion.

3. Take a deep, cleansing belly BREATH (or three).

---

36   https://www.huffpost.com/entry/why-a-pattern-interrupt-i_b_8075800

4. Imagine how it FEELS to be in your favorite happy place. Invoke a lovely, safe, and carefree place either real or imagined. Allow the emotions and feelings of your happy place to infuse your body. What do you see, hear, smell, and feel? Recite one or more favorite positive statements such as, *I'm doing my very best,* or *I feel myself getting better and stronger in each moment.* This step swaps helpful thoughts for unhelpful ones.

5. Finish off this quick exercise with GRATITUDE—an act of recognition, appreciation, and acknowledgment. What are you grateful for the most? Whether it's the ability to continue learning, the resources you have, or just the fact that you're able to breathe deeply and appreciate the moment, it's up to you. Ease into being grateful and thankful.

Don't forget the last step. It's a doozy!

Feeling a sense of gratitude does more than help to derail negative thoughts. It helps generate the "happy" chemicals in the brain, which translate to healthy hormones such as dopamine, serotonin, oxytocin, and endorphins.[37]

The word *gratitude* comes from a Latin word meaning grace. Living in a state of grace is a good thing—for us and everyone around us. This simple FIVE 180 Reset allows you to enter the process in one frame of mind and exit a short time later in one that's different—and improved. Gratitude is always 180 degrees away from negative emotions such as fear, doubt, and worry.

---

37   http://theutopianlife.com/2014/10/14/hacking-into-your-happy-chemicals-dopamine-serotonin-endorphins-oxytocin/

> ### *Positive inner language is a set-up for outer success.*

Here's an extra tip on step #4 of this process. Did you know that the heart sends more signals to the brain than the other way around?[38] Therefore, the feelings you hold deeply (and often) have a profound effect on everything you think, say, and do.

We've discussed the fact that our inner thoughts have an impact on our physical experiences. We feel what we think. But have you given much thought to the actual process? When broken down into fundamental concepts, it's not all that complicated.

Here are the basics of how one process leads to the next.

■ Success algebra

This is a writer-downer.

> ### *Self-talk → Thoughts → Feelings → Actions = Results*[39]

This straightforward equation demonstrates the predictability of the results we achieve in life based on our thought patterns. Negative thought patterns create negative emotions and feelings, which lead to

---

38   https://www.collective-evolution.com/2015/10/30/not-just-brain-to-body-researchers-discover-that-the-heart-sends-signals-to-the-brain/
39   http://www.russellsmall.com/positive-self-talk-affirmations

negative behaviors and actions. Our less than desirable outcomes are then a foregone conclusion.

To solve for results, simply work the equation backward. If the results you experience don't measure up to what you want, go back to the beginning of this calculation. What are you thinking? Remember that up to 96% of your daily thoughts are the same ones you had yesterday... and the day before that... and the day before.

Isn't it time for a change?

> ### *Hit the mental backspace button and delete.*

In this chapter, we've discussed shifting your thoughts in a more positive direction. Awareness of your internal negativity provides an opportunity to insert more of what you want in life.

Repetitive negative thoughts can leave us feeling like victims (this happens automatically). Repetitive positive thoughts can help us feel more like victors (this only happens with focused intention).

It's up to you. You can either take a passive or active role in your future. It can be more of the same or something different.

Repairing your way of thinking is sort of like applying the Find and Replace feature in a word processor. You have to use conscious awareness to find the thoughts and beliefs you'd like to remove and then specify what you want to use as replacements.

A common phrase in the self-help world goes something like this—
"Your mind must arrive at your destination before your life will" (unknown
attribution). Here's my tweaked version for relevance.

> ***Your thoughts must arrive at their***
> ***destination before your results will.***

■ Chapter 5 – Head Work

1. Review your Head Work from Chapter 4. What type of self-
   talk did you notice when you first became aware?

2. Write down the steps from the Strategies for Dealing with
   Negative Self-talk found in this chapter. Put them on an index
   card, notecard, or sticky note. Carry them with you to review
   often. Which steps come easily and which are you likely to
   skip or forget? Practice these steps to make them a smooth
   and consistent response to negative thoughts. Have you committed to making this change? ***Decide*** right now to change
   your response to negative thoughts.

3. Write down the steps for the FIVE 180 Reset. What happened the first time you tried it? Did you feel a sense of calm
   right away, or did you have to practice a few times? Keep your
   written reminder handy so that you follow all five steps. Strat-
   egize now for how you'll remember to use this method when
   stressed. Decide what will make you think of it. (Suggestions:
   At the first sign of stress in the body—tightened shoulders,
   stomach in a knot, etc.—practice thinking of a stop sign or a
   pause button. This initial visual cue can help you to remem-

ber this powerful tool. You may even wish to draw or print out photos of stop signs or pause buttons to post as reminders.)

We've discussed how our thoughts affect our outlook, physical experience, and emotional outlook. In the next chapter, we'll dig into specific words to tweak in your daily dialogue. You'll be surprised at how seemingly benign words may contribute to your derailed health plans.

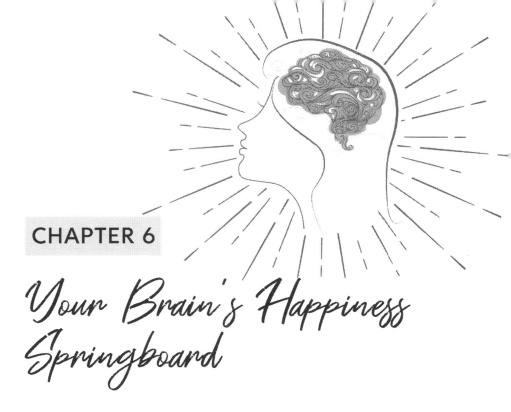

CHAPTER 6

Your Brain's Happiness Springboard

R emoving obvious negative, derogatory, and limiting self-talk makes sense. But what about the chatter that defies logic? Some things we say to ourselves sound okay—at the surface level. However, beneath there lies conflict. Some inner chatter is subtle and deceptive. In this chapter, we'll dig into this often-confusing subject.

Your map is not your MAPP

When it comes to your health goals, where do you want to go? Do you want to improve energy levels, fitness stamina, and perhaps your sleep patterns? What about your sense of connection to others?

It's all about the destination.

Let's imagine that you live in Vermont and want to drive to New Mexico. (For those outside the U.S., that's quite a distance—about 2,151 miles or 3,462 kilometers.) You are a "seat of the pants" kinda person and hop into your car with a song in your heart. You start up your engine, put it into gear, then wonder, "Should I go forward, backward, right, or left?" Subsequently, indecision has you driving aimlessly, never leaving your neighborhood. Frustrated, you decide that you don't really want to go to New Mexico.

That's what happens with no plan to reach your destination.

Now, let's imagine this a different way. You're a meticulous planner and don't trust your GPS. Instead, you map out how to get from Essex, Vermont to Albuquerque, New Mexico and write down every single road, turn, and stop you'll make. You take this giant book of instructions you've now created and start your car. You drive along throwing one completed page after another into the backseat as you go. You're thrilled at your progress… until you arrive at a "road closed" sign. You've got no Plan B. Your instruction book is now obsolete. Because you don't know how to adapt, you turn around and go back home.

Of course, these two examples are opposed and exaggerated. Using no map or guideline isn't useful. A map that's so detailed there's no room for adjustments is pointless, and it doesn't serve as a functional model of goal setting.

Before we get into more particulars about roadblocks and detours, it's time for you to jot down your goals right now. What would you like to achieve in the next 30 days? Note what you *do* want rather than what you *don't* want. Write your goals here, in your journal, or even better—in your *Get Back into Whack Workbook*.

Write down one goal for each of these three categories. Use a pencil. We'll refine as we go.

Health/Nutrition:_____
_____
_____
_____

Self-Growth/Spirituality/Connections: _____
_____
_____
_____

Fitness/Body Movement/Activity: _____
_____
_____
_____

Another reason we use a pencil (or ink with permission to scribble or cross-out) is to highlight that this is not about perfection. It's also not about creating a finite plan. **Goals are a work in progress**. For that matter, life is a work in progress.

Subtle subconscious sabotage

Words can thwart your plans without your permission. Without your conscious awareness, words seed powerful images in your mind, which in turn grow into feelings and emotions. The following list shares words that are not bad, per se. But these words trigger more than what meets the eye (or mind). Beneath the surface, there's cause for concern. Remember that the nonconscious mind is always attentive and listening for instructions. These words may cause the nonconscious mind to stumble over or even sabotage the instructions that you're trying to follow.

I bring them to your attention to give you a reason to pause—a little time to think. Once you've thought about these words, you may choose to remove, replace, or minimize their use in your daily inner and outer dialogue. It's up to you.

■ Words to stumble by

TRY: The very word suggests to your nonconscious mind there's a block or some sort of barrier between what you want and what you'll do to get it. The word try also conjures up feelings and emotions of effort. In the NLP world, we often use the term "efforting." Doesn't that sound difficult? When you say, "I'll try" before something you plan to do, you're telling yourself it's going to be hard, and the likelihood of completing it is slim. The implied thought is that you're already prepared to fail. Your nonconscious mind interprets your desired action as something that would require effort and struggle. Solutions to problems are often blocked from your awareness when the energy of struggle is present. This creates a cycle of self-sabotage.

SHOULD / SHOULDN'T: These terms may imply judgment, blame, or failure. They're spoken with a critical voice. Those struggling to adopt new habits often use these terms in a misguided attempt to stay within constraints. They may say, "I shouldn't eat X," or "I should hit the gym daily." They use should and shouldn't to set nebulous parameters for their healing progress. The truth is, this language impedes progress. The harsh inner critical voice is never a champion for success. And these terms cause the nonconscious mind to create a mental picture of the very things they don't want. TIP: *Consider using "could" instead. (I could go to the gym daily.)*

CAN'T: This word implies that you're unable to have or do what you desire. It suggests that you're helpless or powerless over the situation. It's far more effective and convincing to state your desire as a choice.

For example, *I choose to eat healthy, whole, real foods,* rather than *I can't have processed foods*. Don't paint yourself as a victim.

BROKEN / BAD / BUM: When these terms refer to yourself or a specific body part, they place a negative label that serves no valid purpose. Please don't refer to yourself as broken or to your knee (for example) as bad or bum. When you talk about yourself in this way, your body hears you. Thinking of yourself as malfunctioning or in-adequate has a negative impact. A better suggestion is to always view your body in a state of healing and improvement. For example, *my knee is getting stronger every day*.

BUT: This is a tricky word. It's nearly magical as it can make mean-ings of your sentences disappear. I'm talking about sentences where it's used to join two different thoughts. Here's an example. "I love your new haircut, but I'm not sure about the shade of your high-lights." Would you feel great about the haircut? Or would you dash to a mirror to check out the lousy color job?

The word but often negates (makes meaningless) the words that come before it.

Watch for this sometimes iffy word in your language and the language of others.

It takes a little practice, but switching the word "and" for "but" can yield powerful benefits. But is an exclusive word; it excludes things. And is inclusive; it includes things. Notice the difference in this re-vised sentence. "I love your new haircut, and I'm not sure about the shade of your highlights." Yes, it does sound a bit awkward. However, did you notice the absence of the sting? The second half of the com-ment feels less insulting. Also, watch for this word in your language as you defend your position. "I think that I want to ask for a raise at work, but I'm not sure." Are you unsure about what you think or unsure about how and when to ask for a raise? It's helpful to use words that clarify and strengthen your intent.

TIP: *In some circumstances, you can use the inherent magical properties of this word to your advantage. In your self-talk, if you happened to think, "I blew my healthy eating plan going out to lunch with friends," try this re-wording fix. Add the magical word plus a positive intention and voila! It becomes, "I blew my healthy eating plan going out to lunch with friends, but I'm back on track. I can do this."*

Feel the difference?

I AM + NEGATIVITY: The words, "I am" can be the two most powerful words in the English language. What follows often reflects a deep conviction of who you believe you are (notice I didn't say who you are). Pay attention to *any* negative words that follow your "I am" statements. Do these sound familiar? *I am always late. I am horrible at math. I am overwhelmed or too busy. I am a hot mess*, etc. Each of these statements is a tether holding you back from where you want to go. The switch is obvious. Include encouraging and hopeful declarations after the words I am as often as possible.

WISH / WANT: When it comes to goal-setting in particular, it's critical to refrain from using terms such as wish or want. Just as with the word try, they imply to the nonconscious mind that you don't have the capacity for the desired result. Your mind sees, hears, and feels that your goals are outside your reach. And, for as long as you keep wishing or wanting, your goals will *always* exist outside of your grasp.

LATER / TOMORROW: The nonconscious mind is very intuitive when it comes to increments of time. It doesn't identify with units of measure such as hours, minutes, days, months, etc., at least not in a conscious mind sort of way. So, using words like later or tomorrow have little to no meaning. For best results, use the present tense when goal-setting. Or, if a future date is desired, use a specific one. For example, *I feel strong and confident right now. I am registering for the Hawaii Hapalua half marathon on April 12, 2099.* Use whatever date makes logical sense to you.

IMPOSSIBLE / NEVER: Be careful of using limiting words such as impossible or never—especially in reference to you or your abilities. Your nonconscious mind is listening and knows when your words imply that something is hopeless or fruitless. These words also connect you to the emotions and feelings of helplessness. None of this is supportive. Remember the closed-door thoughts mentioned in Chapter 2? Don't forget to apply these three magic words… up until now.

LABELS: Beware of identifying yourself with negative labels. Think about the negative words you say, referring to some perceived inferiority. Labeling yourself as a lousy cook or a klutz isn't helpful. It's one thing to have an awareness of your skillset; it's another to apply a negative label. Identifying with the labels we assign makes them dangerous. By giving it a label, we may give that notion power, authority, and influence over our behaviors.

I DON'T KNOW: This is another tricky phrase. It's okay not to know something. But if you happen to overuse this term to dismiss someone's question or to avoid thinking about something, it can be problematic. Saying, "I don't know" to a question can actually block you from your intuition.

Consider the following alternatives. *I'd rather not answer that right now. I'd rather not discuss that with you. I'll put some thought into that and make a decision and get back to you.* And, if you really don't know the answer to something, try saying *I don't know right now, but I'm willing to figure it out.*

HAVE TO: We often have to-do lists jam-packed with tasks and schedules that feel outside of our control. But this generalized emo-

tion can lead to feelings of overwhelm and futility. There's a simple
fix for this. Shift your thought patterns from "I have to" to "I get to."
Doesn't that feel different? Of course, this may feel funny at first.
When you tell yourself that you **get to** go to work, it might feel like a
lie. But I challenge you to follow the thought. If you didn't get to go
to work, what would be the alternative? Does your work support your
family, pay for needed items, and keep your financial boat afloat?
There are positives for everything. Even "getting to" fold the laundry
means that you're being a good steward of the clothing items you
own and caring for those who wear and use them. Notice how caring
and being a good steward has a different feeling than the heavy burden of "have to."

DOUBT: This is not actually about a word you use, but rather the
feeling or emotion you unconsciously allow to thwart forward progress. When it comes to achieving goals, even one teensy doubt can
trip you up and cause self-sabotage. It's both something you use and
something used against you.

The best example of the used-against-you type of doubt is the nightly
(or anytime) TV news. Have you noticed that every dire headline in
one way or another plants seeds of doubt? Within the first ten minutes of a news program, you doubt your streets are safe, your political
leaders have brains, and that there are any foods out there that are
toxin-free. For large corporate entities that spend billions on advertis-
ing, doubt is a powerful and intentional tool.

While the opposite—certainty—isn't a solution, consider the possibility that it's okay to have doubts, yet move forward in spite of them.
Or even in tandem with them. Turning doubts into motivation is a
great skill to embrace.

> ## *"The words you speak become the house you live in."*
> —Hafiz

You've now got a firm grasp on how your brain acts as a filter. Your MAPP shapes everything you experience. We've also highlighted your natural tendency toward self-sabotage and negative inner language. The strategic steps outlined in Chapters 2 and 5 continue the process of bringing your awareness to light.

In this next section, we'll tweak what we've already covered about the nonconscious mind for better performance. We'll also discover ways to take advantage of something the brain does naturally and optimize this tendency for faster results.

Changing your mind

When it comes to our health, most of us have at least a general idea of the changes we'd like to make. If I were to ask, you could probably come up with at least three simple nutritional or fitness goals you'd like to achieve such as drinking adequate amounts of water, walking regularly, or getting more veggies into your diet.

Think about it. If you already know what you'd like to achieve but haven't done so yet... what's stopping you? You know the answer. A quick review of subversive self-talk and conflicting beliefs (revealed in prior chapters) shows how they can derail even the greatest of plans. So, how do you move past these hindrances and light a fire under your desire to git 'er done? How do you generate motivation?

This is what I wondered as I wobbled around in my own health journey. When it came to changes that excited me, it was effortless—even painless. I didn't have to plan or conjure up motivation. I just did it. But other goals languished in the murky sea of "someday." I wanted to achieve them, for sure. But the drive to make them happen seemed jammed in neutral. What was going on?

You've probably done this too. You've pushed yourself to follow through with short-term goals. You've efforted and manipulated your emotions to create the drive needed for a limited time. Short bursts of effort can be effective. Self-created willpower is one way to get things done. But it's not a *sustainable* way.

It's likely that you could force your way through a four-week boot camp workout program. For example, I've dragged my way through programs by sheer will. But let's assume we're in this for the long haul. Putting your brainpower to work for you (instead of against you) makes a surprising difference. It makes all the difference between a short-term limited option and a long-term fix.

Why not make it easy on yourself? Enlist the super-accelerated power of your thoughts.

Your top undercover resource

It makes sense to work with your God-given abilities rather than against them. It's logical to work within the natural tendencies of your mind instead of trying to crowbar your way into an artificially manufactured outcome. Let's not work harder than we have to.

Chapter 1 revealed that the conscious mind sets goals, and the nonconscious mind makes them happen. You can tell yourself all day long that you want something better than what you have, but the nonconscious mind needs specificity. What—exactly—do you want? When do you want it? Why do you want it?

Without these details, how does the nonconscious mind know when to spur you into action? And because the nonconscious mind thinks in terms of pictures, feelings, and emotions, how do you "tell" it anything?

Here's a secret that you've probably never heard. There *is* a way to speak directly to the nonconscious mind and give it specific instructions. This should pique your interest, considering that the nonconscious mind is the driving force behind the actions we take.

When it comes to results, I hope you're interested in speed and efficiency. I certainly am. With that in mind, you'll want to pay particular attention to this next bit. The following strategies are the fastest, most effective, and most practical methods to generate limitless motivation. Yes, you can generate motivation.

Let's talk frequencies

This isn't about frequency as in when or how often something happens (although that plays a role later). Right now, I'm referring to the frequencies or electrical currents in our brains. I won't go too deep here. A surface overview is all that's needed to understand this strategy.

There's a link between brain frequencies and how new information is absorbed and modified. This insight can give you a leading edge on how to motivate yourself to take action… and keep that motivation going. Here's just enough background to help you understand what the brain does in these various states of electrical frequency and how they relate to your healing journey.

Our brains cycle through these different frequency states often, and simultaneously, both day and night. Various states can operate at the same time, with one typically being dominant at any given moment.

Here are the primary five brainwave states or brain frequencies. The frequency of each state is measured in cycles per second (Hz). While there is some generalized overlap, the characteristics unique to each are listed below—no need to memorize any of this. A general understanding is all that's needed.

The five brainwave states[40, 41]

   1. **The Beta State** (14-30 Hz)

The Beta state is characterized by our waking consciousness. This is where we experience reason, logic, cognition, and alertness. This is also an excellent state in which to tackle projects or problems as it's a state of full and focused attention.

Beta waves help with logical decision-making. If we tend toward unhelpful thoughts, this state is where negative and persistent self-talk is experienced. There's also the potential for anxiety, fear, and "analysis paralysis" or rumination in the Beta state as well as the nervous system response—fight, flight, or freeze. We spend most of our awake time in this state, and if we're in a critical frame of mind, our negative thoughts can lead to stress, frustration, and worry.

   2. **The Alpha State** (7.5-14 Hz)

The Alpha state is that of deep relaxation. It happens during basic meditation, some soothing fitness activities, and while daydreaming.

---

40   http://www.thetahealing.com/about-thetahealing/thetahealing-theta-state.html
41   http://mentalhealthdaily.com/2014/04/15/5-types-of-brain-waves-frequencies-gamma-beta-alpha-theta-delta/

This is an ideal state to practice and achieve stress reduction meditations and behaviors. You may also know it as the Flow state or Getting into Flow. Flow can move rapidly in and out of states; from Beta into Alpha with dips into Theta.[42]

Professional athletes, musicians, artists, writers, and productive or creative people are said to work at peak performance in this brainwave state. This state is linked to creativity, a deep sense of compassion, spiritual insight, increased awareness, the ability to forgive, and a profound sense of love.

The Alpha state is also sometimes called *the learning state* as it's a favorable brain frequency to incorporate affirmations, visualizations, mantras, memory exercises, or other helpful learning practices. It's also great for problem-solving. This is the state of mind between the awakened state and the nonconscious state of mind. It's where the voice of our inner intuition is most accessible.

3. **The Theta State** (4-7.5 Hz)

This is the state entered in deeper meditation and light dozing, including the healing REM (Rapid Eye Movement) dream state of sleep. Interestingly, the Theta state occurs twice a day naturally. It happens in the brief moments of drifting into sleep at night and upon awakening in the morning. These moments are part of our nonconscious experience. Other than a handful of intentional practices, we can only enter the Theta brainwave state through deliberate practices such as meditation.

Theta is often referred to as a *therapeutic state* as it's where we experience vivid images (great for meditations and visualizations), creativity and new ideas, and discover our sense of intuition and insights.

---

42   https://www.psychologytoday.com/blog/the-playing-field/201402/flow-states-and-creativity

> *"Theta brainwave states have been used in meditation for centuries. Research has proven thirty minutes a day of Theta meditation can dramatically improve a person's overall health and well-being."*[43]

In the period of transition from Alpha to Theta, the brain is in a perfect state for adaptation to new learning. We're aware of our surroundings, yet we're deeply relaxed and open to new thoughts, ideas, insights, and understandings. This broadened awareness state is perfect for deepening connections to intuition. It helps you to feel a greater sense of belonging in this world and a strengthened connection to relationships that align with your spiritual beliefs.

4. **The Delta State** (0.5-4 Hz)

In deep, dreamless sleep, our brainwaves are the slowest. This is the Delta brainwave state. This is an unconscious state, and in it, we're detached from our physical and conscious awareness.

Significant deep healing and physical regeneration happen in the Delta brainwave state. This is one of the main reasons that deep sleep, especially in adequate amounts, is so transformative to physical healing.

5. **The Gamma State** (above 40 Hz)

The Gamma state is a lesser understood brainwave state and is known for high frequencies and spontaneous insights and information processing. This state creates an environment for the absolute highest experience of focus. Some call this The Zone state of intense, single-minded focus in peak exercise.

---

43   http://www.zenlama.com/understanding-the-benefits-of-brainwaves-and-binaural-beats-the-ultimate-quick-start-guide/

I've included these details to clarify how the brain (the mind) process-es information in various states. This understanding points out the differences between states of relaxation and intense focus.

This chapter also reveals what states allow us to feel happy. Notice the "allow" part. Happiness is experienced. It's not manufactured and artificially applied. Happiness is a feeling or emotion that happens little by little as roadblocks, such as negative self-talk are addressed. (There's more to discover about happiness in the chapters ahead—especially Chapter 15.)

In previous chapters, we've established the value of shifting our thought patterns and moving past limited thinking. Now that we un-derstand the characteristics of our various brainwave frequencies, we can see how these states align with desired behaviors and actions.

> *Understanding the need to change negative thought patterns is one thing. Applying that knowledge and putting your foot on the gas is another.*

■ Chapter 6 – Head Work

1. If you haven't already, go back and write down your goals. Do it now. Fewer than 3% of Americans have written goals.[44] So, beat the odds to proven success and get ahead of the curve. The exact steps to reach your goals will change. They're flexi-ble and fluid but the intent of the goals themselves stays firm.

---

44   https://www.briantracy.com/blog/personal-success/success-through-goal-setting-part-1-of-3/

2. What about the Words to Stumble By mentioned in this chapter? Are you surprised at how often you use them? What about how you use them? Notice how routine (and perhaps habitual) it is to use negative words in relation to your health. Here's an exaggerated example. "I try to get better, but nothing works. I shouldn't eat junk food, but my bad knees hurt no matter what I eat." Notice how many negative references this illustrates? From it, you can hear the sense of helplessness and hopelessness this person feels. From this defeated state, she or he would be unlikely to come up with positive solutions or motivation to change. Our thoughts create the state in which we live. How will you choose to create a different state for yourself? How will you choose to create an environment that allows more happiness?

3. When it comes to brainwave states, can you think of activities or behaviors that help you get into the Alpha state? What about the Theta state? Brainstorm a few ways to reach these ideal states of relaxation.

The next chapter is all about stepping on the gas. In particular, I know you'll love the SET Switch Motivation method that can send you from stuck to soaring.

Motivation Mastery: Potholes & Bridges

Here's a perplexing scenario. I once heard a workshop attendee tell the instructor, "Okay, I get what you're saying about the power of my thoughts. From now on, I'll just think positive."

Fortunately, no one laughed.

At first blush, it's reasonable to believe we can simply change the focus of our thoughts as if we can dial in something different. However, it doesn't work that way.

This workshop attendee didn't understand the strength of repeated patterns and the exponential effects of flowing emotions. The following illustrates this frustrating phenomenon further.

The spotlight of the mind illustration

Imagine that you've moved into a tiny house. It's just three small rooms and a cramped attic. You've shoved everything you can into the attic to gain a bit of perspective. In the main room of the house, you plan to put up shelves to organize and highlight your books and favorite objet d'art.

Here's the problem. When you moved, the vertical rails of your shelves were in the way. So, the first thing you did was stuff them in the attic. The horizontal shelves now lean up against the walls of the main room, adding to the mayhem.

This jumbled mess stares you in the face daily.

You feel overwhelmed every time you see the disarray. Shame and embarrassment seep in. You're aware of what needs to be done. You need to dig through the attic and haul the needed parts downstairs. But six long months later, you're still living in a disaster zone.

Why?

Your intentions are good. But here's an example of what can happen when you try to remedy the problem. With flashlight in hand, you navigate your windowless attic. You focus the light to the left where you remember stowing the rails. But a moment later, the beam swerves to the right highlighting boxes, furniture, and other distractions. You suddenly spot the handlebars of an elliptical machine you never used. Instantly, you feel guilty about your botched fitness plans. Then you think of the money wasted on that and more. You notice a box labeled "workout clothes" and feel even worse. Washed in waves of regret, you forget the rails, ignore the boxes, and head back down the stairs in defeat.

The main room's mess still stares you in the face but feeling numb; you turn a blind eye. Your motivation to fix your living room is lost, and a trip to the kitchen sounds like a good idea. You're strangely hungry, even though you just ate dinner.

Now, think of this scenario on repeat (it probably doesn't take much imagination). This sort of thing happens to us all.

> ## *This is exactly how your nonconscious mind works.*

Your mind is like the attic and your MAPP is the focused flashlight beam. Even when you plan to focus on one thing, the light (your focus) instead shifts to another. It's easily distracted and pulled off course by familiar patterns of thought.

One of the primary objectives of the nonconscious mind (revisit Chapter 2 as necessary) is to keep us safe. Keeping the status quo *feels* safe. That means if you want to change to a new behavior or create a new habit, the nonconscious mind will likely step in with ammunition to derail, distract, or even stop you.

When was the last time you started a new exercise program or planned a new way of eating? You may have had the best intentions, but something probably got in the way. You want to fit into your favorite jeans, but the picture you see most in your mind's eye is the unflattering reflection of yourself in a fitting room mirror. Your focus is on what you don't want, rather than on what you do.

The **object** of your focus makes *all* the difference. Repetition seals the deal.

As illustrated here, we may intend to shine our spotlight on what we want, but our focus is a jumpy little thing. It zeros in on our desire for a nanosecond before flitting off to something else. Something negative and possibly soul-crushing. All in an attempt to keep us from taking action.

This is your pattern.

How do I know? It's my pattern, too. Not to mention, it's the pattern of every client I've ever worked with, every friend I've listened to, and every stranger who's shared bits and pieces of their life with me.

What was the last unmet goal you assigned yourself? I'm sure you had every intention of seeing it come to fruition. You had it all planned— strategies in place. With an iron will, you began.

How long you trudged forward varied.

Fortunately, trudging is optional. From here on, you can choose your pace.

Catch the brain wave advantage

Previously, we discussed powering our way through a project or program. We can chant, "I think I can, I think I can" all day long, but creating that elusive motivational spark is a different matter.

Some say that affirmations are the answer. Or perhaps mantras, afformations®[45] (a compelling twist on affirmations), or visualizations provide the fast track toward motivation. In actuality, all of these work. Repetition of positive phrases can boost motivation, and I believe wholeheartedly in their benefits. But they aren't the whole answer.

---

45   https://afformations.com/tas

These methods alone provide inconsistent and limited results. To accelerate the reliability of positive outcomes, add the following SET Switch Motivation to any of the practices listed above. This method adds a booster rocket to your successful launch.

■ SET Switch Motivation

1. **S**tir it up
2. **E**nlist
3. **T**rack

Integrate these juicy steps to any positivity practice, including those mentioned previously (mantras, affirmations, etc.). These added steps amplify your ability and motivation to achieve your goals.

They work *with* your brain to speak its language.

Applying these steps allows your nonconscious mind to see, hear, feel, and understand—with specificity—what it is that you want. This spurs the state of mind that's proven to create success.

Here's an example of how to apply the SET Switch Motivation to a mantra. This simple one is a good place to begin: *I feel stronger and healthier every day.*

Practicing SET Switch Motivation

Step 1: STIR IT UP – Enhance your mantra by making it as vibrant, lively, and energetic as possible. *Stir up* an exciting mental image by adding in vivid descriptions of how a healthy body feels to you, how words of praise and acknowledgment may sound from others, how you'll look at your healthy reflection in a mirror with satisfaction, how healthy foods taste, etc.

Employ anticipatory thinking.

Anticipate and expect your success. Assume things will fall into place and be sure to enlist all of your senses. Make this image as vibrant and rich as possible by amplifying colors, sounds, and especially your emotions. (Vision boards can help stir powerful sensations and feelings.) Feel a sense of gratitude, thankfulness, and appreciation for reaching your goals—as if they've already arrived.

Step 2: ENLIST – For added results, share your healthy mantra (and your goals) with a supportive family member, friend, or health coach. Enlisting an accountability partner makes you answerable to someone besides yourself. It also provides safe and encouraging support and feedback. It's up to you.

Step 3: TRACK – Tracking your success can be as uncomplicated as marking your progress on a calendar, journal, or chart you've created. Jot down each time you complete this practice. Note anything else of importance. Pay attention to changes, progress, and benefits. Repetition and rewards are a vital part of the process—pat yourself on the back for a job well done. Even simple tally marks on paper can help prod motivation and feel rewarding. It's human nature to want to avoid breaking a chain of consistency.

TIP: *This practice can be done at any time of the day. But for greater impact— especially with the visualization process—begin and end your day this way. First thing in the morning and last thing each evening is a prime time to employ the nonconscious mind to work in your favor. This is an "open-minded" time where the critical mind offers the least resistance.*

Combine these strategies with your favorite positivity methods. (You'll find a list of seven dozen Build-a-Better-Brain practices in Chapter

16.) Adding SET Switch Motivation to a consistent positivity practice is like adding jet fuel to your go-cart. It'll kick things into gear in ways you can't yet imagine. The stimulating emotion of desire, a good support system, and monitoring of both your progress and results are proven qualities of a successful plan. Practice them daily.

Avoid progress speed bumps by planning for them in advance. One big bump can come from unfair expectations. Recognize that there's a delay between course corrections and actual outcomes. Be patient. Plan to stick with your new practices for as long as they take. Give your body time to adjust, adapt, and heal.

Another crucial speed bump to consider is the plateau. There's an assumption that nothing is going on during a plateau. Not true! When we've stalled on our forward-moving agenda (whether with weight loss, job-seeking, symptom improvement, etc.) there's usually a GOOD reason. As long as it's not a lack of follow-through, be patient with yourself. Both your body and mind need time to adapt and blossom. New ideas and new programs create an opportunity for change. And change takes time. Don't short-circuit your progress by giving up during a plateau. As long as you're taking positive steps (no matter how small), keep on going.

Sticking to a healthy weight loss plan, for example, is inherently unpredictable. Some lose weight right away, while others may not lose any at all for the first few months. Weight may then drop consistently for a while only to plateau. Again, just stick with it. As long as you're moving in a healthy direction, keep going and remind yourself that your body is making important adjustments even while the surface indicators (i.e., numbers on a scale) may seem stuck.

The cat's out of the bag

Do any of these steps sound like you've heard them before? If you're familiar with *The Secret*, this may sound like principles from what's known as the law of attraction.

Here's my shocking confession. I've neither read the book nor seen the movie.

For a self-help devotee that's quite unusual. While I don't disagree with the law of attraction (that would be analogous to disagreeing with gravity), I'm a proponent of something much greater. I completely agree that what you focus on with energy and enthusiasm is what you attract. And I understand the resonance of our intentions.

But this narrow focus reflects just a fraction of the whole story.

Most "run of the mill" law of attraction programs are based on conscious activities and actions. They don't (fully) address the power and capacity of our nonconscious thoughts. And an even bigger omission is opening ourselves up to what God has planned for us. As creative and capable humans, we're masterfully designed. Our potential on this earth is for so much more than we're experiencing right now. Our personal limitations get in the way.

As a logical and pragmatic person, I gravitate toward practices that work in tandem with God-given tendencies. Meaning I'd rather work *with* the flow than against it. From that perspective, if we lack motivation and the nonconscious mind generates motivation, why not begin there?

Ignoring the role the nonconscious mind plays in motivation is like wishing for warmth from an unplugged space heater.

This is partially why I felt drawn toward the linguistic discipline of NLP long before I'd heard of *The Secret*. I read my first NLP book in 2002 and was intrigued right away. I knew that getting my success psychology into alignment took more than conscious practices.

From there, I read more books, attended seminars and workshops, and have taken hundreds of hours of classroom training. I'm interested in all things related to the mind, brain health, neuroscience, behavioral psychology, success philosophies, and more. I not only want to see my clients heal through physical means (nutrition and fitness); I want to see them embrace the healthy habits that make their success a lifelong inevitability.

So far, everything covered in this book about motivation has focused on our conscious intentions. Because we know that this approach leaves about 90% or more of the mind's potential untapped, it's time to step it up. It's time to activate the nonconscious mind.

Motivation takes a quantum leap

Get ready to be surprised.

Do you know what occurs when the conscious and nonconscious minds are aligned? To launch your capacity to succeed into the stratosphere, bring your conscious goals, and nonconscious resources together. Light the fuse and stand back.

Tap into this amazing alignment by accessing the Theta (therapeutic) brainwave state. This is where renewable sources of motivation are generated.

A quick Theta state summary:

- Allows deep relaxation of both mind and body
- Boosts the immune system
- Fosters a heightened sense of creativity
- Cultivates a sharpened sense of problem-solving
- Is the most commonly accessed state for peak performance
- Is changeable, growable, adaptable, and malleable

■ Hop over the gate into the Theta state

It would be great to snap our fingers and instantly switch from a conscious brainwave state (Beta) to nonconscious brainwave states (such as Alpha or Theta). While shifting from one to the other takes an approach different from a finger snap, the following intentional practices can help. I call them gateway practices.

- Meditation (both active and passive)
- Some particular body movement and fitness activities
- Hypnosis
- Deep meditative prayer
- Moving meditations such as yoga, tai chi, qigong
- Guided imagery recordings
- Brain entrainment recordings

Even repetitive motion and creative activities can be soothing enough to allow the conscious mind to slip into the very helpful Alpha state. These include gentle, calming, artistic, or handicraft activities such as:

- Knitting
- Crocheting
- Hand sewing/quilting
- Woodworking
- Sculpting
- Painting
- Coloring/drawing
- Soothing physical activities such as getting a massage, taking a shower, relaxing in a water jet tub, etc.

Surprised?

Many of these practices are familiar, easy, and no-brainers. Literally. They take no thought which is exactly what we're looking for. You're probably doing some of them already and had no idea of the brain-wave benefits.

Now that you know, which ones will you implement today?

The sequence of success

Accessing the most efficient path for your brain's function is your key to finding renewable motivation. Did you get that part? Your motivation can become a renewable resource. It's not a nebulous intangible thing that only materializes when the stars align. Rather, it's a predictable, replicable result of applying the principles described in this book.

Once your positive practices are in place (amplified by SET Switch Motivation), then add the final component. Apply your favorite gateway practice creating a focused partnership of the conscious and nonconscious mind.

Here's how.

If you're fond of affirmations or afformations®, consider repeating them as you walk, meditate, or while enjoying a mindless craft such as coloring or doodling. Multiply the benefits of your efforts. Once you've strategically put these practices into place, your desired results will sharpen into focus.

> ### *A clear and well-defined mental picture generates clear and well-defined actions.*

Get creative and adopt your own success routines. Try several on for size and see what suits you best. While there are often shortcuts to most practices, give them a good rehearsal first. Let your brain wander and adapt. As you ease into these practices, you'll naturally gravitate towards the ones that work best for you.

Don't forget your unfair advantage. Unlike others around you, you're reading this book. In these pages, you're given a well-worn path to follow made smooth by my hard-earned footsteps. I promise to point out peak efficiency and effectiveness signposts along the way.

You may also wish to work one-on-one with a specialized practitioner who can help customize your routines. Whether you contact me or find a practitioner on your own, this single step can boost your efforts in ways you cannot imagine at this time. Working with someone else can speed up the process of crystallizing your plans.

■ Chapter 7 – Head Work

1. What self-sabotaging behaviors came to mind when you read the Spotlight of the Mind Illustration? Did you recognize the gap between something you planned to do and what actually happened? Use this evidence for your benefit. Go back and review your goals listed in Chapter 6. View them from your new understanding of how self-sabotage ensues. Brainstorm ways to overcome or avoid this limiting pattern.

2. Where will you apply SET Switch Motivation first? Write out the steps and review them as you make this method a daily practice.

3. What gateway activities appeal to you most? Consider adding a few to your relaxation practices and experiment. Discover which ones are most effective for you. Of course, feel free to add your own. You're the best judge of what relaxes, soothes, inspires, and invigorates your soul.

You probably say the word "stress" every day. Whether you're referring to experiences or feelings, stress is everywhere.

Many people feel that they just have to live with it. I share a different viewpoint in this next chapter… and it's a good thing. Good for both brain and body.

CHAPTER 8

Stress: My Story & the AWOL Factor

Taking the broad topic of stress and breaking it down into bite-sized chunks is eye-opening. Through my healing process shared in this chapter, you get to tag along and see how specific discoveries about stress changed the trajectory of my journey (and potentially yours too).

Hidden symptoms provoked by stress

Stress is a big deal. A very big deal. It negatively affects every aspect of our lives, from emotional wellness to physical health. There's hidden collateral damage to think about too. Stress clouds our perceptions and abilities to focus, adapt to change, and recognize opportunities.

I've talked about my healing story for years now. I've detailed it in my book *FibroWHYalgia*, magazines, my blog and website Rebuilding-Wellness.com, and in various interviews on TV, radio, and in print. Stress played a significant role in my chronic health symptoms, but a full understanding of *why* didn't come along until much later. My nascent beliefs about healing took time and experimentation to sprout.

■ My personal path to rebuilding wellness

Although I had no idea at the time, my healing journey taught me fundamental lessons, that I'll use the rest of my life. In my exhaustive search for a diagnosis, I pursued every doctor and every traditional medical protocol I could find. At my core, I'm a natural-born rule follower. I did what I was told. I waited and waited. I'm still a rule follower at heart, but back then I discovered something shocking.

My tendency to wait for permission to act got me nowhere. I had to begin taking action on my own, which at first, felt wrong. My beliefs about waiting and about taking action conflicted. It sounds silly, but it's a much more complex matter. I learned that these beliefs were about my identity. About who I believed myself to be.

Moments of conflict provide an excellent opportunity for growth. I call them pivot points. At a memorable doctor's appointment, I saw (with new clarity) that I was getting nowhere. After years of visits and dozens of prescriptions, I was shocked to discover that my doctor didn't actually know the answers to my questions. I realized that I was in charge. My unique collection of symptoms were mine alone, and it was clearly up to me to suss it out.

That discovery created a powerful identity shift. From then on, I became someone who tenaciously sought out truths about healing. I uncovered untruths about what I'd been told. I took action and did whatever I needed to make my transformative health goals a reality.

> ### *Identities (and our beliefs about them) can be either limiting or liberating.*

Identities, by the way, are formed at the nonconscious level. It's not as if I consciously recognized the shift and said, "I'm now an action taker rather than a bench warmer." I simply moved forward propelled by a new (unrecognized) inner drive that urged me on.

That's how our identities and beliefs work. They provide kindling (emotions and feelings) that start the fire within us. Yes, they're that powerful.

Once I'd fought my way through the medical system to confirm my diagnosis, I knew I had to put up my dukes and find solutions. My rheumatologist said to my face, "It doesn't matter what you eat." But my gut instinct said otherwise. I wish I'd known Dr. Sara Gottfried then.

> ### *"The food you eat can be either the safest most powerful form of medicine or the slowest form of poison."*
> —Dr. Sara Gottfried, *The Hormone Reset Diet*

Later, my research confirmed this to be true. I dove in head-first. I incorporated healthy, whole, nutrient-dense, and fiber-rich foods into my daily meals. Yes, real *nutrition!* As a mealtime Guinea pig, I experimented with specific macronutrient and micronutrient ratios looking for balance. I found nutrients that made a significant difference to my health—both in whole food and in high-quality supplement form.

From my kitchen escapades, I learned what foods strengthened my immune system and what ones weakened it. I removed processed, artificial, and chemically-manufactured foods, replacing them with fresh, living, whole, nutritious foods. I created my own low-inflammatory food diet long before I'd ever heard of such a thing.

> ### *All I knew then was that real foods rewarded me with more energy, clearer thinking, less pain, and better digestion.*

After nailing down a few mealtime basics, I tiptoed into the exercise arena. To put it simply, I just plain felt like moving my body. I was starting to feel better, and a low-key body movement activity felt like a natural next step. I bought a cheap-o piece of gym equipment (in the clearance department at Target for $29) and created my own routine. I did this at home after dinner, when the kids settled in for the evening. Because it was low intensity, it didn't interfere with my sleep. (At least it didn't make my then awful sleep patterns any worse.)

My body responded with more energy and strength. I felt a foreign (but welcomed) interest in more physical activities. I checked out DVDs (and VHS tapes!) at my library, teaching me new ways to stretch, move, and challenge myself. Later, I added T-Tapp[46] routines and joined a local fitness center to amp up my regimen. I revised my schedule to hit the gym after work. The uniquely tailored weight-lifting and cardio machine workout routine I discovered was perfect for my needs. Within a short six months, there was a significant noticeable shift in my health. I felt great, slept well, and had the energy I

---

46   https://www.t-tapp.com/

needed to get through my day. I developed a strengthened core in many powerful ways.

Later, I learned that body movement stimulates cognitive clarity. Getting the body moving clears away the mental fog that prevents us from seeing solutions or options.

Healthy nutrition fortified my immune system allowing me to heal from the inside out. But nutrition alone can't fix all ills. Exercise worked its magic in similar yet different ways. I had no idea that, through exercise, I was detoxifying my body, building core strength, elevating my mood, practicing the skill of pacing, inviting mental clarity, and creating positivity for the future. I didn't know that I was creating a kick-butt immune system. I merely enjoyed the friendships made at the gym and continued to show up.

It really was that simple.

Within a year, I felt healthier than I had in my entire adult life. ALL of my symptoms fell away. I thought I'd cracked the complicated fibromyalgia health code. Could it be as practical as diet and exercise? My body continued to improve as my strength increased. I felt better and better every day.

Until….

■ The only consistency you can count on is inconsistency

Three years later, my daily routines changed before, during, and after an epic family trip abroad. After that trip, symptoms didn't creep up on me; they blindfolded me and took me hostage. My back and neck felt trapped in a vice grip of pain. Insomnia returned and compounded the fatigue that had taken root. Doubt, anger, frustration, and an oppressive sense of pointlessness followed me like a gray cloud.

I'd worked so hard to get well! If what I'd done didn't stick, then what was it all about? Were my time and effort all for nothing?

Pain has a way of channeling your thoughts. You can either choose to focus on the futility of it all (and on the pain itself) or on the way out— even if you don't know the way. I did a lot of soul-searching. I had to get honest with myself. What catapulted me backward, and what was my mental state at the time? Uncovering the raw and ugly emotions beneath the surface wasn't fun. It's human nature to tamp down and ignore what we don't want to see. But once I took a glimpse, I got the surprise of my life.

I always thought I was an even-keeled, centered, compassionate, and kind person. What I recognized is that while I may have been any or all of those things at times to others, I wasn't *any* of those things to myself. My inner voice back then was merciless. Relentlessly so. I held myself responsible for everything that went wrong in life and for everything and everyone around me. I had to get to the core of why I felt compelled to be the peace-keeper of the world. At first, my only success was increased frustration.

At that point, I knew only one thing. I'd enjoyed several years of a symptom-free life, and I wanted it back! I had a direct comparison to what it was like, and I wasn't willing to settle. I had to get a handle on the stress in my life.

The family trip I mentioned was stressful. Super-stressful. While it had a good measure of fun, it also had a lot of anxiety, pressure, and drama. I recognized that I was a worrier at heart. I worried about everything and everyone. I had to face my anxieties head-on and admit the toll this pattern took on my body.

So, the dynamic duo of diet and exercise can't fix everything? Darn. It turns out they're two slices of the wellness pie, but not the whole pie. The third component—what I refer to as Emotional Wellness— is the pan, the crust, and even most of the filling that makes up the complete pie. I could no longer ignore what my body had to say.

> ***Stress has a far greater impact on health than food and fitness alone can ever fix.***

Stress management: the absentee puzzle piece

Back to the drawing board. More study and more research. Of course, I jumped back into my healthy eating and gym routine. But something was missing. My symptoms diminished rather quickly, but they didn't completely go away. I researched studies on the effects of stress on health-challenged individuals. I came up empty-handed.

I branched out to other stress-related topics and found management protocols. I tried most that didn't strike me as either too far-fetched or too woo woo. I boosted my prayer life (always a good thing), tried out meditation practices, and became serious about faithfully and consistently using the free tool, Emotional Freedom Technique[47] (EFT) also called Tapping. I'd been Tapping on and off for many years, but it was time to assess its practicality and put it to the test.

Guess where I met the most success?

Prayer is about talking and expressing yourself while meditation is about listening to that still, small voice for inner guidance. I deepened my prayer life and crashed and burned when it came to meditation.

---

47   http://eft.mercola.com/

Of course, that's an oversimplification, but structured, solitary meditation and I didn't mesh. Prayer is a two-way street. I talk and listen.
Prayer is always my primary go-to solution for stress.

Meditation is commonly thought of as sitting still, clearing your mind,
and listening. With that expectation, a successful meditation practice
can be a tough nut to crack for busy people. How could I settle my
overactive monkey mind?

I'm grateful to share that my understanding of how meditation works
was just plain wrong. I learned that I don't have to clear my mind or
my busy schedule to feel successful. There are multiple ways to meditate. Saying "om" in a pretzel lotus position isn't for everyone. It's
taken some perseverance, but I've found moving meditations, guided
imagery, and passive meditations to be more my style.

When it comes to "on the spot" stress management, my favorite tool
for fast relief is Tapping.[48] If you've read my book *FibroWHYalgia*,
you've read about my experiences with it and the benefits I've received. I use it almost daily and have practiced it with clients and
others for more than 18 years. I've added other stress management
protocols to my arsenal of healthy practices, yet Tapping[49] is one I
return to again and again. There are now a lot of exciting research
studies available on Tapping that weren't available even ten years
ago. Tapping is shown to help lower cortisol levels (often referred to
as the body's stress hormone)[50] and is also proven to lower the negative effects of the stress response on the amygdala area of the brain.[51]

Of course, effort is never wasted on eating well and moving the body
in healthy ways. In fact, after my relapse, I discovered something
quite powerful. I saw a direct correlation between my overall health

---

48   https://www.prohealth.com/library/practical-guide-to-eft-tapping-for-fibromyalgia-35545
49   https://rebuildingwellness.com/tapping-fibromyalgia/
50   http://www.thetappingsolution.com/science-and-research/
51   http://www.eftuniverse.com/index.php?option=com_content&view=article&id=11893

and the rate at which I recovered. Because of the core strength I'd built with healthy foods and body movement, my rebound to better health didn't take all that long. Here's a winning equation.

Strong core health = faster recovery

I'm glad to prove myself wrong when it helps to propel me forward. I was petrified about my relapse being permanent. Fortunately, it was a temporary freak-out as it just wasn't true. I now view it as a significant flare, and I had to find a way out. Once I added stress management practices (including thinking differently) to my restored nutrition and fitness regimen, my health bounced back. Emotional wellness protocols allowed my stress levels to stabilize, then diminish.

I advocate what I call **The Restoration Trio**.[52] I've personally experienced root-level healing benefits from—

1. Healthy Nutrition
2. Healthy Body Movement
3. Emotional Wellness

True healing requires a combination of all three. Each is mandatory, and none can be slighted. The body needs nutrition, body movement, and emotional wellness practices to serve as catalysts to balance and wholeness.

(For a handy downloadable one-page guide detailing the healing benefits of the Restoration Trio, go to https://RebuildingWellness.com/trio.)

Each of these categories is an umbrella term that covers a lot of ground. Healthy nutrition may refer to dietary changes such as add-

---

52   https://rebuildingwellness.com/fibromyalgia-energy-balance/

ing nutrient-dense foods and removing inflammatory foods. It can also include meal planning, cooking skills, short-term detoxes, and using high-quality supplements.

The healthy body movement category may include moving in ways that stretch, tone, and support the structure of the body. Inactivity is a leading cause of health risks such as heart disease, cancer, and diabetes.[53] Moving the body in healthy ways can also cover range of motion and proper posture mechanics. Understanding your unique physical endurance levels and limitations is key.

The emotional wellness component is the largest umbrella of all. It's a broad category that includes emotional intelligence, accountability, self-talk, fatigue and energy, anxiety-reducing practices, relationships, meditative protocols, restorative sleep, and much more.

Weave them all together to produce the strongest treatment possible for any health challenge. Benefits may include improvements in sleep quality, digestion, oral health, anxiety levels, range of motion, body and organ toxicity, mood stability, a greater sense of well-being, balance, and mental clarity.

Want that and more?

First, here are a few tips on what may be holding you back.

A quick bit about epigenetics

Even many years after my healing transformation took place, I continued to research a topic that piqued my interest more than a decade ago—*epigenetics*. While this isn't the place for a comprehensive look

---

53   https://www.reuters.com/article/us-health-fitness/a-quarter-of-adults-are-too-inactive-putting-health-at-risk-idUSKCN1LK2RR

into this fascinating subject, it's vital to share the exciting benefits it has to offer.

When the human genome project was completed in 2003, scientists were left with far more questions than answers. They expected to find a complete genetic blueprint to the human body. Instead, they learned that rather than a basic blueprint, the body is created in a way that's constantly changing, evolving, and adapting to its surroundings.

> ***There's no static blueprint***
> ***to the human body.***

In this ever-changing environment, external factors have a much greater influence over our health than ever imagined. This external influence—called the epigenome (meaning above the genes)—has a greater impact on health than anything you're born with.

Less than 10% (some research shows less than 2%) of human disease is a result of genetic destiny. Therefore, a full 95% (or more) of chronic disease manifestation comes from epigenetic factors.[54]

Epigenetic factors tell our genes to turn on and off. They tell our bodies how to function. Therefore, they influence not only the creation of disease (and syndromes), but they also provide the solutions to healing or reversing them.

What are these critical components?

Epigenetic factors include:

---

54   https://thehealthsciencesacademy.org/about/ (Genetic Adaptations to Nutrition textbook, 2015)

- Everything you eat, drink, breathe, and touch
- How you feel (emotions)
- What you do (behaviors)
- What you think and believe (patterns of thought)
- How you live (your environment)
- What you perceive (either real or imagined)

Taking this into consideration helps to make sense of how we become sick. Once this understanding is in place, it's a matter of taking authentic action on cleaning up our external factors. What we put in and on our body matters. Our thoughts and mental patterns matter. Our connections matter. And, what we believe matters.

The key takeaway here is that the role that genetics plays in our health outcomes has been oversold in the past. My favorite medical researcher (and TV show host of *Know the Cause*) Doug Kaufmann reports, *"We used to tell women that if their mother or grandmother had breast cancer, their risk of breast cancer was very high. That isn't true because we now know that DNA plays a role in only 5-10% of breast cancers."*[55]

Do you see how exciting this is?

We hold our health potential in our own hands! We have control over what we eat, drink, think, and do. We govern much more authority over our future than previously believed. The bold statement, *"Your DNA is not your destiny"* was splashed across the cover of TIME magazine as far back as 2010 and explained in detail by Dr. Joseph Mercola.[56]

Next up, we'll tackle the most pervasive influence on our overall health.

---

55   http://www.knowthecause.com/index.php/doug-s-blog/4836-the-danger-lies-in-observing-the-effect-and-believing-it-is-the-cause
56   https://articles.mercola.com/sites/articles/archive/2010/01/23/why-your-dna-isnt-your-destiny.aspx

The penalty box of stress

Stress doesn't have one specific cause and one specific solution. If it did, we'd fix it and be done. Stress, like yeast, feeds on its surroundings and multiplies upon itself. Stress magnifies conflicts or problems in any area of life, including business, personal, financial, and relationship circumstances. Chronic stress leads to brain challenges that trickle down to the physical body.

Increased stress begets increased symptoms. Stress math is pretty simple:

More Stress = More Pain

Like mosquitoes to malaria, stress is intrinsically linked to chronic health challenges. Pain, fatigue, cognitive impairments, and intestinal challenges all reflect the stress levels you're currently experiencing. Under chronic stress, the digestive system fluctuates between near dormancy (constipated or sluggish) and wildly overactive (I'll leave the details to your imagination).

Under stress, the body's muscles seize up in pain while the brain falls into the trap of looping, repetitive, unfocused, and non-productive negative thoughts.

Familiar, right?

But what if you feel your stressful circumstances have no remedy? For example, you may find your time stretched thin when caring for the special needs of a loved one. Or perhaps you feel the relentless weight of financial pressures. Stressful circumstances will always peak and wane. Does this mean we have to sit down, shut up, and accept the symptoms that follow? I'm here to tell ya, that's a no.

My intention for this book is to mirror back to you the fallacy of that sort of thinking. Resignation is never the first step in any healing journey.

I want to encourage you to read this book as an *action* guide. I want you to take action **now**. Learn to deal with stress in healthy ways using the tools outlined in the remaining chapters. I hope you feel inspired to put your newfound knowledge into practice and find solutions.

Stress management isn't optional.

Rather than balance, you may feel that you're in a state of imbalance or "dis-ease" (literally meaning a lack of ease). Fluctuating between feeling stressed out, and a temporary calm is common. But that doesn't make it acceptable.

Living in a chronic state of stress has become a global pandemic. The physical impact is systemic. The adrenals, thyroid, immune system, digestive system, brain function, and more are impaired. Mentally, the impact is just as profound. Stress contributes to depression, cognitive dysfunction, anxiety issues, and personality disorders.

While there is a helpful kind of stress—eustress[57]—the focus here is on the chronic type that generates negative results. Eustress is short-termed, spurs you to action, and has positive results. Good stress is a platform for growth.

Good stress is not the type that feeds chronic illness.

---

57   https://rebuildingwellness.com/stress-good/

What fertilizer do you use in your mental garden?

Stress or relaxation. Which is most familiar? If you're not sure, consider the thoughts that flit through your mind as you wait at a traffic light or in line at a store. Are you more likely to think about the argument you had with a significant other or revel in thoughts of delight over your last visit to your masseuse?

No judgment here. It's just a question. In case you're wondering, it's human nature to lean toward the worrisome side of things.

To-do lists, work, finances, relationship issues, and other mental stressors take an emotional toll. You may not consider the impact on the physical body. Food sensitivities, medication side effects, biotoxin exposures, tick bites, heavy metals, injuries, and infections can all contribute to a problem that's at the heart of systemic dysfunction.

■ The aftermath of inflammation

Inflammation is the underlying root cause of nearly all chronic illnesses.[58] The level of inflammation in your digestive tract is a barometer of your overall health status. The more inflammation, the more the likelihood of systemic dysfunction and disease advancement.

Stress burdens the body with compounding symptoms. The cascade effect of stress-induced inflammation is key to this concept. Once the body is impaired by inflammation, pain is just one of the many symptoms to follow.

---

58   http://articles.mercola.com/sites/articles/archive/2013/03/07/inflammation-triggers-disease-symptoms.aspx

The strong bond between stress and inflammation forms links to pain, digestive disorders (including leaky gut and yeast/candida/mycotoxin overgrowth), cognitive dysfunction, and more. Each flows like a catastrophic waterfall from one pool of symptoms to the next.

> ## *Understanding WHY inflammation happens is the key to stopping the progression.*

Reducing inflammation is a topic that could fill a library of books. The study of how to stimulate autophagy[59] (your body's ability to dampen inflammation) is a growing field of research. The basics include removing inflammatory foods, managing stress, and helping the body to detoxify naturally.

Next up? We'll isolate the study of stress and how it specifically affects the physical body. You'll be equally surprised by what it's doing to you as by what you can do about it.

Stress doesn't have to leave you feeling like you're on a nonstop downhill toboggan run. I'll share a few techniques that can stop stress in its tracks.

Before jumping into the next chapter, take a moment to step outside the box. Outside of *your* box, specifically. Consider how you view yourself and your probability to heal. Do you feel you're a victim of stress (and other factors) and that nothing can be done? How do you perceive your healing potential?

View your observations without judgment. No arguments. No denial.

---

59   http://fitness.mercola.com/sites/fitness/archive/2016/03/11/autophagy.aspx?

> ***"You never change things by fighting***
> ***against the existing reality."***
> —Buckminster Fuller

■ Chapter 8 – Head Work

1. Do you relate to my healing story? To what parts? Have you partially recovered from some of your symptoms or eliminated some? Finding the sweet spot of the Restoration Trio can help. What parts of the trio are lacking in your recovery plan? Jot down your discoveries and make changes, if necessary, to your goals listed in Chapter 6.

2. In what ways does stress add to your pain levels? Does it add to other symptoms too? Be specific as you consider this topic. The effects of stress can be obvious and disguised. In which of the following areas do you experience the most stress: health, finances, relationships, career, education, personal development, spiritual development, social life?

3. In what ways do you believe your body is inflamed? Read my article, Symptoms of Systemic Dysfunction,[60] and review the signs of inflammation. (For your convenience, I've included this list as an excerpt in the Appendix.) Which ones relate to you? Investigate a few ideas on what areas of your life need focus as it relates to this problem.

---

60   https://www.prohealth.com/library/do-you-have-these-fibromyalgia-symptoms-of-systemic-dysfunction-37277

Coming up, you'll discover more tidbits and truths regarding stress and how it affects your body. Read it, paying attention to your personal triggers and patterns of behavior.

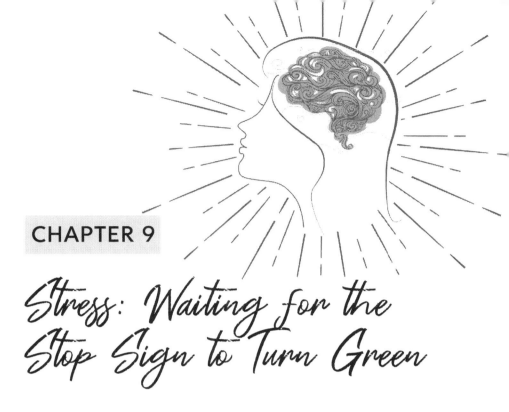

CHAPTER 9

Stress: Waiting for the Stop Sign to Turn Green

Nobody likes stress.

It breeds crazy, mind-spinning thoughts. Thoughts such as, "I'm overwhelmed with everything I need to do, but I'm not getting anything done." Or, unresolved looping thoughts on money, relationships, finances, declining health, and more.

Spinning thoughts create a vortex of worries about what you don't want. Think about that. Stress tells your mind to create a tornado of thoughts and they're nearly all negative.

One sign of being overly stressed is the feeling as if someone hit your brain's pause button. You may stare into space, your thoughts bouncing but not landing on anything in particular. It's a brief, mental blank.

That's a picture of an overwhelmed brain.

Have you ever sat in your car at a stop sign waiting for it to turn green? (Re-read that if it sounds correct to you.) What about pointing a remote at your kids and hitting "mute" because the TV was too loud to hear them? When you find yourself disengaged from the world—even if momentarily—it's time to do something.

There's a vast difference between living in an emotional hurricane and feeling like you've got it together with fair weather in sight. The difference comes from your point of view.

You already know about the advantage of working with the nonconscious mind. So now it's time to focus more on the physical side of things. Stress has an impact on every cell of your body. And the constant overflow of stress must be held in check.

That overflow ends now.

Once you discover what's in this chapter, you'll think differently. You'll notice the physical impact of your thoughts, which will spur changes in how you act. You'll make different choices leading to improved health.

The reality of stress can't be ignored. Your body is at war. Every day, there's a battle between outside stressors and the defenses your body is trying to maintain.

Your body is under attack, and it's no wonder you're exhausted!

Stress: limbic and neocortex short-circuitry

When we're trying to make decisions, stress can cause all sorts of misfires. The limbic system wants instant action, but the neocortex looks ahead to the downstream consequences of the action. When we can't decide (indecision is one symptom of stress) we become engaged in battle with neither side willing to raise the white flag.

Here's a paraphrased definition of **STRESS**: *Stress happens when what's expected of you is greater than your ability or opportunity to deal with it. This leads to an "out of control" experience that feels overwhelming.*

Did you know that stress also impacts our ability to judge time accurately?

Anxiety caused by stress distorts our perception of time[61] so that we may either over or under exaggerate how much time has passed while under stress. Additionally, we lose the ability to plan and organize projects. We feel only the weight of "now." Under stress, we can't conceptualize an orderly to-do list to complete in a step-by-step fashion. Instead, we *feel* the burden or pressure of everything that needs to be done—all at once.

Stress creates a negative tunnel vision. Under stress, options diminish, opportunities are obscured, and hope dwindles. Stress doesn't allow for open-minded, solution-driven thinking. It's not surprising that descriptive phrases such as massive, mountainous, heavy, or a boatload are often used to describe our burdens and responsibilities.

Some of us wear "overwhelm" like a second skin.

---

61   https://pdfs.semanticscholar.org/b32a/616ae26046faaade852eb224790b7e855fe2.pdf

Don't miss this point. When it comes to stress and overwhelm, our bodies *feel* it. The tide of pressure changes from a tiny wave to a tsunami when there's no end in sight. Chronic stress triggers chronic health challenges.

Chronic stress (referred to as Red Mind[62] by Wallace J. Nichols) causes the body to consistently pump out high levels of cortisol. Among other symptoms, this triggers short tempers, fuzzy thinking, an exaggerated startle reflex,[63] and an inability to see the big picture. It also leads to chronic health conditions such as diabetes, unwanted weight gain, heart disease, and cancers.

Stress and your overwhelmed body

Multiple systems perform basic operations of the body. The one that governs our stress response is called the autonomic nervous system (the ANS). It sounds mechanized and robot-like, but the way it's influenced by thoughts and emotions demonstrates a purely human experience.

The two parts of the ANS relative to this discussion are the *sympathetic nervous system* and the *parasympathetic nervous system*.

Here's what happens under stress.

Physically, stress causes increased blood pressure, heart rate, respiratory rate, and decreased digestive function. Added together, that's bad news for anyone trying to heal. These reactions represent the sympathetic nervous system at work, also referred to as the fight, flight, or freeze[64] response.

---

62   http://www.wallacejnichols.org/101/803/current-biology-red-mind-blue-mind.html
63   https://rebuildingwellness.com/startle-reflex-fibromyalgia/
64   https://rebuildingwellness.com/fibro-pain-freeze/

Chronic health challenges stem from staying in this unhealthy state for prolonged periods. This is chronic stress at its worst. In short, we tense up our muscles and hold our breath.

Sound familiar?

The sympathetic nervous system is activated by a perceived crisis. Note this crucial distinction. We need only to *perceive* the situation as a crisis.

In the sympathetic state, the body's responses are to—

> *INCREASE* – heart rate, sweating, muscle strength, pupil di-lation, lung dilation (expansion), constriction of the vascular system, constricted muscles, and adrenal stimulus (secret-ing norepinephrine and epinephrine), and stress hormone* production

> *DECREASE* – digestion, mucosal production (nose and mouth), organ functions of the liver, kidneys, gallbladder, and the reproductive system

It's important to note that hormones are like traffic signals in the complex com-munication system of the body. They tell the body how to process and react. They stimulate the organs to function (or not). They regulate all sorts of tasks that keep us healthy, including triggering our emotions.

The sympathetic nervous system also stimulates piloerection. In-trigued? This means it can make the tiny little hairs on your body stand on end. (This information is probably more interesting than useful.)

If you've had more than a handshake from chronic illness, then you're likely familiar with many of these symptoms. Like a cabinet-rotting water leak under your kitchen sink, consistent exposure to these symptoms erodes the foundation of your health.

Your body may feel like one big bruise.

If you think that putting the brakes on these symptoms is impossible, keep reading. I'll soon share stress-busting protocols that I encourage you to put to the test.

The rescue response

A state of pure relaxation eliminates stress. More to the point, it eliminates the body's negative responses to stress. Relaxation is nature's stress antidote. "Re-lax" literally means to loosen up, again and again. When the body experiences a relaxed state, the parasympathetic nervous system comes to the rescue. It calms the body by lowering blood pressure, heart rate, respiratory rate, and allowing a return to healthy digestion.

> **The parasympathetic nervous system kicks the body's healing process into gear.**

The body has a built-in system designed to restore balance—*homeostasis*. It's the state of "all's well."

The parasympathetic nervous system is your body's way of policing after a riot of stress. It restores calm and establishes order. It induces body functions that clean up after themselves like street sweepers following a parade. Once the floats, marching bands, and sash-wearing beauty queens have gone by, the cleanup crew spiffs up and sets things to right. The parasympathetic system works in this way to restore whole-body balance.

In the parasympathetic state, the body's responses are to—

> *INCREASE* – mucosal production (nasal and oral—returning to normal levels), healthy organ production for liver, bladder, kidneys, stimulate healthy digestion, and healthy hormone production

> *DECREASE* – heart rate, lung stimulus (returning them to normal function), pupil dilation (returning them to normal), constriction of the vascular system

TIP: *A helpful way to remember which nervous system response is the one to restore balance is to think of* parasympathetic *and the word* parachute. *They're both lifesavers!*

The sympathetic and parasympathetic systems are commonly referred to as the stress response and the relaxation (or rest and digest) response. Now that you know how these responses affect the body under stress, you're ready for what's next.

This following nugget of truth completely rocked my world.

■ The power of opposites

You may or may not have noticed, but the stress response and the relaxation response are polar opposites. They're not slightly different from each other; they're opposed. Each response of the autonomic nervous system has an opposite response.

Therefore, the two systems do not function simultaneously.

> ### The body's stress response and relaxation response CANNOT engage at the same time.

Why is this a big deal?

The body cannot fire off and stimulate opposite responses at the same time. Your digestion cannot *both* slow down and speed up. The lining of your nose can't be stimulated by your body's responses to dry out and to be runny at the same time. Your heart rate cannot be both rapid and sluggish.

You already know that you can't feel relaxed when you're stressed out and anxious over life's circumstances. However, have you thought about the converse reaction? Can you feel stressed out at the same time that you're feeling calm, relaxed, and in charge of your own life?

Nope.

I hope you recognize the rosy bud of hope in this premise. Creating a state of relaxation is **the key** to reducing stress. Stress and relaxation are an either/or proposition—not both.

The relaxation response opens the door to a state of healing. It opens the gate, puts down the drawbridge, and hands you the key. In a state of relaxation, the body increases its receptivity to other positive outcomes. Therefore, creating a regular relaxation practice is critical.

> ## *Relaxation provides a permission slip to heal.*

Stress is a normal part of daily life. But a chronically stressed body breeds inflammation and the potential for disease.

As I'm sure you've noticed, the stress response fires off all on its own— whether we want it to or not. Stress is ongoing, so doing nothing is like standing on railroad tracks, closing your eyes, and hoping the train doesn't hit you.

> ## *The stress response isn't optional. But, inviting the relaxation response is.*

Eliciting the relaxation response takes some effort. It doesn't happen automatically. At least, not at first. It takes practice before it becomes second nature.

I learned all of this at the time I was trying to climb out of my significant flare. Coming to grips with the importance of stress management, I took every opportunity to practice new techniques. For example, I signed up for a tai chi class to learn a little bit about body movement and to strengthen my much-needed social connections. But no one was surprised more than I to experience health benefits. I'll never forget my first relaxation response ah-ha moment. I'd been enjoying the tai chi class for several weeks. One day, as I focused on the instructor trying to mimic her pace, I lost myself in the moment. I was watching my hands doing a "float like clouds" move, and I felt strangely at peace. My spinning thoughts paused. My body felt calm, and miracle of miracles, I forgot that I was in pain. All too soon, my "real world" returned. But I'd had a glimpse of what could be.

I wondered if that could happen temporarily? What could make it last?

In short order, I discovered that it doesn't take hours of meditation or other challenging practices. The great thing about getting into a relaxed state is that the benefits multiply the more you put them into practice. Even better? The more you do them; the benefits linger longer. When the rescue response is applied—consistently and daily—the brain's tendency toward the stress response is changed.

Do you see how this puts you in the driver's seat?

> ***"Research out of Harvard has demonstrated that meditation changes the structure of the brain. A consistent meditation practice for 30 minutes daily over the course of 8 weeks results in measurable changes in brain volume in the hippocampus—the area of the brain involved in learning and memory."***
> —Dr. Kristen Willeumier, Neuroscientist

Deep breathing by the numbers

Take hold of the wheel.

When dealing with chronic health challenges—and especially pain—it's typical to hold our breath or consistently take short, shallow breaths. Unfortunately, the actual act of holding our breath triggers more of the stress response.

It's an un-fun cycle. The natural response to stress—holding your breath—*causes* more stress. Taking deep, slow belly breaths gives the body the space it needs to trigger the relaxation response. This allows you to experience mental clarity and renewed energy. Make it a daily prescription. Deep breathing practices can help you feel more centered, relaxed, and resilient to the stressors that life throws your way. Deep breathing practices create the environment for better insight and improved ability to avoid distractions and helps you to become a laser-focused problem solver.

Try these on for size.

Breathing Technique Option 1) This is super simple. Just count ten breaths. Take a deep breath in through your nose, and then breathe out slowly through your mouth. Do this nine more times. Breathing IN activates the sympathetic nervous system (in a good way when it's balanced) and breathing OUT activates the parasympathetic.

If you like, do another set of ten or as many sets as needed to relax. This is a good practice to establish before falling asleep. Besides keeping count, you may wish to visualize and say empowering words as you inhale/exhale such as Peace/Release, Light/Let go, Relax/ Relief, etc. TIP: *Placing one hand on your heart and the other on your stomach helps to intensify relaxation.*

Once you feel centered and balanced doing this basic breathing practice, you may wish to increase the relaxation response by changing the exhalation time as described next.

Breathing Technique Option 2) Experiment with calming breathing techniques where the exhale is even just a few counts longer than the inhale.[65] As an example, try this 4-7-8 exercise.

1. Inhale slowly through the nose while counting to four.
2. Hold your breath for a count of seven.
3. Exhale slowly through the mouth for a count of eight.

Breathing Technique Option 3) There are so many variations to try. As an ancient practice, different cultures suggest different methods. You may choose to inhale for a count of seven, hold your breath for a short bit, then exhale for a count of eleven. Or you may choose alternate nostril breathing. It sounds (and even looks) a little complicated, but it's not. According to Dr. Paula Watkins, this method of breathing activates the parasympathetic nervous system, enhances respiratory strength and endurance, and improves attention and fine motor performance.[66]

Go ahead and experiment.

Caution: If at any time, you feel a little bit dizzy, stop. Permit your breathing to regulate naturally. Then you can decide whether to reduce the frequency of your deep breathing practice or decrease the length of time you do it. Simply focus on noticing your breaths, expanding your abdomen (diaphragmatic breathing), and allowing your body the opportunity to feel the soothing effects.

---

65 http://www.mindbodygreen.com/0-4386/A-Simple-Breathing-Exercise-to-Calm-Your-Mind-Body.html
66 https://www.mindbodygreen.com/0-12936/3-reasons-everyone-should-try-alternate-nostril-breathing.html

There are other benefits too. Deep breathing minimizes the stress hormone, cortisol, and limits its Napoleonic march through your body. It has the ability to stimulate the vagus nerve, thereby reducing inflammation.[67] And, here's a surprise—deep breathing practices positively influence healthy gut bacteria and the immune system. That means, it can improve healthy digestion and fight off colds and flu.[68]

Consider employing a deep breathing practice before meals. Even better, pair it with prayer. This practice can help you optimize your digestion, absorption of nutrients, and satisfaction of your mealtime choices.

Getting a handle on the stress in your life and knowing what to do about it brings you to a crossroads. You're at a place now where you can put these practices into use and find yourself propelled forward in unfathomable ways.

Or you can choose to stay where you are.

■ Chapter 9 – Head Work

1. Review the ways that stress impacts the body. With the polar opposite effect in mind, how do you view your body's reactions? In the past, when you felt stress, what was your go-to behavior? Decide from now on, what your response will be instead.

2. List three practices you can implement to manage your stress levels.

---

67 https://www.iahe.com/docs/articles/6_Ways_to_Instantly_Stimulate_Your_Vagus_Nerve_to_Relieve_Inflammation.pdf
68 https://www.npr.org/2010/12/06/131734718/just-breathe-body-has-a-built-in-stress-reliever

3. Plan to implement a deep breathing strategy into your daily life today. Create a micro habit[69] by linking your new deep breathing practice to something you already do daily such as getting dressed, brushing your teeth, or fastening the seatbelt of your car.

Before making that decision, take a look at this next chapter. Review the ADAPT and GROW technique. Notice how it provides a basic roadmap to navigate through life's problems. Like a map or blueprint, it guides you through challenges that otherwise feel frustrating or confusing. This strategy exposes a no-nonsense path toward solutions. That's why I like to think of it as a success blueprint for life.

69   https://qz.com/877795/how-to-create-new-good-habits-according-to-stanford-psychologist-b-j-fogg/

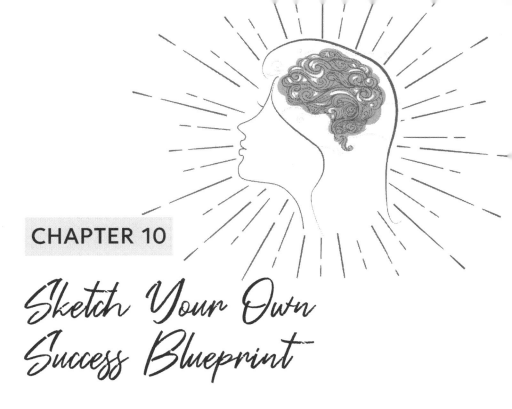

Sketch Your Own Success Blueprint

Do you know what sets you apart from other success seekers? Yes, reading this book is a great start. But even before that decision, you demonstrated the willingness to stretch yourself into something unknown. You tried one healing treatment and then another. You found some remedies to be successful and others less than.

It's all good.

What truly sets you apart, is that you understand what creates success. You might not think you know it… but you do.

> *True success comes to those who decide, adapt, and expand into change.*

Ready for change?

Change is always going to crop up. It's a constant we can count on. How we choose to react makes a difference. Do we pick up our toys and go home? Or do we keep swinging for the bleachers? And, by the way, we don't have to slug it out in everything. It's okay to pick and choose where we expend our valuable energy.

If we don't embrace change, we become rigid and unresourceful. Change, by its very nature is challenging.

I used to view change as the enemy—something to avoid at all costs. I believed in the nirvana of a changeless existence. A perfect job, a perfect marriage, perfect children, etc. I viewed change as either a threat to what I had or as a reflection of my blemished life.

Either way—I didn't want it.

I'm human. Change still makes me uncomfortable. But at some level of acceptance, I know that it's supposed to. I understand that the agitation factor of discomfort is the very thing lighting a fire under me to take action.

I've learned that even discontent can be a good thing. A subtle feeling of discontentment occurs when we recognize that the status quo is no longer acceptable. Discontentment indicates that change is needed. Viewing change as a limitation feels threatening and brings a sense of fear. Viewing change through the lens of optimism feels hopeful and brings eager anticipation of the future.

Studying change (habit development, in particular) is my passion. I devour books, papers, studies, online programs, and documentaries on behavioral psychology as it relates to brain health, change, and habit formation. In a book I mentioned previously, *The Power of Habit*, author Charles Duhigg explains that some habits create themselves, but intentional habits require at least some planning. His Cue-Routine-Reward diagram of habit change[70] makes a vague topic, both tangible and repeatable.

The basics of Duhigg's Cue-Routine-Reward goes something like this:

> **Cue:** The stimulus that causes us to act. One example would be an alarm clock buzzer that causes us to hop out of bed and begin our morning schedule.

> **Routine:** The routine habits, practices, or behaviors that follow a specific cue. In this example, the routine may be getting showered, dressed, fed, and organized to get to work.

> **Reward:** The positive result of the routine. The reward may seem counterintuitive in this example about getting to work (especially if you're not fond of your job). But that's only if we look at the short-term result. Taking a longer and wider viewpoint, we may recognize that getting to work on time keeps us employed and able to provide for ourselves and our family.

To begin new and healthy habits, it makes sense to create a new one that works within this proven framework. No wheel reinvention necessary. We often muddle things up by trying to make basic things impossibly complicated. For example, why declare "I'm going to get to the gym six days a week by 5:00 am," if you never go now and you're not naturally an early riser? Guess how you'd feel at the jarring sound of that 4:30 am alarm. Brutal.

---

70   https://charlesduhigg.com/wp-content/uploads/2014/04/Flowchart-How-to-Change-a-Habit.pdf

Start small. Make it simple.

First, link the desired behavior to the one *you already do*. Referred to as chaining or stacking, decide to insert a new behavior that pairs well with an action that's already a habit.

For example, if you remove your office shoes and clothes after work, why not lace up your walking shoes right away? Consider doing this rather than sliding into flip-flops or slippers. Remind yourself of the powerful physical and emotional benefits of a short walk before dinner. It's a perfect way to clear your head for the evening tasks at hand. It's an effective transition between work and home responsibilities. Walking improves muscle tone, lowers blood pressure, and improves digestive function for the meal ahead. It also sets you up for an easier wind-down later on and eventual restorative sleep.

Wanting results doesn't work. For those with health challenges, it's not as simple as wanting to get better or, even worse, not wanting it enough. Wanting is a nebulous factor to discard.

By expanding into the changes around us, we create our own levels of success.

As a good example, review how your MAPP operates. Your focus is influenced by the patterns you've already established. From those patterns, a blueprint is designed for you to follow each day. ***You automatically use patterns from your past to filter everything you see today.***

It's a mental matching game. Your brain wonders, "Does what I see (or hear, taste, touch, feel, etc.) match what I already know?"

Putting the filters of your MAPP into context

Let's say that Cathy has a prejudice against dogs. She believes all dogs are rambunctious, slobbery, and destructive. At some point in time (either consciously or nonconsciously), she created this belief and now views all dogs through this filter. With this in mind, what would be the likelihood of her becoming attracted to a man who talks incessantly about the antics of his three Labradoodles? If she did meet him, what doggie behaviors would she see?

Our MAPP is the director of our focus. The things we may hold as true are learned experiences masquerading as truths. Discerning this difference cracks open the door to possibilities. This is the path to positive change.

■ Step-by-step ADAPT and GROW technique

To identify the exact steps needed to create successful change, I've outlined a strategic process I use with clients called the ADAPT and GROW technique. It's a clear-cut blueprint to outline the steps needed for any desired change. Accurately following a blueprint increases the likelihood of success.

A—AWARENESS

Start at the beginning: Increased awareness gives us the flexibility of choice. Once we're aware of a problem, we can choose to address it or make changes. Becoming aware allows us to become masters of creating what we want rather than victims of what we don't want.

To begin this step, observe your day-to-day activities, looking for patterns. Are there problems that show up with nagging persistence? Do you see a general theme to your recurring worries or frustrations?

In this phase, just observe your life and thoughts from a detached perspective. Try to stay "above" the fray of negative emotions that are likely tied to your fears. Establish a sense of unbiased curiosity about the problem. What do you notice? What would you like to happen instead? What's your desired outcome? For now, just notice and become aware.

D—DECISION

Make it concrete: This sounds like a no-brainer, but don't skip this step. After becoming aware but before taking action, you must make a conscious and intentional *decision.* The Latin definition of decision is to cut off from[71] or to do something different from what you're now doing. This step is about deeply rooting this decision.

The distinction is critical. Being interested in something is a far cry from making it happen. Do you want to dabble with the idea or commit to doing something about it?

The emotion of wanting isn't enough. It won't provide adequate motivation to tip the scales toward forward action. Interest isn't an action.

---

71   https://www.etymonline.com/word/decision

TIP: *Write it down! Take the extra step to put pen to paper and create your declaration statement. Nothing fancy needed. Jot down your intention, the date, and a few words on WHY it's important to you. Understanding your "big why" gives you a successful edge. Ask yourself powerful why questions. Why do you want this? Why will it benefit you and those around you?*

Don't forget to sign your John Hancock at the bottom. There's a primary kinesthetic (touching and feeling) correlation between the act of writing and your brain. Writing by hand, uses your brain in different ways than typing. It's connected to improved memory, accessing the RAS,[72] and other benefits.[73] Your brain and body interpret a **sensory commitment** *to signing this document. Put your declaration in a place that's relevant to you—either private or public. Tuck it away in your journal, Bible, nightstand drawer or post it on your fridge, at your workstation, or on your bathroom mirror.*

After making this decision, the following is a natural next step.

A—ACTION

Create the spark: Now that you've made the all-powerful decision, it's time for action. Get the ball rolling. Consider these questions. Do you need to know anything more about "the problem" before you move forward? Do you need to know more about your desired outcome? For example, does it involve anyone else other than you? Does it require

---

72   https://www.ragan.com/infographic-how-writing-affects-your-brain/
73   http://www.forbes.com/sites/nancyolson/2016/05/15/three-ways-that-writing-with-a-pen-positively-affects-your-brain/#1ab6383e1b93

additional tools, assets, or resources? This step may involve research (but not too much), some investigation into potential solutions, and gathering additional help.

TIP: *You do NOT need to know the solution at this point! Ambiguity about what, exactly, you plan to do may feel uncomfortable, but trust in your ability to see it through.*

This step is about taking sufficient initiative to do what's necessary. For me, I love to read, watch documentaries, look up articles, and find trusted research sources and practitioners. You may wish to talk to others and ask for suggestions or referrals. Reaching out to supportive practitioners and working with a mentor or coach may be the next step that you need.

Don't forget the obvious. Research is well and good, but this step is about action. I've been the queen of analysis paralysis, so don't make this mistake. If you're like me, it may go against your nature, but do it anyway. Find the spark. Leap. Do something. Take ONE small action step right away (aka NOW). Taking authentic action is more important than feeling "sure" that the step you take is the right one. You may or may not ever feel sure. Put one foot in front of the other. This makes the difference between success and stagnation.

There's plenty of time for making adjustments later.

TIP: *Remember that one powerful way to spark action is to link your desired action with something you already do. For example, if you want to start a deep breathing regimen, link it to something you already practice daily such as a bath or shower, flossing your teeth, pouring a cup of tea or coffee, driving, etc.*

P—PLAN

Set up the how-to: Now it's time to work the plan you've created. Apply your discoveries from previous steps. What did you learn in that first step? What else do you need? Create an action plan that includes a basic outline of what you propose to do until you've made the desired change.

Did you know that intention beats motivation[74] when it comes to driving desired behavior? You've already made the decision (thereby setting the intention), so creating the plan is the icing on the cake.

Define when to implement this change. And, where will you do it? Be specific. Include options for flexibility and use this if/then formula to help. Brainstorm ways your plans could derail (stuff happens). Then come up with alternative solutions (i.e., if I intend to walk in the morning and it rains, then I'll do stretches at home instead).

Define at least the first couple of steps. The subsequent steps along the way will change, so it's not

---

74 https://onlinelibrary.wiley.com/doi/abs/10.1348/135910702169420

practical (or even logical) to try and nail everything down. This is a common mistake.

> ***Believing that you need to know all the steps in your plan might prevent you from taking even one.***

Some tackle this planning process on their own, but most of us can use outside feedback. The objectivity provided by an outsider can prove invaluable. Isolation can skew our focus or lead us to believe we lack potential or have limited opportunities.

Create your support team. Break down your tactical approach into small steps and gather needed support. This is how the plan becomes a vivid, living thing rather than a dream or a nebulous "want." The small, and maybe even subtle, steps taken toward a goal can generate a successful feeling that bathes the brain in dopamine, often referred to as the success hormone.[75] The philosophy of micro-steps leading to continuous improvement (also called kaizen[76]) can pave the way to sought-after success.

It's also a good idea to put cognitive priming[77] into place. This is the practice of activating the brain with vivid images of what it will look like when

75   https://www.psychologytoday.com/blog/the-truisms-wellness/201610/the-science-accomplishing-your-goals
76   https://www.kaizen.com/what-is-kaizen.html
77   https://www.ncbi.nlm.nih.gov/pmc/articles/PMC2376275/

you've made the change that you desire. How will it look, feel, and sound when you achieve it?

If it helps, go ahead and reverse-engineer your plan. Instead of starting with the problem, begin with your desired outcome, and work backward. Sketch out a timeline for your goal and then break down the steps needed to accomplish it into doable chunks.

This is a work-in-progress. Embrace your eraser. Use a pencil to create a flexible document designed for change and continuous adaptation.

TIP: *Don't let your control-freak side get the best of you. You'll get more mileage from your efforts by developing WHY you want to achieve this goal rather than from detailing HOW to get there.*

T—TRAILBLAZING

Take it out for a spin: This is my favorite step. This is where you get to take what you've learned so far and tailor it to meet *your* needs. What methods and practices work best for you?

Your path to success gets its definition from repeated action. You may forge your own trail or follow in the footsteps of others (straying off the beaten path when necessary). It's your call.

TIP: *There's only one certainty here—your plan won't go as expected. That's a good thing. Take what you've learned, enjoy the detour, and keep moving forward. Viewing the hiccups along the way as temporary detours or speed bumps rather than roadblocks makes all the difference to your success. This single mindset shift separates the (successful) men from the boys. Or women from the girls... or whatever. You follow the drift.*

Now that you've embraced the ADAPT portion of this technique, are you done? No-sir-ee-bob.

Once you begin to adapt to change, there's an essential next step. As each change becomes a habit, it's time to GROW. It's time to expand into your new circumstance.

G – Get on with life

R – Repeat what's working

O – Observe circumstances with detachment

W – Welcome new ideas and intuitions with gratitude

The growth phase is every bit as necessary as adapting.

From your new perspective after adaptation, what looks, feels, or sounds different? What's working? What might not work as well? What do you need to forgive or let go of? Are more changes needed to make this new healthy habit your own?

Use the ADAPT and GROW technique to foster positive change and adopt healthy habits. Be patient and observant. Habits take time to groom. Like raising a puppy, habits need attention and monitoring during the early days to reinforce the right behaviors. Soon enough, you'll have a loyal companion at your side.

> *"The changes might not show up in a week or a month, but consistent practice over time can turn you into a completely different person."*
> —Dawson Church, author of *Mind to Matter*

What about a blueprint for deleting an unhealthy habit?

If there's an undesired mindless behavior you'd rather remove, a bit of set-up helps first. Any behavior done mindlessly becomes a habit. Habits can't be deleted. They must be replaced.

Let's say you want to reduce your soda consumption. If you grab one from the fridge, for example, and drink half of it before you even notice, that's a mindless habit. It takes conscious awareness to change it. And, by its very nature, this habit is sub or beneath your conscious awareness.

The first step is to bring this behavior to the attention of the conscious mind. You could put sticky notes on the fridge door or on the sodas themselves to get your attention. You could also remove them or move them to a different place to break the routine.

You'll also want to define the habit you want to install instead. This must be pre-selected in advance. Perhaps you plan to replace the soda with a bottle or glass of water. Or you plan to go outside for a moment, do a few stretches, or cuddle your pet. Can you march in place during the length of one TV commercial once per day? The point is to do something quick and easy. Make the replacement a small thing, and it'll soon enough become a no-brainer.

From there, you can add to the process. Use the ADAPT and GROW technique to bolster your current healthy habits and add new ones.

Here's more information on a roadblock mentioned earlier.

New behaviors are always challenged.

Have you ever noticed that when you try something new, you may have quick success and then something happens? Or perhaps there's an obstruction right at the starting gate?

Either way—it's a GOOD thing!

New ideas are always tested. And, challenges are an integral part of the process. They provide our brains with the opportunity to reinforce and strengthen our neural pathways. This reinforcement is part of how we can change the structure of our brain to implement new ideas. Reinforcement that includes struggle has been proven very effective at this process, according to Dr. Lara Boyd[78] of the University of British Columbia.

She also states that while the struggle is good, struggle that frustrates you isn't. Keep a positive outlook, and keep moving forward. Don't allow temporary challenges to derail your plans to create permanent healthy habits.

---

78   http://www.totallearningcenter.com/5403-2/

> ***"Progress is evolutionary***
> ***rather than revolutionary."***
> —BJ Gallagher

■ Chapter 10 – Head Work

1. What life changes in the past threw you a curveball? Which ones were the most frightening or felt the most threatening? Ponder how you felt when the change initially occurred. Notice, in particular, how you probably could not see the possibilities for benefits from the change. Think about how your thought patterns kept you stuck amid that change. Notice if those thought patterns repeat at other times, even when the change isn't as drastic.

2. Write down at least three ways that unexpected change has brought you positive results. Consider changes in all areas of life.

3. Write down the steps of the ADAPT and GROW technique. Brainstorm goals or plans that you'd like to implement using this specific plan. (Review your goals outlined in Chapter 6.) From this list, choose one to implement first.

Now that you have a grasp on methods to move through problems and struggles, we'll next deal with change. How do you put your plans into action and cultivate them?

The following chapter outlines the process of successful change in an easy-to-follow format by sharing a helpful sample case study.

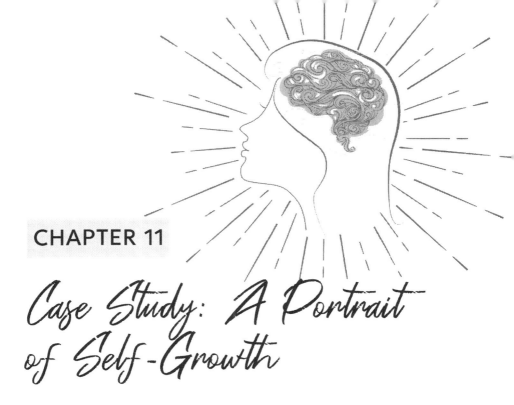

Case Study: A Portrait of Self-Growth

It's one thing to read through the steps of any given method and another to apply it to yourself and your situations. Pay attention to the following case study. Notice the client's reactions to each step and how she responded. Would you respond in the same way?

Roadmap to change

The ADAPT and GROW technique looks simple, doesn't it? That's good. And it may be even easier than you think. Sometimes, just the act of plotting out a few steps allows you to see options and solutions that were there all along. You may find yourself skipping forward through the process much faster than anticipated simply by being aware of the process.

Let's see it in action. The following case study demonstrates the ADAPT and GROW technique in a step-by-step format.

For a clear illustration, I've chosen a busy woman's challenge of set-ting a consistent bedtime as the problem to overcome. Getting either more or higher-quality sleep is a fairly universal concern. The follow-ing example uses a fictional client, Callie. Of course, much of this information is based on an amalgam of my experience with actual clients.

■ Callie's ADAPT a Regular Bedtime Routine Case Study

Step A: How **Aware** is Callie of her sleep challenge?

Upon initial questioning, Callie states, "I don't really see a consistent bedtime as a big problem. After all, I get to bed at a decent hour most of the time."

(*Hopefully, you're already aware that the actual "problem" isn't her bedtime. The true underlying hold-up is her erroneous belief that she's getting adequate sleep. Broaching the subject of her bedtime is an example of a gateway topic, as men-tioned in Chapter 3. An earlier bedtime is an acceptable subject that will meet with less resistance from Callie than deeper subjects that are not yet within her aware-ness. This process of tip-toeing through a gateway topic is designed to uncover what's truly going on.*)

As a sleep pattern homework assignment, I ask Callie to envision a sense of curiosity. I encourage her to pay attention to how she feels upon waking, during the workday, and at bedtime. What signals does she see, hear, or feel throughout the day that indicates she's tired? What cue tells her it's time for bed? Is it an actual time or is it task-re-lated, meaning that it occurs once things are done? Next, I ask her to get specific about what "most of the time" means for her. When does she actually go to bed each night? She's to track this for at least ten days and share her findings with me at our next session.

Callie soon reports several key discoveries. She points out that she's often very groggy in the mornings and feels somewhat nauseous for the first hour or so after waking. She realizes that she depends on caffeine or sugar (or both) to jumpstart her day. This occurred ten out of ten mornings. This had never come to her conscious thought before, and she had a vague notion that "everyone does this." She believed everyone uses some sort of stimulant to wake up.

That is until she took an informal poll at work. She asked her co-workers how they felt upon waking. Some reported feeling tired and pressing the snooze button often. But others said they were usually up before their alarms. Their sense of grogginess was fleeting if present at all. Callie's curiosity about the definition of "normal" sleep was aroused.

This spurred other observations.

Next, she reports that her daytime nausea sometimes sticks around most of the day. Even more, she states that headaches, digestive troubles, and a generalized sense of "overwhelm" are constant occurrences.

Lastly, Callie admits that her bedtime schedule was a lot more erratic than she'd thought. Her evenings were somewhat unpredictable with random interruptions such as phone calls, family tasks, and an endless array of incomplete household chores. Once aware, she observed a wide disparity between the times she planned on getting to bed, and when it actually happened. In reality, she often collapsed into bed well after midnight with a night or two of "crashing" at 9:00 pm thrown in for balance.

Coincidentally (more on this later), Callie caught the final 30 minutes of a documentary revealing the physical impact of sleep deprivation. She wondered about the possibility that some of her symptoms were related to lack of sleep. When I asked which ones bothered her the most, she became noticeably agitated and impatient with the topic.

I pointed out that there's no right or wrong answer. We were simply working through the speculation and discovery step of the process. I asked her to jot down more of her symptoms for further evaluation.

Clearly, the impact of her new awareness struck a nerve.

Once aware, Callie couldn't ignore the problem. In her thoughts, her problem shifted from a minor annoyance to something needing attention. She recognized that there's a potential health risk to her current behavior, which is why she felt irritated. Before, it was easier to avoid this issue when she told herself it was "no big deal."

> ### *It's human nature to default to the status quo.*

People don't feel compelled to rock the boat unless pushed by something uncomfortable.

This is the very reason why, by the way, some people don't want restaurants to list nutrition information on their menus. While some are already aware of the importance of this information, others are not. They prefer (perhaps not consciously) to stay in a state of "not knowing." Meaning, they prefer to make their menu selections without the clutter of statistical data regarding their meal options. If they're unaware, for example, they can't be held responsible (even to themselves) for making healthier food choices. And, they won't feel the internal pressure of making a "good" or "bad" selection. This isn't about right or wrong. It's just an observation of human behavior as it relates to awareness.

Step D: It's time for Callie to make a **Decision**.

At our next visit, Callie demonstrated a readiness to discuss potential ties between her symptoms and lack of sleep. She reported a fascination with her research. She mentioned these main symptoms of concern: nausea, inability to focus, delayed reflex reactions, digestive dysfunction, and poor memory.

With noticeable excitement, she said, "I want to see if consistent sleep can help improve these symptoms. Who knows? Maybe it can even improve others I'm not aware of?"

Yippee—Callie made a decision!

I asked her to write a declaration of this statement, which she signed and dated. She wrote, "I, Callie, decide to make a regular bedtime a priority in my life. I'm tired (literally!) of not feeling my best and want more from life. I'll set a consistent bedtime, plan for better sleep, and accept the consequences of this decision as neutral feedback for me to learn more."

Well said, Callie.

Step A: Time to spark **Action**.

Callie made it clear that setting a regular bedtime was something that she truly wanted. That's a great start.

So, now what?

I gave Callie more assignments to put her newfound awareness to use. It was time to shift beyond the desire for change and make the change a reality.

Since the topic of sleep deprivation was at the top of mind, I seized the momentum. I asked her to research and report back to me three quick facts regarding the lack of sleep. Specifically, I asked her to identify three that were new and/or surprising to her. (NOTE: I could have easily handed her a list of sleep deprivation facts since it's a topic I often share in articles and lectures. But an essential element to uncover here is a personal relationship between Cassie and the discoveries. This occurs when A) she's accountable to make the discoveries herself, and B) she prioritizes her findings to the top three based on evaluations of her personal interests.)

Because Cassie was now open to new ideas, I also mentioned how nutritional deficiencies and dehydration could contribute to her early morning nausea. She committed to doing more research on this area of study.

Finally, I asked Callie to investigate different ways to incorporate bedtime rituals. What sort of routines appeal to her? What types of activities sound doable and practical?

Step P: Time to craft a **PLAN**

When Callie reported her new findings at her next session, her implementation steps became clear.

She eagerly shared with me her startling research discoveries. She saw a causal link between serious health challenges and sleep deprivation. She was shocked to learn that sleep-deprived people share similar reflexes and reaction times with those who are intoxicated.[79] She real-

---

79   http://www.ncbi.nlm.nih.gov/pmc/articles/PMC1739867/

ized that in her every day commutes to and from work, she was putting herself and others at risk with her "drowsy driving" behaviors.[80]

This information served as a catalyst to help Callie not only see the importance of sleep but to make a personal commitment to change. All on her own, she reported adopting some nutritional changes as well as drinking more water for better hydration. She had already experienced improvement in her early morning nausea.

This early success fueled Callie's desire to proceed.

Together, we listed her favorite relaxation activities and created an "unwind" sequence to practice before bed. We assigned an approximate time to each item so she'd know how long each could take. Then, we added up the total and settled on an ideal timeline of about 45 minutes for her nighttime ritual.

Her list included stretching, deep breathing, meditation, music, diffusing essential oils, reading, and writing. This personalized routine was tailor-made to her interests as listed below:

- Stretching and a few yoga-type poses done while listening to her favorite soothing relaxation music and diffusing a sleep-inducing essential oil blend
- While stretching, she practices deep breathing, meditative relaxation techniques, and prayer
- Writing in her gratitude journal
- Reading from inspirational, devotional, funny, or heartwarming books (she shifted her personal favorites—exciting mysteries and legal thrillers—to daytime reading)
- Sipping clean, pure, filtered water throughout the day

---

80   http://drowsydriving.org/about/facts-and-stats/

I asked Callie to define her level of commitment to the plan we'd arranged. She said, "No problem… I'm committed 100%. I've got this."

Step T: Time for **TRAILBLAZING**

Callie found her Unwind Routine to be reasonably effortless once she got into the swing of it. At first, she procrastinated and dragged her feet. Bedtime seemed too early, and she feared that other things wouldn't get done. She soon realized that she needed to give herself permission to "spend time on me."

Before our work together, she perceived this sort of activity as selfish. She thought it would take time away from her family. With her new awareness, she had a clear understanding of the importance of this routine. She increasingly found it easier to set boundaries—both with her family and with her inclination toward sabotage. She was surprised at how clarity of mind helped her to get more done than she had in the past.

Callie discovered that the practice of relaxation is more of an art than a science. She wasn't used to going to bed early (unless she was in a fatigue/crash cycle) so it took time and patience to adjust. She learned to accept that how quickly she fell asleep didn't reflect the sole value of the unwind practice.

Soon, she began to tweak her routine. She found that 30 minutes, rather than 45, was optimum for her. She became very diligent about turning off her digital devices at least 30 minutes before bed and then turning out the light and hitting the hay at her pre-arranged time. If she chose to read longer or swap out a different soothing activity such as a long soak in the bath, she adjusted her start time accordingly.

Callie was encouraged to find more benefits than just better sleep. Her meditation practice left her feeling more centered, focused, and calm in many ways. She was more organized in the mornings, more productive at work, and felt a greater sense of patience with others. She was intrigued to learn that in addition to relaxation benefits, prayer and meditation helped with problem-solving, planning, introspective objectivity, and more.

From her stretching exercises, her body gained muscle tone, increased flexibility, and improved digestive function. She also realized that her body had a Pavlov-like reaction to her relaxation music and aromatherapy practices. Through repetition, she felt her heart rate lower, muscles relax, and a deep sense of calm spread throughout her body on cue. Hearing her favorite music and enjoying the scent of her favorite essential oils triggered this healing reaction even before completing the routine.

She was particularly surprised by the impact of her aromatherapy practice. These preferred soothing, relaxing scents became a favorite part of her routine. She instinctually took deep, calming breaths as soon as she used the oils. (TIP: *Essential oils—through our sense of smell— speak directly to and calms the limbic system.*[81]) Encouraged, she found ways to incorporate diffusing pure essential oils throughout the day (both at home and work) for relaxation, focus, invigoration, and for lifting her mood. She also added essential oils to her self-massage and bathing routines.

At first, she paid conscious attention to follow the steps of her routine pragmatically. Over time, the habit became second nature and no longer took thought or effort.

Now I'd like to back up a little bit. Do you remember Callie's "coincidence" of seeing that documentary on sleep? That was her RAS in

81   https://www.medicalnewstoday.com/articles/10884.php

action. (You may wish to review Chapter 1.) Her Reticular Activating System (RAS) directed her attention to the documentary once she focused her brain's powerful sense of curiosity on looking for and finding more information on the topic of sleep.

The RAS is great at making strategic connections in what we notice in life. Whether you call them synchronicities or coincidences, the information, and resources you seek, show up when needed. It happens as a result of choosing to become curious or interested in something and then deciding to follow-through.

I prefer to think of these occurrences as God-orchestrated Divine appointments. For Callie, once she became engaged in the process of our work together, she noticed that magazine articles, TV commercials, books at the store, and talk in the breakroom at work often seemed to focus on self-care topics (or the lack thereof). She was amazed at how much information there was to support her efforts.

Once Callie used the ADAPT method to create her Unwind Routine, I next encouraged her to GROW into her new-found benefits. She let go of the former behavior patterns that kept her stuck. She continued to search for (and then let go of) thoughts and behaviors that did not promote her desired results. With a deep sense of gratitude, we looked for other areas of her life that worked well but could use a few tweaks. By looking forward, we reinforced her new plans and magnified her success.

> **The ADAPT process is doing;**
> **the GROW process is living.**

The intent is to create a lifestyle that's always changing, growing, learning, and expanding. Now that's something for which to be grateful!

NOTE: *I purposely used the relevant topic of sleep as an example. The problem of sleep deprivation affects about 50-70 million adults in the U.S. alone.*[82] *Besides the benefits listed above, it's essential to understand that adequate sleep provides the body with the opportunity to rebuild, repair, and regenerate at a cellular level. Our metabolism, immune system, and detoxification processes all get a boost while we sleep. The body gets what it needs to heal from restorative rest—especially from the Rapid Eye Movement (REM) cycles of deep sleep.*

BONUS TIP: *In a lecture I attended, Dr. Kristen Willeumier, Neuroscientist, shared that every hour of sleep before midnight is worth two after midnight. A regular sleep pattern is fostered by getting to bed before midnight,*[83] *and a well-rested body is fortified to deal with stress, drama, change, conflict, and other anxiety-provoking occurrences.*

> ***To turn on your creativity, focus, and problem-solving switch, get better sleep.***

Oh, and be sure to hydrate, too.

■ Chapter 11 – Head Work

1. After reading this case study, were any of her results unexpected? Did Callie have discoveries or epiphanies that surprised you? Consider that as you implement change, you're often able to see things from a different angle than before you

---

82 https://www.ncbi.nlm.nih.gov/pubmed/20669438
83 https://premeditatedleftovers.com/naturally-frugal-living/reasons-sleeping-before-midnight/

began. What problems would you like to be able to view from a different angle?

2.   Review the problems list you made from the previous question. Write down the steps for the ADAPT and GROW technique. Then consider those steps as they'd apply to the problems you'd like to solve and the goals you'd like to achieve. Choose one and move on to the next question in this chapter's Head Work.

3.   Complete the first two steps of the ADAPT technique in detail. Don't skimp on the time or thought put into this part of the plan. After these steps have been fleshed out, take a moment to consider what comes next. What action steps come to mind first? Don't complicate things by analyzing what's "right" or wondering what may happen down the road. Jot down your thoughts and take the next obvious step.

These tips are so fundamental they're in danger of being overlooked or discounted. Drinking adequate amounts of pure, clean, filtered water and getting better, quality sleep are two vital practices that should be first on anyone's health goals list.

There's still more to uncover about the fascinating topic of habit change. Next, we'll dig into the Four Phases of Growth as well as a powerful healing analogy that will give meaning to your journey.

Navigate Smooth Seas or Squalls

Y ou've probably never thought about it, but learning comes in
distinct phases. Many of us never even step into the elusive final
phase, where something we've learned becomes a habit.

To transform what you've learned so far into a habit, and set your
sails for success, tackle this chapter with a highlighter and your favorite warm mug in hand.

Land ho—awesome info ahead!

Habit change: the four phases of growth

This will likely be new to you. Learning (including habit formation)
occurs in four distinct phases. I read about these phases about a doz-

en years ago in a book written by an NLP expert and thought, "Why isn't this taught in schools?" The practicality of these teachings get to the heart of how and why we think and behave as we do.

■ A brief narrative on NLP

If not in schools, at least NLP is gaining popularity in the business world and the private sector. I saw this recently in a PR Newswire article. *"In the last 35 years, NLP has gained immense global recognition, becoming an impactful tool for personal change and to alter behavioral patterns to achieve desired goals in one's professional as well as personal lives."*[84]

A quick word on programming. The neuro-linguistic side of things is obvious. We get that it's about the brain and language. But the programming part is easily misunderstood. It sounds weird or perhaps even dangerous. I view it as an unfortunate naming choice, but I can see how in the '70s it reflected the hey-day of personal computers and the brilliance of programming.

In reality, the programming part of NLP is all about using our personal skills to our best advantage. Understanding how we think and how we make words and pictures in our minds tells us a lot. Using these skills, we can set our sights on what we want to achieve. A central tenet of these teachings is to study the words, phrases, and linguistic patterns in yourself and others. In this way, we gain valuable insight that gives us a leg up on our interactions with the world.

The original intention of the word *programming* was to bring awareness to our mental patterns. Once we're aware of our internal programming, we can change it. It's worth noting that when working

---

84   http://www.prnewswire.co.in/news-releases/sonalika-group-venturing-into-a-new-horizon-of-training-in-neuro-linguistic-programming-to-bring-inner-transformation-to-conduct-a-free-two-day-similar-session-on-march-24-and-25-in-new-delhi-676806103.html

with an NLP practitioner, there's nothing done *to* you. It's a "done with you" relationship.

Many practitioners have adopted other definitions for the acronym to reflect the overall intention of the study. I'm particularly fond of both Natural Language Patterns and Neuro-Linguistic Psychology. Some simply refer to it as the science of cognitive re-patterning.

Whatever you want to call it, the lessons in this area of research can change how you think. Profound ah-ha moments develop from new understandings. Granting clarity to ill-defined notions, this fascinating field of study continues to intrigue and interest me.

The Four Phases of Growth outlined below serve as one example. While they're pulled from research sources pre-dating the NLP inception era,[85] this outline is often used in NLP trainings as it shares a clear picture of the learning process. Assigning a concrete definition to vague ideas helps us to become more intentional about our actions. Once we know what the steps are, we can assess where we stand and where we want to go.

These phases relate to gaining competence in any desired behavior.

The Four Phases of Growth (or Competence)

In any learning environment, change passes through these stages.

Phase 1) Unconscious Incompetence:

> *We don't know what we don't know.*
> In other words, we're unaware of what we don't know.

---

85   https://trainingindustry.com/wiki/strategy-alignment-and-planning/the-four-stages-of-competence/

Phase 2) Conscious Incompetence:

We're aware of what we don't know.
We may have an inkling that we know little or at least not everything about a particular subject.

Phase 3) Conscious Competence:

We're aware of what we want and take intentional action towards it.
This is the phase where effort is applied to make change emerge. It's the beginning of habit formation.

Phase 4) Unconscious Competence:

Conscious awareness is no longer needed to drive desired behavior.
The shift from Phase 3 to Phase 4 occurs when we're so accustomed to doing the desired behavior that it no longer takes conscious thought or effort. We've now created a nonconscious habit or routine.

It's common to become stuck in the endless loop of Phase 3, Conscious Competence. We're aware of what we want, we know the first step of what to do, yet we unwittingly backslide into self-sabotage, stalled progress, or derailments and interruptions. We're held in the orbit of Phase 3 and can't quite get the propulsion needed to pull away into Phase 4, Unconscious Competence.

In the behavioral science world, Phase 4 is also known as automaticity.[86] It's the ability to do something "in your sleep" or "on autopilot." It's where the desired behavior becomes a no-brainer.

---

86   http://www.learninginfo.org/automaticity.htm

> ### *You can't unknow what you now know!*

Now that you see it in print, how are you doing? If this was new to you, can you recognize the difference between the phases? When it comes to healthy habit creation, to truly make them a no-brainer, are you stuck in the pitfalls of Phase 3?

If so, you're gonna love what's ahead.

Clarity through stories

Esoteric and cloudy concepts become clear through the effective use of analogy. This method makes vivid mental pictures which speak directly to the nonconscious mind. Great examples occur throughout historical texts. The Bible makes good use of this style of writing using storytelling and parables to share in-depth philosophies.

Here's a story I created to help clients embrace their ability to change and to enlist support along the way.

■ The Smooth Sailing analogy

Take into account that a sailboat is designed for efficiency and performance.

- The **boat** itself represents you. It symbolizes your physical self, including your genetics. It embodies all that you are (past and present), including your physical injuries, challenges, specific diagnoses, etc.

- The **mast** represents what you do with your body. It symbolizes the foods you eat, supplements, and medications you may take, the treatments you choose, and the fitness activities you do to stay in shape.

- The **rudder** represents the input and influence that others have over you. Those who may affect, shape, or change your journey. This may include family, friends, colleagues, health practitioners, authors, speakers, etc.

What's left?

- The **sails** represent your emotional intelligence. This symbolizes the direction, power, and effectiveness of *staying on course*. What thoughts guide your intended route? What's the focus of your intentions? What mental practices do you consistently follow to assure your success?

> *Only you can put the wind*
> *in your own sails.*

You may eat well, take quality supplements, surround yourself with supportive people, and even invest in great health practitioners. But unless the negative, stagnating, monkey-mind patterns are redirected, your boat continues to follow the unplanned path… aimless on an uncharted course.

> *Don't allow the unintended*
> *life to set you adrift.*

As Lewis Carroll, the author of *Alice's Adventures in Wonderland* said, *"If you don't know where you're going any road will get you there."*

Using the natural energy of *intentional* wind in your sails, you can chart your course for any desired destination. Without the sails, you're effectively floating in a glorified bathtub. With brute strength, you could drop in some oars and paddle. But why make it more difficult than necessary?

Forward momentum comes from either the sweat of your brow or from sitting back and harnessing the power of what's already available to you. I hope this comparison portrays the differences in effort.

Willpower requires neither willingness nor power

When it comes to "eating right," clients may say, "Just give me a list of what to eat. None of that mindset stuff for me." While I respect their intentions, I point out this not-so-obvious concept; a diet, by nature, is temporary. White-knuckling your way through dietary changes zaps the supply of your limited willpower. It's a short-term solution for a long-term problem. What I want for you is lasting change.

Change that takes place at the conscious level (using effort and willpower) isn't sustainable for the long haul. Change that takes advantage of the inner workings of the nonconscious mind is.

Having great willpower, by the way, has nothing to do with a superior character. The reverse is also true. Lack of willpower doesn't reveal some shameful personal flaw. Willpower is a conscious-mind construct. It takes awareness and effort to put it into place.

And, speaking of effort, if you're dealing with a health challenge, your body's resources are already compromised. When the sympathetic nervous system is bombarded all day long with signals of a malfunctioning body, overwhelm will show up on your doorstep. In the fight, flight, or freeze response, the body's experience of anxiety is amplified. This is where decision fatigue[87] (the mental exhaustion that comes from too many decisions and too little resources) comes into play. We make thousands of micro-decisions every day. According to some sources as many as 35,000.[88] No wonder we're tired!

Due to its energy-draining properties, chronic illness wears down your reserves, including your ability to generate and sustain willpower. This is why *trying* (efforting) to make healthy changes from conscious-level thinking is exhausting—not to mention unproductive.

Don't make it so hard. Give yourself a break. Work *with* your brain in the way that it's designed to work best.

Remember that the most dominant thoughts in the nonconscious mind will *always* prevail over time. If your conscious mind wants broccoli and kale, but your nonconscious mind holds the belief that a salad equals deprivation, then look out. There's an uphill battle ahead. Getting to the root of this belief allows you to pull the weeds of distraction and plant the seeds of desired outcomes.

Laying the groundwork of healthy motivation creates a lasting pattern for future goals. My goal is to work through this process with clients so they can go solo. They'll soon have what they need to keep themselves on course.

I'm happy to prepare them to leave the harbor. But I'm even happier to watch them pack up what they've learned and set sail.

---

87   http://jamesclear.com/willpower-decision-fatigue
88   http://go.roberts.edu/leadingedge/the-great-choices-of-strategic-leaders

> **"Smooth seas do not
> make skillful sailors."**
> —African Proverb

■ Chapter 12 – Head Work

1. What phase of the Four Phases of Growth do you find yourself getting stuck in the most? Decide to beat inertia! Implement the Head Work following each chapter and notice how taking authentic action helps to rock your way out of "stuckness."

2. After reading the Smooth Sailing analogy, what do you think about your "sails?" What choices can you make to harness this part of your health journey? Write down at least three ways you can support your plans through changes in how you think, and by shifting to a positive focus.

3. Brainstorm and jot down at least five decisions you can make in advance to reduce decision fatigue. Don't overthink this— keep 'em simple.

Next, we'll dig into the methods of making change happen. Do you start with dipping a toe into the pool or dive right in? Real-life studies can give us ideas about our motivations and hesitations. This next chapter provides some compelling—and revealing—data from my client case studies.

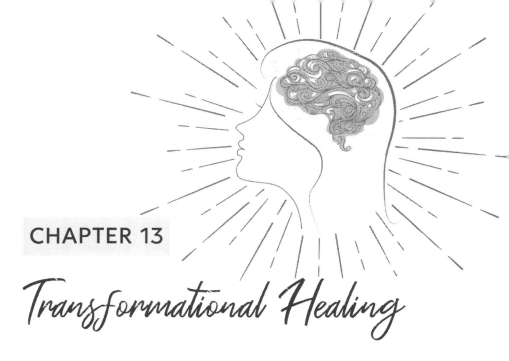

CHAPTER 13

Transformational Healing

Have you ever felt inspired after reading an intensely personal account of someone's trials and triumphs? Or have you felt motivated to make a better life for yourself after seeing an inspirational movie or documentary? A book that fits that bill for me is *Unbroken* by Laura Hillenbrand (I highly encourage you to skip the movie and read the book). Understanding the challenges of others at a profound level can have a lasting impact.

The unthinkable hardships suffered by Louis Zamperini, detailed in this biography, will leave a permanent mark on your psyche long after the final page. I don't know about you, but I find stories about healing from the inside out to be profoundly moving. Some turn their stories of tragedy into the very spark that drives them forward.

That's exactly what I want for you. I want you to fuel your own transformation with the strategies you've learned. It's time for you to **Get Back into Whack**!

> ### *You're the author of your own transformation story.*

Are you familiar with the term, *post-traumatic growth?*[89] I experienced it on a personal level long before I knew there was a name for it. It means: finding a significant positive change after a period of loss or struggle.

Has this ever happened to you? As we've discussed, change is often unplanned and downright scary. Yet, unexpected change can be the catalyst for some of the most profound and powerful personal growth phases of your life. Change never comes from within the comfort zone. *The impetus for change comes from the agitation of discomfort.*

My own story serves as an example. Nineteen years ago, it wouldn't have crossed my mind that I had the potential to heal much less write a book about it. Back then, my only focus was on crawling out of the abyss of near disability. I felt my cane would always be a permanent presence at my side. Most of the time, I just wanted to give up and give in. My eventual healing wasn't attributable to any particular skill or drive within me. I possess no amazing or even measly superpowers. I had no power at all—of my own.

I was just a mom trying to hold it all together.

I had no idea that I'd soon rebuild my health, restore relationships, and define a life's passion beyond my wildest expectations. But I did have faith in my Heavenly Father, and I felt the support of His faith in me.

This is my wish for you too.

---

89   http://www.livehappy.com/science/positive-psychology/science-post-traumatic-growth

I hope you feel the abiding comfort and assurance that comes with a belief in God's plan for you. You're not in this alone.

So, what now?

Change–that first scary step

It would be a crying shame for you to have read this far and not have taken action at all. I don't want any credit (or blame) for tears shed due to a lack of progress. It's time to take stock. Have you got what it takes to make changes in your life? (The answer is yes, you do.)

Whatever you feel to be true, please know that it's probably not as hard as you think. Don't overcomplicate things. There's a new wave of habit change research that states small, tiny changes are more effective, doable, implementable, and have a higher rate of stick-with-it-potential than trying to make drastic changes.[90] What may seem inconsequential is anything but.

> *When it comes to change—*
> *small is the new big.*

Get creative. Give it a test drive. Make your *Get Back into Whack* plan a flexible and tailor-made process that suits you (pun intended). There are as many ways to change as there are desired changes. I white-knuckled my way through nutritional and fitness changes assuming that it was supposed to be difficult and unpleasant.

Take a wild guess at the nature of my mental focus? You guessed it. I constantly thought, "Looky here at how hard this is."

---

90 http://stephenguise.com/small-steps-ultimate-guide/

My Negative Nancy focus *amplified* the difficulty. Although it was done in ignorance, my focus made things a pain in the patootie. It's no surprise that it took me years of progress and backsliding to slog my way into a settled pattern.

For you, it needn't be a picture of frustration. You're starting (or continuing) in a far better place than I did.

Wherever you are in your health journey, wipe the slate and begin anew.

Select a small, healing practice to adopt. Choose to hydrate yourself daily. Choose to move your body in some way. Choose to consume more vegetables. It's your call.

Don't forget that you're the captain of your support team. What kind of backup do you need? Ask for and invite others to help. As you set off down the path, choose the fork in the road that appeals to your sense of comfort and challenge. Are you a self-starter who's fine with dangling your own carrot? Or do you find it easier to stay on track with an accountability buddy—someone to walk beside you, pointing out the pitfalls, and cheering you on to success?

It's up to you.

Whatever you do, don't skimp on support. Even if you're self-motivated, you can still benefit from touching base with someone else now and then. Remember that you don't have to know all the steps in advance. Step 3 of the **ADAPT** and **GROW** technique emphasizes that only the first, or the first few, steps need definition at the start.

Another thing to consider. We're all programmed to resist change. Change doesn't feel pleasant. Yet, if given the opportunity to sign up for transformation, we're all in. I'd like you to consider that they're two sides of the same door. Change leads to transformation. From here on, when you think of or read anything about change, keep an open mind to the transformation waiting on the other side.

Get ready to step over the threshold.

It's all about control, right?

When I wrote my book, *FibroWHYalgia*, the working title was "Spiraling Into Control." Like it? I sure did. I was quite enamored with it. I liked the energized feeling that it gave me. I wanted to share that feeling of self-empowerment with others. It felt compelling, and I couldn't wait to launch my book into the world.

I'm fond of spirals. I love how they frequently appear in nature. Spiral seashells, flowers, and tightly curled ferns remind me of God's everlasting presence in the natural healing process. I often use spiral images in my lectures, articles, and guided meditations with clients because they beautifully describe the healing journey. They illustrate the key point that healing is not a linear (point A to point B) process. I was drawn to the beauty of spirals long before I learned that I wasn't the only one. The symbol of the Nautilus is often used in ancient texts to represent problem-solving skills and the sacred healing journey.[91]

Interesting, eh?

---

91 http://galacticconnection.com/spirals-their-ancient-meaning-and-symbolism/

> ### *Just as there are no straight lines in nature, there are no straight paths in the spiral journey.*

Getting back to my point. The "Spiraling Into" part of my book title was fine, but the word "control" didn't really apply. The more I wrote and studied, the more I discovered this erroneous viewpoint. Healing has more to do with acceptance—the absence of control—than with control. True healing begins when we learn to accept, adapt, and expand into change. Healing happens when we let go of expectations. Conversely, it doesn't happen when we seek to control them.

I eventually discovered that I had to accept that I was okay no matter what the outcome. When in chronic unrelenting pain, that level of acceptance is hard-won. I understand that. Over time, I realized that even in my painful body, I was precisely where I needed to be to listen, learn, and put my discoveries into practice. After embracing this stage of acceptance, I had to adapt to new ideas and concepts.

Finally, I had to let go of the notion that my body was diseased or damaged and broken. Searching for a "fix" is in itself defining yourself as malfunctioning. Don't get me wrong. My poor body function was far from optimal. But I recognized why my previous efforts hadn't worked. By shining a light on my body's failings, I stayed stuck in despair. My constant view of what I perceived as brokenness held me back.

Shifting away from "what's broken" and toward the "how to heal" mindset meant turning away from the familiar. I had to ditch medical authorities who shared the belief that healing was an impossibility. I even had to turn away from my own local fibromyalgia support group that shared instructions on how to handle my future disability status (as if a future of disability were set in stone). I had to turn away from well-meaning friends, too, who weren't in alignment with my new-found path of positive discoveries.

I zeroed in on forward motion. I viewed every thought and experience through a dual lens—either positive or negative. Just two options. This simplified view helped me to sift and sort. If a thought, emotion, relationship, or behavior caused my plans to stagnate, or worse, move backward—I dropped it. If it propelled me forward, I multiplied it. (More on this practice I call Change or Chains later in this chapter.)

As you know, *spiraling down* into despair, self-sabotage, or relapse is easy. Falling takes next to no effort at all. Falling can happen without conscious awareness. On the other hand, *spiraling up* into new ideas, thoughts, processes, techniques, and healthy relationships takes intentional practice. There's no getting around that. Any new behavior takes at least some effort… at first.

Spiraling *up* takes conscious intention and action.

I'm pleased to share that there's hidden treasure on the other side of this action. Initial effort turns to effortlessness when repeated. Repetition of spiraling up helps to harness the wind in our sails.

Here's one of my absolute favorite quotes describing this process.

> ***"All change is hard at the beginning, messy in the middle, and gorgeous at the end."***
> —Robin Sharma

Things can really get muddled and mired in the middle.

Consider this advance warning. If you pursue a difficult change, there will be a point (somewhere in the middle) where you will question the process. You may even question your judgment. You'll wonder if you made a good decision and if you'll be able to follow it through. You'll wonder whether or not others will support you or any one of a hundred other concerns. You may envision disaster scenarios.

Your thoughts may whisper to you, *I should just give up now before I'm in too deep.*

The anxiety level of this stage may be a blip on the scale or off the charts. But know this: trying to parse it out isn't the main thing. Write the following quote onto a sticky note and place it where you'll see it often—

> **When all's said and done, it's not the analysis of my fears but the decision to move beyond them that truly counts.**

Negative thoughts, fears, and worry feed a downward spiral. As an antidote, application of any of the Build-a-Better-Brain practices found in Chapter 16 fuel an upward spiral.

Contrary to what you may think, fear isn't the enemy. Fear is a natural survival instinct. Did you know that there are only two innate fears? We're born with the fear of loud noises and the fear of falling.[92] That's it. All other fears are either created or learned. Chew on that for a minute. Now that you know that the vast majority of your fears are adopted through life, would you like to lessen the grip they have over you?

---

92   https://www.cnn.com/2015/10/29/health/science-of-fear/index.html

This next section will help. Creating resourceful strategies in advance puts you in charge. From a place of strength, you can stay on track, stay flexible through change, and transition into that upward spiral with ease.

> **"Of all the liars in the world,**
> **sometimes the worst are our own fears."**
> —Rudyard Kipling

Client case study summary

I originally planned to include several case studies in this book detailing the actual progress made by my clients. I know how empowering it can be to step into the shoes of those who've struggled with similar circumstances.

But when I compiled my list, I found something very interesting. It shouldn't have surprised me, but it did.

Clients come to me with differing circumstances. They're challenged by a myriad of things. But when all is said and done, the underlying roots of their struggles fit into far fewer categories than you may think. I knew there were similarities, but until now, I hadn't distilled them down to a brief list. I'll share a synopsis of these underlying issues shortly.

But first, here's a summary of what clients state they're looking for from me:

■ Typical client preliminary concerns

- Nutritional guidance and support (either "just tell me what to eat" or "show me a few recipes and let me figure out what to eat")
- Pain relief/chronic pain management (joint, muscle, skeletal)
- Sleep/insomnia issues
- Support regarding combative/antagonistic co-workers, spouses, family members, etc.
- Work-related stress and anxieties
- Weight loss
- Blood sugar regulation
- Support for inflammation and digestive issues (IBS, SIBO, leaky gut, candida, mycotoxin, yeast overgrowth, etc.)
- Concern over recent lab results (obesity, high inflammation markers, thyroid/hormonal dysfunction, high blood pressure, diabetes or pre-diabetes warnings, etc.)
- Wanting to solve the "I just think negatively" mindset
- Needing to feel better physically to get a better job or improve job skills
- Needing support with cravings, emotional eating, and/or binging behaviors
- Looking for nutritional supplement recommendations and support
- Meal planning and budgeting support
- Exercise suggestions and support
- They don't actually want to see me at all but arrive at my office at a friend or family member's urging (or influence)

As you can see, they come for a wide variety of reasons. They connect with me at a pivot point in their lives. They're fed up and frustrated. They're afraid that if nothing changes, what else will fall apart? And, they recognize they're not getting results on their own, and it's not for lack of trying. That's exactly what support is for.

But here's what's really going on.

Even though clients come with diverse concerns, there is one surprising and unifying truth. When asked, clients can easily tell me multiple, basic things they can do to achieve what they want. They say, "I need to eat more veggies, or get rid of my Diet Coke habit, or get out and walk."

Seems simple, right?

They're not as much confused about what to do (although there is *some* of that), but they're more confused about HOW to do it. And how to stay on track. They need guidance and encouragement to get through the bumpy parts of the journey.

And here's something even deeper.

While they come to me with a "surface" problem, they also believe they have a secret core problem. One they haven't spoken out loud. One that's incredibly personal and impossible to solve. One that no one else on the planet shares. I remember feeling this way too. The more I believed my problem was unique, the more alone I felt.

Perhaps isolation keeps chronic illnesses sufferers cocooned from further pain. But it also shields them from options to heal.

After my recovery and in my early days of coaching, I kept this in mind. I vividly remembered the sting of loneliness in my pain. (Loneliness has little to do with being alone, by the way.) Later, I witnessed this same isolation and pain in the eyes of my clients. Consistent patterns emerged, and I was onto something. Excitement and enthusiasm flowed as I began to document these core problems.

With an abundance of naiveté, I set out to do more research on what I'd found. My findings were far from isolated. The phenomenon of feeling alone, odd, not fitting the mold, and different from others is shockingly common. When in crisis, that which we try to hide the most is what unifies us.

This applicable quote says it nicely.

> *"What's most personal*
> *is most universal."*
> —Carl R. Rogers

The following underlying client issues represent a Reader's Digest version of what I hear most often. Some are derivative of others, but I've listed each to illustrate the sum total of these truths.

■ The brutal truth of common underlying client issues

- Beliefs of being broken, unfixable, different, and/or unworthy (and that this "uniqueness" means that no one else could understand or help)
- Belief that there's ONE main soul-crushing thing that's unfixable, broken, or deficient
- *Negative self-talk that's scathingly cruel*
- Fear of not belonging or not being accepted for who they are
- Anxiety over family issues and familial unspoken rules or secrets
- A distorted and skewed body image (and firm beliefs about what their body is capable or incapable of)

- A belief that trying something new only means they'll fail later
- A belief that trying something new means having to give up something else
- A belief that something crucial (but unidentifiable) is missing in their lives or their character
- A belief that there's ONE elusive way to get well (and it's somehow hidden from or denied them)
- A universal belief that any or all of these factors are sufficient evidential proof to condemn them to a life of isolation and loneliness (they don't belong)

As if the above statements aren't disturbing enough, take a look at what Lissa Rankin, MD has to say about this last point.

> ***"Loneliness is as dangerous for your health as smoking 15 cigarettes per day."***
> —Lissa Rankin[93]

As you can see, fear and limiting beliefs are common experiences in the human landscape. But ferreting them out in isolation is a challenge. It helps to enlist the objective viewpoint of someone adept at recognizing and eliminating them.

The collective truth of unbelievably harsh inner self-talk is one of the hallmarks of chronic illness. Whether the derisive self-talk came first and contributed to the development of chronic illness or the self-talk is a result of the illness doesn't matter.

The point is that both are present.

---

93   https://www.youtube.com/watch?v=s2hLhWSlOl0

I'm always saddened, and sometimes even shocked, at the ruthless ways my clients speak to themselves. It's as if they believe they can somehow change their behaviors by being "mean enough."

> *If meanness worked, we would already have the goals we set for ourselves.*

When it comes to talking to ourselves, there's no shortage of harsh words. What IS in short supply is kindness, acceptance, patience, empathy, objective insight, and self-compassion.

Advanced strategies and thought-pattern review

- In Chapter 1, we discussed your MAPP and how your filters can help you identify familiar patterns in your life. This provides a basis for understanding your mind and how it works.

- In Chapter 5, we mentioned the impact of self-talk on achieving your goals and plans. The FIVE 180 Reset is one method to help counteract negative self-talk and negative feelings in general. As a pattern interrupt, it provides an opportunity for exacting choice over your thoughts.

- By adding the powerful ADAPT and GROW technique (detailed in Chapters 10 and 11), you have a dependable recipe for effective problem-solving.

When a problem behavior or a negative thought comes to mind, put these strategies into action. Try them on for size. First, consider the fact that your mind's filters are probably skewing what you see or hear. Next, apply the simple FIVE 180 Reset method. Quick and easy.

Later, as you're planning out goals and desired outcomes, apply the ADAPT and GROW technique to create your plan for success.

■ Uncork that bottleneck

These strategies provide another useful benefit. When it comes to doing something new or trying to get something done, do you sometimes feel stuck? Do you feel as if you have no options?

It's common to feel that all the signs you read along your journey say either "road closed" or "detour." Limited choices lead to frustration and feelings of futility. Applying these strategies helps to alleviate this bottleneck by reducing the stress response on both the body and mind. This, in turn, opens up the floodgates of new ideas.

Once the stress response is ratcheted down (or eliminated), new or innovative options come to mind more freely. Fresh options become visible.

New thoughts spur new solutions.

■ P.S.

The last lines (the postscript) of a letter can pack a powerful punch. As a postscript to this topic, I encourage you to add the Change or Chains process after the FIVE 180 Reset method. It can amplify positive results and help restructure your thoughts.

It's a clear-cut process where the explanation of it is longer than the practice itself, so don't get bogged down here.

After you've completed the FIVE 180 Reset method, take a brief moment to reflect on the initial frustrating thought. In very simplistic terms, was it negative or positive? Did it support what you want from life or not? (Hint: if it were positive, you likely wouldn't have needed a mental reset.)

Since the thought was powerful enough to prompt taking action, think for a moment about that power. What kind of emotions and actions do negative thoughts create? Probably not the actions you want to take.

Imagine this. You're standing in line at the grocery store, already late for an appointment. As you inch to the front of the line, the cashier turns her back and takes a personal call on her cell. Your patience is on thin ice. Thankfully, you practice the FIVE 180 Reset method and soon feel a sense of calm settle in. Once you get to the front of the queue, you're in command of what you choose to say (or not to say). You're operating from a position of authority and are in charge of your reaction.

Before applying the FIVE 180 Reset method, what would you have been thinking? Perhaps something such as "She's so rude! Because of her selfishness, I'm going to be late." These thoughts could likely stimulate elevated blood pressure and increased anxiety (perpetuating the negative health consequences of the situation).

Observe the emotional and physiological power of this circumstance. Simple thoughts can crank up your body's stress response. Thoughts can wind you up or calm you down. They have the power to create momentum, one way or the other. They encourage forward motion or stagnation (no momentum at all).

■ The Change or Chains process

Notice that forward motion feels like positive CHANGE—a world of possibilities. In contrast, stagnation, or staying stuck, feels like being shackled or tethered with CHAINS. In the simplest of terms, our thoughts launch us forward or keep us stuck. They're helpful, or they're not.

Becoming skilled at this identification takes practice.

> *Thoughts can be negative wolves disguised in positive sheepskin.*

Just because a thought may seem positive doesn't make it so. Practice a little self-awareness. Do your thoughts give you hesitation or pause in any way? If they hinder you, choose to move on. There's no merit to dwelling on whether or not they're true. The validity isn't the point.

Simply make a "note to self" on whether they're positive or negative. Do they help you feel there's an openness for CHANGE in your future? Or do they leave you feeling CHAINED to your current circumstances?

> *Moving forward embraces change while staying stuck chains you to the status quo.*

After practicing the FIVE 180 Reset, notice the intention behind your original thoughts and compare them to what you truly want from life. Apply the Change or Chains concept.

Do you have the results you want, or are you making consistent progress toward them? (How much progress is irrelevant.) If not, use the Change or Chains process to clarify what's holding you back. Notice the feelings of either hopeful possibility or of being stuck. Decide to embrace the thought or drop it and replace it with something better.

Are you now ready to put on a cape and discover your brain's superpowers?

You're equipped with a great foundation. Focused empowering thoughts build the neural pathways in your brain that align with success. You now have what it takes to strengthen your mental muscle. Continue building strength in these areas by adopting your favorite superpower traits featured in the next chapter. Grab a pen. You'll want to jot down notes next to the ones that feel especially soul-affirming to you.

■ Chapter 13 – Head Work

1. Do you tend to have a Negative Nancy in your head? Does that voice shift your focus to the potential for failure? Does it distract you from considering opportunities for success? If your Negative Nancy has anything to say about the potential outcomes of this book so far, jot them down now. Hold off on reviewing this list until after you've read Chapters 14 and 15. For now, just write down your negative thoughts. They need to be heard.

2. Review the steps provided in the Advanced Strategies and Thought Pattern Review section. All of these steps should be familiar at this point. Identify what step may challenge you the most. Is it noticing your inner self-talk in the first place? Or perhaps it's deciding what you'd rather think instead.

Whatever it is, focus on that step in particular and decide to make the solution for it into a habit.

3. The Change or Chains process is deceptively simple. It doesn't take long to do, and putting it into practice can be quite an eye-opener. Each time you find yourself feeling tense, stressed, nervous, or knots in your stomach, reflect on the triggering thoughts. Notice if there's a pattern. Do you often have thoughts that make you feel isolated or alone? What about feeling broken or that you somehow don't measure up? Notice these patterns and choose statements that lead you toward a changed future rather than a chained past.

Have you ever thought that your personality is just what you're born with? I hope the chapters you've read so far put that misnomer to rest. In the next chapter, you'll get an idea of how your traits can add a positive spin to your personal characteristics. Get ready to discover your superpowers.

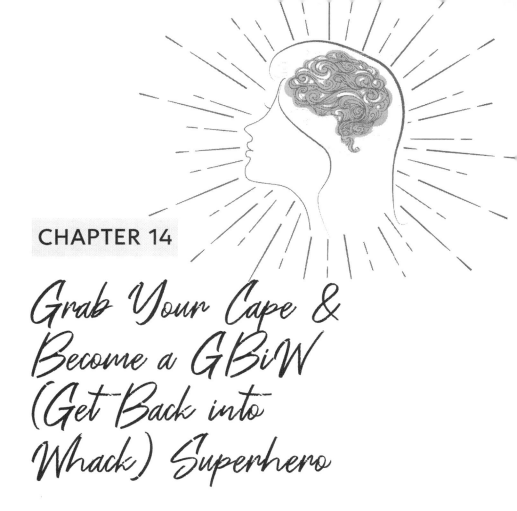

CHAPTER 14

Grab Your Cape & Become a GBiW (Get Back into Whack) Superhero

Not everyone can be a superhero. At least not the Marvel comic type. But we can become kick-butt superheroes in our own sphere of influence. By adopting the following traits and deciding to show up authentically as ourselves in the world, we become superheroes in our own lives and the lives of others.

20 superpower traits to flex
your brain muscles

Can you rewire your brain from negativity to positivity? Absolutely! Studies show that with repetition and consistent application of positive thought patterns, the brain's neuroplasticity tendency can adapt by creating new neural pathways.[94] This, by the way, is available to all. Our brains can adapt and improve at any age.

It's remarkable news for those who feel stuck and unable to change. Development and growth of any (or all) of the superpower traits listed below help to move the needle toward a positive healing outcome.

Reinforce these traits for healing success. Some may appeal to you more than others. That's okay. As you reflect on them, notice the ones that give you a positive inner buzz. Start there and allow others to grow over time. Many of these traits naturally overlap, cascading from one to the next.

Some may feel partially redundant. That's the beauty of the English language. Words elicit powerful images, physical sensations, and emotions. And, I want to make sure that the right ones are harnessed for *you*.

Here's how Mark Twain describes finding just the right word: *"The difference between the almost right word and the right word is like the difference between a lightning bug and the lightning."*

Discover your "lightning" trait. The one or ones that feed your soul. They're in no particular order.

---

94   http://bigthink.com/think-tank/brain-exercise

■ Superpower traits

• A sense of CURIOSITY

Curiosity allows your perception of a problem to change. It allows for a healthy sense of space or detachment from the circumstance. Curiosity may lead to overcoming adversity by shifting the focus from "problem to solution." When inner self-talk centers around blame, shame, or helplessness, it reinforces the belief that solutions exist outside of your control. When self-talk centers around hopelessness, it reinforces the belief that there are no solutions and there's no way out. In either scenario (living in the past or future), the beauty and clarity of the present moment are lost. Developing a sense of curiosity creates that "way out" by shifting the perspective.

Becoming curious about why something is the way it is opens the door for discovery. And, please keep this tip in mind. Understanding the "why" of things is your job. But when it comes to "how," turn it over to God.

Why not begin now? Become curious about the positive changes in store for you as you finish this book. Write, repeat, and meditate on phrases such as—

"I wonder how I'll put what I've learned into practice?"
"I wonder where I'll find the most success?"
"I like the idea that healing is possible for me."
"I'm curious about how the resources I need always show up for me."
"I'm interested in watching this specific problem work out for me."

As you develop the curiosity to anticipate a change in your life, allow space for results that are better than what you'd predict. From my experience, God often exceeds my expectations by revealing solutions

and answers that never would have occurred to me. Allowing this extra space leaves me feeling eager to see how things will resolve.

Try this one on for size—

"I like the idea that God has a solution to this problem, and I love to
be surprised at how it unfolds."

- **A sense of OBJECTIVITY**

Objectivity is a natural offshoot of curiosity. Looking at a problem
or a potential solution with a sense of wonder and curiosity provides
a crucial perspective of detachment. That little bit of distance gives
you the valuable breathing space needed to see things in a new light.

Distance also allows you to detach yourself from emotions or judgments that may cloud your perspective. Choosing to view a situation
with curiosity and objectivity not only tells your nonconscious mind
that a solution is possible, but it also implies an openness towards
finding it.

From the center of chaos, your view of available options is narrow
and obscured. Applying objectivity to difficult or critical situations
widens your viewpoint and increases your potential for success.

- **A sense of GRIT**

The word grit can bring to mind anything from John Wayne to the
residue on the bottom of your well-worn flip-flops. The definition I'm
referring to here is the characteristic that gives you the extra push you
need to keep going. This Marvin Phillips quote comes to mind—"*The
difference between try and triumph is a little umph!*"

That's grit.

Grit gives you the nudge for one last try before calling it quits. Grit allows you to withstand adversity yet stay aligned with your morals and goals. It's not about perfection, but rather persistence.

Two of my favorite characteristics related to grit are tenacity and passion. Grit added to the mix creates an unbeatable, unstoppable, and unflappable person who perseveres. If you'd like to learn more, check out Angela Lee Duckworth's TED talk on Grit.[95]

- **A sense of GRACE**

Developing a sense of grace is about finding the strength to be flexible. Strength is often confused with the tendency to be rigid. Grace allows freedom within the boundaries of your expectations. Things don't always go as planned. Having the grace to accept yourself as human (not infallible) is a learned skill.

Perhaps you're like me. I used to chastise myself for silly things such as losing something or missing a turn when driving to an important appointment. My inner world had a slim margin for error. From this obscured point of view, it's nearly impossible to see the humor in your own weaknesses.

I remember the moment this shifted for me. In a business meeting, I realized that a suggestion I'd just made (with fervor) was less than practical. I laughed out loud and said, "Who am I kidding? I don't know if that'll work or not. And if anyone else has a better idea, I'm listening."

It had been a contentious meeting, and my willingness to laugh at myself broke the ice. Even more, I learned that I didn't always have to have it all together. Revealing my weakness and a willingness to laugh about it developed a stronger bond with the group.

---

95   https://www.ted.com/speakers/angela_lee_duckworth

Viewing disappointment or failure as a fundamental part of life provides an open door for grace to enter. (TIP: *If the word failure pops up in your head, replace it with the phrase, "learning experience." And for more suggestions, check out the entry for a sense of FLEXIBILITY below.*)

We can barely comprehend God's grace for us, let alone our own sense of grace for our actions and others. To me, grace always evokes a sense of expansion or space. If nothing else, it reminds me to breathe.

Here's a favorite quote from the author Suzanne Woods Fisher: *"We fail in the work of grace and love when there is too much of us and not enough of God."*

- **A sense of FORGIVENESS**

Forgiveness is one of the most commonly discussed subjects in my work with clients. For many, anger and resentment boils beneath the surface for wrongs done to them.

I get it. Life is unfair.

Unfortunately, holding on to lethal emotions allows disease to fester and spread. Ignored emotions don't disappear—they're stored in our bodies. There's a reason why chiropractors and massage therapists often say, "issues are in the tissues."

Negative thoughts also have an effect. Bitterness burrows deep into our physical neurology with pain being one of the most obvious indicators. While there are lots of ways to work through the process of forgiveness, here's the first misconception I'd like to clear up. Forgiving someone is *not* the same thing as condoning their behavior. Forgiveness isn't about them at all. You get to decide if they're even involved in the process.

Forgiveness is about *you*. Forgiveness is about letting go of a past wrong and moving on… for *your* sake. Forgiving someone is one thing. Staying in a relationship with them is another. You get to make that choice.

Here's another often missed element of forgiveness. Put yourself at the top of the list of those to forgive. It's not uncommon to hold ourselves accountable for perceived failings that we may or may not have had any control over. And, it's not just for the living. We can forgive those who've passed on.

Either way, it's time to let go.

Prayer, meditation, journaling, and getting outside support can help to reveal bottled-up situations that warrant self-compassion and forgiveness. What can you let go of right now? Make the effort to move forward.

Don't waste one more precious moment. Forgiving yourself and others may be the single most powerful healing step you take from this book.

> *"I don't forgive people because I 'm weak. I forgive them because I 'm strong enough to know that people make mistakes."*
> —Marilyn Monroe

- **A sense of SUSPENDED DISBELIEF**

Have you ever seen a product demonstration at a tradeshow of something you already own? If so, you easily agreed or disagreed with the sales pitch depending on personal experience. But think about this. If you owned it already and considered it rubbish, how open would you be to hear about new potential uses for the product? Probably not very.

A mind that already believes it knows something isn't open to new ideas.

We don't intentionally walk around with closed minds, but our previous experiences create what we perceive to be true. Skepticism, doubt, and disbelief easily slide into cynicism, suspicion, and distrust.

Maybe you're familiar with the skeptic's annoying cousin, the know-it-all? A know-it-all, by definition, has no mental room for anything other than what's already there. Besides being highly irritating to everyone else, a know-it-all is quite stuck. Without new growth, it's impossible to find solutions.

Certainty can be a good thing, but a healthy willingness to question the status quo has its place. Here's a favorite Mark Twain quote on the subject: *"It ain't what you don't know that gets you in trouble. It's what you know for sure that just ain't so."*

Not fully comprehending something can be a positive thing. In the coaching classroom trainings I've attended, we clap and celebrate when a student says, "I'm confused." We do this for two reasons.

The first is to honor the fact that we're further along in the process than we may think. We can't be confused about something we know absolutely nothing about. For example, if we know nothing about performing heart surgery, we'd never complain that we're confused about it. We wouldn't fret over not knowing how to knit major arteries back together. We only recognize what we don't know.

Being confused about something means that we know at least *something* about it.

The second reason we applaud the state of confusion is to celebrate where we are—the precipice point. A state of confusion often precedes an amazing breakthrough. If you're confused—congratulations! You're exactly where you need to be to turn the corner and experience the epiphany ahead.

Ready for a breakthrough? Suspend your disbelief, applaud confusion, and keep pressing forward.

- **A sense of POSSIBILITY**

You may feel that this is the same thing as a sense of suspended belief. But there's an important distinction. A sense of suspended disbelief *begins* with the notion of disbelief. There's a firm obstacle that must be overcome.

A sense of possibility may or may not begin with an obstacle.

A sense of possibility has a tingly feeling to it. It feels light and unencumbered. It's filled with hope and anticipation. It feels juicy. It may even feel exciting and a little bit like forbidden fruit. It depends on how closed off you are to believing you can have what you want.

Do you believe that a healthy, whole body is available to you? Do you believe that healing is part of your present and future?

I encourage you to invite the sense of possibility into your vocabulary today. Focus on what's possible (rather than on what's not) and see how you navigate the waters of chronic illness with the wind in your sails.

- **A sense of POSITIVITY**

From my clients, I often hear variations of these statements—"I can't change how I think. I'm just a negative person. It's who I am."

That's not 100% true. When it comes to our mental forecast, we're all partly negative and partly positive. But which is the bigger part? *That's* the indicator of success. How far we lean toward the positive side of things can mean the difference between reaching for desired results and staying stuck in bitter disappointment.

Negative thought patterns may develop from observing behaviors of those around you. Or negativity may spread from environmental exposures or circumstances. In any case, negative thoughts arrive uninvited. We don't coax ourselves to be negative. Flipping the switch from a negative to a positive nature takes deliberate intention and practice. It takes constant monitoring. The principles outlined in this book are designed to help you do just that. Through intentional practices, you can adopt a more positive mindset.

In the meantime, keep this in mind:

You are NOT your thoughts.

You are not the sum total of the thoughts, ideas, and perceptions that flit through your mind. If they happen to be negative, it doesn't mean that *you* are negative. It merely means that your MAPP is running on autopilot, bringing to mind familiar and well-worn negative thoughts and feelings.

That negative voice in your head is *not* you. It plays like a tape recorder in your mind and doesn't offer any new or original thoughts.

Thoughts can change. We can create new patterns and develop new neural pathways of positivity. You can jumpstart this process by adopting any of your favorite Build-a-Better-Brain practices as listed in Chapter 16. They provide the guided path to making a positive outlook a reality.

With repetition and incremental application of any of these practices, your new and improved statement can be, "I'm just a positive person. It's who I am!"

- **A sense of EMPOWERMENT**

A sense of empowerment can help you blaze past the doubts and fears that keep you hamstrung. This is more than simple motivation. A sense of empowerment prompts the awareness that you're capable and that you have the means to tackle any given task.

Feeling empowered is often accompanied by a sense of feeling equipped.

The emotions that accompany a sense of empowerment mature into confidence. This expansive feeling nudges out lower energy emotions such as fear, anxiety, and insecurity. Feeling empowered can help you to take on a difficult task and see it through to its denouement.

(Please note that a sense of empowerment is different from a sense of entitlement. Feeling empowered is an *earned* confidence. Those who feel entitled also award themselves with confidence, but this feeling is hollow and one-dimensional. It's assumed without merit.)

- **A sense of WHY**

Successful outcomes begin by clearly defining what you want to achieve. And nothing crystalizes that sense of clarity like a strong emotional tie attached to the end goal. Emotions invoke a visceral feeling to our desires. Feelings stick with us without effort.

This all comes from developing a sense of *why*.

Once we've defined *why* we want to achieve a goal (accompanied by a vivid mental picture linked to elevated emotions), we're likely to keep the goal at the forefront of our conscious awareness.

Emotions amp up our goals, making them feel bigger and brighter. They become fabulously real. Goals that bring up intense images and emotions come naturally. Your sense of why may steer you either toward your goal or away from not achieving it. Both paths have merit. They help us to feel encouraged and inspired to take action as well as driven to continue.

Cultivating a strong sense of *why* serves up a big payoff. A sense of why blends the power of images, emotions, and imagination to engage your feelings of motivation.

One quick note of caution; You know I'm all about the WHY. After all, I titled my book, FibroWHYalgia. *Understanding why I got sick was an important component of my healing journey. However, when it comes to some topics such as limiting beliefs, unwanted behaviors, and looking into past emotional hurts, looking for the why can possibly stunt your progress. For example, wanting to know why we bite our nails is less helpful than knowing that we want to stop. Digging around for the why can serve as a distraction and a way to procrastinate, especially when analyzing someone else's behavior. In these cases, WHY can be a sticking point. Instead, stop treating yourself and others as a project. Place your focus on ridding unhealthy behaviors rather than on digging for why they occur. Forward motion is the productive path.*

• A sense of INTEGRITY

What does integrity have to do with your personal goals? More than what meets the eye. Surprisingly, many of us are not all that aware of our core values. We've never taken the time to articulate what's truly important to us. This lack of awareness leads to incongruency when it comes to goal-setting.

Taking the time to assess and jot down your values is a worthwhile investment. Even better, enlist the help of a practitioner to go even deeper. When you're clear about what matters to you, compare your values list to the outcome of your goals. Review them for compatibility. Goals aligned with personal values stand a much higher chance of achievement. (You'll find further steps to assess practical application of core values in the *Get Back into Whack Workbook*.)

Integrity is more than just a set of rules. Understanding what's important to you helps to develop the core of who you are. It takes little to no effort to stay in alignment with actions and behaviors that fall within your personal code of ethics. It makes things easier.

Use your sense of integrity as a measuring stick. When setting a specific goal, analyze your options by comparing them. Do they fall within your standards?

Here's a quick example. Once I learned the truth about the harmful chemicals, additives, and artificial ingredients inherent in processed foods, I no longer saw them as real (or even desirable) foods. My values changed when it came to my nutritional options.

My food choices reflect my personal integrity. This has nothing, by the way, to do with perfection. There's no such thing as "perfect." I just do my best. I understand the role that my personal integrity plays.

My nutritional choices either build me up or tear me down. The decision-making process becomes simplified.

Our core values differ. There's no right or wrong. The point is that by crystalizing what's valuable to **you**, you'll fortify your sense of integrity.

- **A sense of COMMUNITY**

You weren't created to live and take action as a lone wolf. By nature, you need the assistance of a supportive community to flourish. Strong relationships and a sense of community even impact your overall health and longevity factors.[96] Do you belong to a religious congregation, social organization, fitness club, or to a community support group?

They can bolster you with much-needed guidance and encouragement.

Building a sense of community paves a two-way street. You benefit from the collective group, and everyone gains when what you have to offer is shared. Lending a helping hand fulfills your needs for social connections. What can you do for others? Whether it's volunteering[97] your time, making donations, or participating in a prayer group, these links strengthen your health resources as well as others.

Compassion is a great co-op to a sense of community. Developing compassion for others helps you to feel you've walked a mile in their shoes. By expressing compassion, you increase the ability for others to hear and understand your needs.

---

96   http://www.health.harvard.edu/newsletter_article/the-health-benefits-of-strong-relationships
97   https://articles.mercola.com/sites/articles/archive/2018/03/15/volunteer-work.aspx

> *"We rise by lifting others."*
> —Robert Ingersoll

- **A sense of GENEROSITY**

I'm sure you've heard the adage, "It's better to give than to receive," and it's true. A generous nature nourishes the soul. But did you know that giving freely promotes physical benefits too? Heartfelt charitable giving, volunteering, donating, lending a hand, and any type of altruism without seeking a return gives you that sought-after warm, fuzzy feeling inside.

That feeling is one indicator that your body is humming along at optimum levels. It's firing on all cylinders. Feeling good about your benevolent actions generates a cascade of positive chemical reactions in the body. A generous nature douses the body in that powerhouse of the feel-good hormone—oxytocin.[98]

Losing yourself in generosity creates a grateful feeling that leads to an inner sense of peace. Generosity, by the way, is truly contagious. Try it for yourself. See if you can out-give your friends, family, co-workers, and others. The ripple effect from your actions benefits you and extends well beyond your reach.

- **A sense of ACCOUNTABILITY**

Studies consistently prove that outside factors have a powerful (and positive) influence over goal achievement. By enlisting outside sup-

---

98   https://www.psychologytoday.com/us/blog/the-moral-molecule/200911/the-science-generosity

port, your goals not only stand a greater chance of coming to fruition but desired outcomes multiply with greater speed and efficiency.[99]

Have you ever set an intention to hit the gym first thing in the morning and then reneged on the commitment? Have you noticed that you're less likely to bail on the commitments you make to others than ones made to yourself? Even if you're self-motivated, it's productive to enlist a supportive nudge from a respected outside source.

The role of this compatible relationship always makes me think of bowling alley bumper pads. For young or unskilled bowlers, using a bumper pad in the lane's gutter keeps the ball within bounds. When they're in place, the ball has a good chance of knocking down at least a few pins. In the same way, an accountability partner provides support, encouragement, and feedback to guide you on course.

They can keep you out of the gutter of despair and feeling like you want to wave a white flag. An accountability partner can make the difference between giving up and crossing the finish line.

Some accountability practices can be self-guided. Tracking is my favorite accountability tool for fitness goals, mindfulness practices, food-related plans, and much more. Track your goals, progress, setbacks, achievements, and anything else related to your plan. Being able to physically see your progress—on paper or in a digital format—helps you to discover patterns of pitfalls and success.

> ### *Using a tracking strategy can provide that "stick with it" breakthrough you're looking for.*

---

99   http://www.huffingtonpost.com/vanessa-van-edwards/the-science-of-goal-setting_b_6335764.html

Track your progress in a notebook, calendar, app, or whatever method you prefer. Don't overcomplicate it. Easy-to-use free apps such as Lose it and My Fitness Pal makes food tracking easy. To solidify your results, recruit outside accountability from a friend, neighbor, or family member. Even better, hire a coach or mentor.

Don't forget Fido!

Your pet's physical need to get out and smell the roses is a great way to help you do the same. A wagging tail can demonstrate not only love but also an invitation to a mutually beneficial partnership. If you don't have a walkable pet, might I suggest visiting your local animal rescue shelter? Perhaps you'll find a furry friend who's looking for a person to rescue. Or offer to walk a neighbor's dog. Either way, the benefits are multiplied.

- **A sense of INTUITION**

How familiar are you with your sense of intuition? Do you feel in touch? Have you checked in with your gut instinct lately?

The digestive tract houses your body's enteric nervous system. This interconnected structure contains possibly more neurons than the spinal cord.[100] The innate intelligence that exists in this system is highly reactive to thoughts, feelings, and emotions. The correlation between emotions and intuition has been well-documented for centuries.

With this in mind, the phrase "gut feelings" becomes clearer.

There's a wide spectrum of connectedness to experience. Some feel a stronger sense of inner guidance than others. They trust their gut instincts and frequently "check-in" to assess how they feel about things.

---

100   https://www.ncbi.nlm.nih.gov/books/NBK11097/

If this doesn't describe you, don't worry.

You may not feel this inner alignment at all. Not all that long ago, intuition seemed like a foreign language to me. I recall a yoga class instructor who said, "Now, breathe deeply and connect to your intuition. What's your inner guide saying to you?"

My only thought was, "Run!"

Out of embarrassment (and perhaps curiosity), I stayed put. I felt as if the rest of the class was privy to something to which I hadn't a clue. Everyone else looked so peaceful and serene, and I felt anything but. I wondered, "How do I get connected?"

Quieting the monkey mind is a great place to start. In the silence that accompanies prayer, meditation, and deep breathing, you may feel a sense of calm. Your intuition may whisper to you during moving meditation practices such as tai chi, qigong, and restorative yoga. It's not only the circumstances. Your intuition has always had something to say. The opportunity to hear it comes from taking the quiet pause to listen.

A deepened spiritual life fosters this inner sense of knowing. Most of us do have a feeling of yes or no. We naturally lean toward choices we want to make and away from those we want to avoid. But we may have learned over time to ignore this inner sense and instead make no decision at all. If that's you, it may take some time and practice to reconnect.

Re-establishing a relationship with your sense of intuition builds trust. You can feed and nurture your intuition through meditative practices that strengthen this bond. The scientifically proven methods from Heartmath[101] can help.

---

101   https://www.heartmath.com/blog/articles/new-guided-heart-meditations/

Open the door to your intuition and let it step inside. Feed it what it needs to flourish—respect and recognition. When you feel the nudge to think of a friend, call him or her. If a sales pitch makes your stomach flop rather than flip, walk away. If you feel energized by a new thought, idea, or concept, move forward to learn more.

Intuition is also sometimes referred to as heart intelligence.[102] Close your eyes, put your hand over your heart, and check-in. When your intuition feels invited and respected, it shows up more often.

Here are some qualities that may help you to recognize your intuitive voice:

1. It speaks first, but very softly
2. It may feel more like a nudge or a gentle push toward something
3. It may be a small gentle whisper
4. It's unconditionally loving and is never critical
5. It may encourage curiosity or stepping into the unknown
6. It's never controversial, pushy, or attention-seeking

Your intuition connects at both the conscious and nonconscious levels. The inner voice that comes from God fosters a spiritual core that transcends all others.

Our God-given inner voice has much to say. That is, when we're quiet enough to listen.

• A sense of FLEXIBILITY

We've talked a lot about adaptation and expansion, but I'd like to reinforce one main component of it. This is about getting up, dusting

---

102   https://www.heartmath.org/articles-of-the-heart/heartmath-tools-techniques/heart-agent-transformation/

yourself off, and getting back in the saddle after a tumble. Your willingness to get back on the horse comes from how you interpret the
fall in the first place.

If something doesn't go as planned, do you sulk or get angry? Do you
feel disappointed in yourself? These common emotions are the an-
tithesis of those who practice a "radically successful" lifestyle.[103] For
them, a setback is a mere hiccup and not viewed as a failure.

There's a famous self-help quote that states, *"There's no failure. Only
feedback."*

Can you see how this turns the tables on the standard definition of
failure? A strong determination to stay flexible already presupposes
that there will be setbacks and plans that go awry. Try to view them as
speedbumps rather than roadblocks. A winning strategy is to decide
at the get-go that you'll do what it takes to work around, past, over, or
under the inevitable setbacks.

Here's another truism that applies to the negotiation process. It states,
"The person with the most flexibility wins." Flexibility allows for adaptation, regrouping, reassessing, and reevaluating. A rigid person is likely
to overlook available possibilities to remedy a situation strictly because he or she is closed off from options. A sense of flexibility allows
for freedom in any negotiation process as well as creating freedom in
your own health journey.

Flexibility also builds resilience. A sense of flexibility allows you to
rebound from disappointment gracefully. With enough flexibility and
resilience, you may not only endure, but have the potential to thrive
after hardships, crises, and trauma.

---

103   http://www.forbes.com/sites/davidkwilliams/2013/07/31/the-one-thing-successful-
people-dont-do-and-9-famous-examples/#2cd5189171bb

• **A sense of PEACE**

Developing a sense of true inner peace provides an intriguing journey. We may invite a sense of peace, but it arrives at its own pace. It arrives when it's darned good and ready.

I've felt a profound sense of peace at the beach, in the car singing Christmas carols, and certainly while holding my grandchildren. These may seem cliché. I've also felt peace when I've made a tough decision that may or may not be popular with others. I've felt peace upon completion of an arduous task such as writing a heavily researched article, a religious poem, or after finishing writing a book.

Peace can show up at unexpected crossroads. When it comes to our health plans, a sense of peace helps us to learn as much (if not more) from the detours along the way as we do from the straight and narrow path.

A genuine sense of peace can't be manipulated. Cultivating peace takes intentional and focused practice. It takes a willingness to let go. You may wish to study the concept of Blue Mind[104] from Wallace J. Nichols.

If you're not sure of what peace is, you're probably well aware of what it isn't. A sense of peace cannot exist within anxiety or fear. Worrying is like praying for what we *don't* want. Worrying robs us of the ability to feel peace at all according to professional speaker, Isabelle Mercier. In her lectures, she suggests that we adopt a zero-tolerance policy when it comes to accepting the daily onslaught of worrisome thoughts. In her TED talk[105] on the subject of worry, she relays this sage advice from her mother, *"If you don't have time to say no to what you don't want, you'll never have the time for what you do want."*

---

104   http://wallacejnichols.org/
105   https://www.youtube.com/watch?v=--mY5ruEhqI

She points out that according to research, 92% of our worries will either never happen at all or have already happened. Sadly, the staggering pressure of that worry keeps us from living the life we're meant to live.

Is it time to embrace a sense of peace by redirecting your focus away from worry? Decide to break the pattern of worry right now and adopt (and adapt to) a sense of peace.

> ***"Worry is a misuse of the imagination."***
> —Dan Zadra

- **A sense of BLISS**

In this definition, bliss differs somewhat from peace. While peace is the absence of fear, anxiety, and worry, peace can also feel like a state of no feeling at all. It can be a transcendent existence of empty space and utter calm.

Bliss, on the other hand, has an abundance of feelings and emotions. The positive feelings of bliss add an emotional layer on top of the feeling of peace. It adds cheer, gladness, joy, delight, blessings, and anticipated hope. A sense of self-transcendent awe[106] can invite this blissful feeling. Feel your body awash in the powerful beauty of God's creations—sunrises, sunsets, oceans, forests, deserts, vistas, flowers, creatures, etc. Feel the sense of bliss and wonder in every cell of your body. *Feel* AWE-some.

One of my favorite positivity acronyms is HOPE (Hold On, Pain Ends). Could you benefit from hearing that daily? Dire circumstances

---

106   https://www.researchgate.net/publication/324651280_Awe_A_Self-Transcendent_and_
Sometimes_Transformative_Emotion

don't last forever—hallelujah! Change is just around the corner. It may not arrive according to the timetable we expect, but when we're flexible and able to adapt, change lifts us from our present circumstances and elevates us to what's next.

> *"There was never a night or a problem that could defeat sunrise or hope."*
> —Bernard Williams

- **A sense of FREEDOM & EXPANSION**

Freedom and expansion provide space for acceptance of who we are. When we're traveling the path of who we are and know what we're placed on this planet to do (our passionate purpose), we can feel this freedom in every cell of our body. Guided by our sense of quiet direction, freedom both adds and deletes. It adds creativity, expansion, and a sense of wonder. It deletes the burden of perfection.

We grow into an expanded sense of freedom by incorporating the Build-a-Better-Brain (Chapter 16) practices listed in this book. Sample many of them. Put a select few into daily practice. Be choosy. Add the ones that feed your soul and don't be afraid to try new ones along the way. Adopting a sense of freedom and expansion is a changing, flowing practice.

- **A sense of HUMOR**

Do you hone your sense of humor? Do you intentionally focus on keeping it in shape? Doing so has clinically proven health benefits.

A developed sense of humor strengthens the immune system, attracts new social connections, improves the metabolism, and sends a shower of happy hormones throughout the body.

And, that's just a fraction of the physical payoffs.

A sense of humor fosters the ability to practice one of the main healing principles of this book. The beneficial side effects of humor allow you to ADAPT to your surroundings and situations with grace and ease.

> ### *Humor paves your way to*
> ### *roll with the punches.*

I discovered this delightful quote from the witty Dr. Seuss after I'd completed writing this book—and long after I'd selected the title for it. As you'll see, it's quite apropos.

"Nonsense wakes up the brain cells. And it helps to develop a sense of humor, which is awfully important in this day and age. Humor has a tremendous place in this sordid world. It's more than just a matter of laughing. If you can see things out of whack, then you can see how things can be in whack."

■ Superpower traits summary

Are you ready to put these traits to work for you? When you do, you'll have a multi-dimensional map ready to follow. As a bonus, the next time some well-intentioned person says, "You just need to be positive," you can simply smile and nod in response. Because you know exactly how to make that become a reality.

> **"Change your thoughts,**
> **and you change your world."**
> —Norman Vincent Peale

■ Chapter 14 – Head Work

1. Review the superpower traits and place an X by the ones you relate to most and believe you already possess (to any degree). Re-read these entries and focus on how they make you feel at a physical level. Engage deeply in the emotions, ideas, and thoughts these traits bring to mind. Notice a deep sense of gratitude as you identify with these traits.

2. Review the superpower traits and circle the ones you'd like to develop. Who do they remind you of? What person (known personally to you or publicly known) exemplifies these traits? Write down the characteristics of the person(s) you'd like to emulate. Make a list of the superpower traits you'd like to adopt and review them daily.

3. Create a visualization practice incorporating your superpower traits. Imagine yourself (employing all senses—sight, sound, touch, smell, taste, AND emotion) deepening your experience with the traits that are familiar to you. View yourself adopting the traits you admire in others and see yourself shifting to think, feel, and act as they do.

＊

Whew! After this extensive chapter, you probably feel like you know everything there is to know about superpower traits. But wait... there's more. Just like the late-night Ginsu Knives salesman says. *"... if you act now, more bonuses to follow."* They're waiting patiently in Chapter 15. No credit card needed.

CHAPTER 15

Inspirational Clarity

What inspires you to take action? What motivates you and makes you tap dance in the right direction? Or, what makes you lose steam and drag your feet? Motivation seems to be a now-you-see-it / now-you-don't kind of thing. And, what's the deal with willpower? Sometimes it's there and at others—poof—it's just gone.

Searching for these feelings may leave you feeling like Indiana Jones traipsing through deserts in search of the Holy Grail. Motivation and willpower can be elusive at best.

But when we're searching, we're seriously looking to feel better about our actions and choices. We want to feel good.

All in all, we want to feel happy, right?

You're in the right place to dig into all three weighty topics. By the end of this chapter, you may feel that you hold the Holy Grail (of emotions) within your grasp.

The missing traits

Upon review of your personal goals and the superpower traits mentioned in the previous chapter, you may find a few crucial missing elements.

Happiness * Motivation * Willpower

They're suspiciously absent from the list—for a good reason. They're important enough to deserve a new chapter all their own.

For most of us, our understanding of how to generate these feelings is inaccurate. We get it backward or sideways. Unfortunately, this cattywampus approach leaves us feeling deficient or lacking in some way... the opposite of how we want to feel.

Let's start with happiness and motivation.

Many of us mistakenly believe that when some cosmic or magical chain of events happens, *then* we'll feel happy or motivated. What this means is that we're putting the responsibility for how we feel into something that's entirely outside of our control. **As long as we believe that our circumstances are someone else's responsibility, we're imprisoned in our own world of helplessness**. Happiness and satisfaction will always be out of reach.

How tragic!

If you feel this way, then it's no wonder you feel like a cork floating down the river of life. Each morning, same day—different scenery. No direction. No ability to change. And, no hope of paddling anywhere on your own.

This is often referred to as an if/then scenario, which we touched on in Chapter 10. Here are a few examples.

> IF I win the lottery, THEN I'll feel happy.
> IF I buy new running shoes, THEN I'll feel motivated to go to the gym.
> IF I start my diet tomorrow, THEN I'll feel like "I'm good."
> IF my family/spouse/boss praises me, THEN I'll feel better about myself.

These statements are false (even though they may feel true). Cause and effect are listed in reverse order. No outside event or circumstance can make us *feel* happiness or motivation. We may experience a surface-level temporary boost in mood, but the subsequent crash is definitely not worth it.

We want to experience lasting happiness despite our circumstances, don't we? And we want to feel energized and motivated to achieve our goals even when our health isn't at its best. I don't believe this is too much to ask, so let's figure out the source.

> ### *A genuine sense of happiness or motivation comes from within. It must be an inside job first.*

If you recall, the nonconscious mind is quite literal. Close your eyes and imagine the thought, "I want happiness." Did it work? Do you have happiness or even feel it? No. You've just expressed "wanting it." Remember, the act of wanting tells your nonconscious mind that it's out of reach. **The mental image created is of something at arm's length or further away from you.**

To feel happiness, let go of the word "want." Practice the feeling of having happiness now (even if you're pretending). Recall times where you felt bliss, peace, joy, and happiness. Make it a mental and full-sensory experience. Vividly imagine it as if it were happening *now*.

> ### *Happiness is a choice, not an outcome.*

Deriving a sense of happiness from your choices is a decision that you make, not something that you figure out or grow into. When you've decided to be happy with who you are and what you do, the need for approval from others becomes superfluous. Approval is nice, but it's not necessary to generate a sense of happiness.

Remind yourself often of how happy and satisfied you are with your own choices.

The states of happiness and motivation come naturally as a *result* of taking action. Doing things that help us feel happy, surrounding ourselves with supportive and positive people, and implementing any of the Build-a-Better-Brain practices found in the next chapter helps to fortify a sense of happiness within.

Doing things that help you to *feel* happy helps you to *be* happy.

Getting this process in the proper order puts you in charge. Notice that both happiness and motivation are results. Taking inspired action initiates an energetic boost that generates feelings of motivation. When lined up in order, everything else falls gracefully into place.

Just as with happiness, motivation isn't something you do or don't have. Motivation is a result of taking action—*whether you feel like it or not*. Taking action is an accomplishment that inspires motivation.

> ***Success builds upon success. Which, in turn, builds more motivation.***

Speaking of not feeling like it, here's a quick motivation hack. Stand up. Or simply sit up straight. Imagine your spine as a linear string of pearls. Positive emotions can be driven by shifting your physiology. Now that your posture is aligned straighten, stretch, smile, and reach your arms up in victory over your troubles. Wave your hands. Grin. Listen to heart-pumping music and dance if you like. Do what it takes to shift your emotional gears.

But wait. I hear you say, "Isn't this just a 'fake it 'til you make it' strategy?"

My response is, "Who cares?" Whether it is or isn't doesn't matter. To your body, these actions *feel* sincere. Your body interprets positive posture and movement as feel-good motivation, and that's what counts. The benefits of practicing this often add up and multiply results.

Now that you know how to generate happiness and motivation, the weighty subject of willpower is at hand. Generating willpower is similar to the strategies used for happiness and motivation, with one key difference. **Willpower is a finite resource**. Contrary to what you may have heard, there's not an unlimited supply. It's also not true that some have it in spades while others come up lacking.

It's a good thing we can wisely use and manage our limited avail-ability of willpower by planning out a few steps in advance. Similar to generating motivation and happiness, recall times of achievement and feeling good about your decisions. Amplify these feelings by in-cluding all of your senses.

Decision fatigue (mentioned in Chapter 12), dovetails beautifully into the topic of willpower. Why? Making choices takes willpower, but habits don't. Making our daily health activities into habits frees up headspace and our limited resource of willpower.

The subject of *automaticity* (creating no-brainer habits) is a focus for behavioral researcher Dr. Susan Peirce Thompson of Bright Line Eating.[107] She successfully guides others through the creation of food plans that become second nature. When behaviors become rote, there's an increased probability of them sticking through the long-term. Her program boasts an unparalleled success rate mainly due to this key principle.

Use your willpower effectively. Similar to an allowance, it's wise not to spend it all in one place. Spread it out across your day by planning as much as possible in advance. Make a list first thing in the morning (or at night before bed) of everything you need to for the day. Write down what you'll eat, wear, get done at work, which workout you'll do, what errands you'll run, etc. Map it out.

This map allows you to navigate rather than ruminate. It's much eas-ier to read and follow directions than to dither about every option. The decisions are then already made, reducing the need for willpow-er. Even easy-to-make decisions can be exhausting as they add up. Don't get caught at 5:00 pm without a plan in place for dinner. It's not a good time to rely on the remnants of willpower you may have

---

107   https://www.usatoday.com/story/sponsor-story/bright-line-eating/2018/01/19/
dieting-and-willpower/109609286/

left. Because your stores of willpower are fresh in the morning, use this fact to your advantage. Outline your plans first thing.

Now you're better-equipped to generate and handle the esoteric feelings of happiness, motivation, and willpower. Next, we'll become more grounded with logical and predictable high-performance arithmetic.

More success math and the value of opposites

Jot this down. The equation for success is 10% conscious thoughts and planning, and 90% nonconscious calibrations. Some believe this ratio is closer to 5/95.

Does that equation help you see the value of where to place your focus? I hope so.

Viewing the nonconscious mind as your autopilot feature makes strategically choosing your internal programming even more important. Use your entire mind—your mindset and your emotional intelligence—[108] for peak performance and results.

In Chapter 9, we reviewed the body's autonomic nervous system (ANS) responses: stress and relaxation. As equal and opposite forces, they cannot fire off simultaneously.

Did you know that emotions have opposites too?

Negative emotions can trigger the stress response. One way to harness these feelings (for our benefit rather than detriment) is to consider their equal and opposite emotions.

---

108   https://dailyhealthpost.com/emotional-intelligence/

The broad emotion of fear, for example, is the opposite of gratitude and appreciation. Scientific studies have linked the power of practicing gratitude with healthier relationships, a greater sense of happiness, and an improved perception of optimism.[109] A gratitude practice can strategically shift your focus away from what you don't want and toward what you do want in life.

A sense of gratitude and thankfulness impacts the body by neutralizing anger, resentment, fear, anxiety, and more. Getting into a state of gratitude may be the fastest way to get into a physical state of healing. Feelings of gratitude cannot co-exist with fear-based emotions.

In my book, *FibroWHYalgia*, I discussed what I call "theme streams." By noticing common threads in life, paying attention to positive occurrences or ideas of interest, your MAPP draws them into clearer view.

Similar themes in life are attention-grabbing. I hope the theme of equal and opposing states grabs you and holds on. Want to change how you're feeling? Think of the opposite state. The state of stress cannot co-exist with the state of relaxation. The state of fear cannot co-exist with the state of gratitude.

Want more examples? You cannot simultaneously feel annoyed while feeling deep appreciation. Deprivation and lack cannot co-exist with feelings of abundance and plenty. Feeling stressed can't harmonize with feeling blessed.

These aren't simple platitudes, so don't mistakenly dismiss them as trite. Instead, consider the benefits and put this method to work for you. Strategically calibrate your mind's autopilot feature.

---

109   http://www.health.harvard.edu/newsletter_article/in-praise-of-gratitude

Clients often ask *how* to shift their thinking. They want to know how to move away from fear, hopelessness, anxiety, and despair. I've made many suggestions so far with more to come. For now, ponder the effective principle of equal and opposing states.

Take the leap. To move away from fear, leap into gratitude. To banish deprivation and scarcity, look for and dwell on a richness of resources. Amp up the emotions on the positive side of things. How does gratitude look, feel, and sound? Delight in it.

Discover great satisfaction in the equal and opposing forces of grabbing and letting go. Grab onto new ideas and let go of notions that no longer serve you. The old must be left behind to make room for the new. The decision to embrace a new belief provides you with a pivot point. A time to make a radical shift in a new direction. A time to turn from one way of thinking and head toward another.

I'm grateful that you've come this far. I hope that you've embraced at least a few new ideas which can become pivot points of your own. Gratitude is always a great starting point.

> **"Gratitude is not only the greatest of virtues but the parent of all the others."**
> —Marcus Tullius Cicero

Power questions (to provoke action)

I can't let you finish this chapter without elbowing you from your chair. I want you to take action. Use these questions to create your pivot point moments.

- Have you considered your current circumstance as an opportunity to experience post-traumatic growth?

- Do you fall prey to analysis paralysis? Instead, look for that "stepping off point" in whatever situation has you feeling stuck.

- Do you find yourself falling into the downward spiral of negative self-talk? First notice, then take needed action to change direction.

- Do you love to start new things but rarely finish? Or have trouble starting something new? Pay attention to your tendencies and anticipate ways to create different future outcomes.

- What do you tell yourself about your options? Your inner thoughts are likely to go toward either lack or abundance. Intentionally choose abundance.

Look for practices and techniques listed in these chapters to help you deal with unhelpful self-talk and stop it in its tracks. Meditate on what—in particular—holds you back. Don't overthink this. Use what you've learned here to come up with workarounds to help you push through the "messy parts" of making change happen. As always, this may take outside support. You're not meant to do absolutely everything on your own.

It's time to switch gears and decide that your life can change. Write out in detail how your life will look as you apply the healthy improvements you have planned.

■ Chapter 15 – Head Work

1. List at least three benefits of implementing a gratitude/appreciation practice. Decide and jot down how you will implement this practice right away.

2. Which of the three missing traits (happiness, motivation, or willpower) eludes you the most? Using the tips and strategies provided, create a game plan for developing these much-needed emotions and add it to your calendar.

3. How will you deliberately decide to use your nonconscious mind as an autopilot feature? Success math shows that you'll achieve far more with your internal mental reprogramming than with any other external effort. Which methods appeal to you the most?

We've finally reached the chapter I've referred to over and over in this book. Its contents warrant well-deserved hoopla if I do say so. The Build-a-Better-Brain practices offered on the following pages have the power to transform your life. Seriously. Why wait? Flip the page and then flip your script.

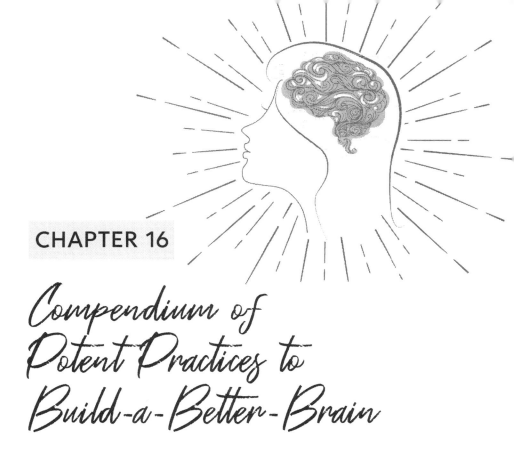

CHAPTER 16

Compendium of Potent Practices to Build-a-Better-Brain

What NOW?

I've mentioned a few times that most people can quickly come up with at least three things they could do to improve their health. What to do isn't always the problem. The bigger question is… why aren't they?

After reading the previous chapters, you're now equipped to answer that question. You understand that personal roadblocks, negative self-talk, and sabotaging beliefs are common factors that keep us from taking action toward our goals. You also may recall that taking strategic action, regardless of what hinders you, is the fastest path to success. Taking that step—large or small—is what matters.

> ## *The simplest path to success is to take action now and then figure things out as you go.*

We're nearing the end of this book. By now, you probably have a broad game plan in mind. All that's required are the first few nuanced steps and a decision to keep the momentum going.

Take that step in faith. It doesn't matter what step. Just start. Remember that there's always more than one way to approach a problem.

> ## *Lighting any spark to ignite action is more important than deciding which spark to light.*

Below you'll find dozens of practices from which to choose. Want to accelerate the process of reaching your goals? It's simple. Stack them. By applying more than one, you can expand and strengthen your desired outcomes.

Know this for certain: **the body is designed to heal**. Approaching the healing process from multiple angles can speed up the process. The following practices are sure to spark new ideas.

On your mark, get set...

For both the mind and body to **Get Back into Whack**, here's a list of to-do practices. Some you'll fall in love with immediately. Others, you may have to take out on a few practice dates first. Some may hold no appeal whatsoever. That's fine too.

Think of your healing mindset as a journey. One sit up won't give you six-pack abs, and one meditation won't remove your anxiety for life.

Choose what interests you. *And then keep on going.*

Here are three steps to apply the Build-a-Better-Brain practice of your choice. Don't trip over the last one.

    a.   Choose a practice, implement it, experiment with it
    b.   Evaluate your body and mind's response, comfort, and results
    c.   Rinse and repeat

Seven dozen potent Build-a-Better-Brain practices:

1.   **Prayer.**[110] Always a primary go-to practice. Take the time to share your troubles and fears with the One who loves beyond measure.
2.   **Meditation.**[111] Any form of meditation is beneficial. Practice daily.
3.   **Nutrition.**[112] Choose whole, natural, nutrient-dense, fiber-rich foods.

---

110   https://www.huffpost.com/entry/prayer-improves-health_b_9018194
111   https://www.healthline.com/nutrition/12-benefits-of-meditation
112   https://rebuildingwellness.com/fibro-diet-1-start/

4.   **Guided meditation.**[113] An easy-to-follow practice for stress management, relaxation, visualizations, etc.

5.   **Self-hypnosis.**[114] Teach yourself ways to become present and relax. Learn how to hone and improve lifestyle skills. Plant healthy seeds.

6.   **Self-care.**[115] Practice kindness, setting boundaries, taking a break, getting enough sleep, etc.

7.   **Yoga.**[116] Restorative yoga is my favorite.

8.   **Tai chi**[117] and **qigong.**[118] Enjoy these moving forms of meditation that are beneficial for all—including those with limited mobility concerns.

9.   **Celebrate success.** Celebrate ALL progress. Don't skimp. Remind yourself often and honor how far you've come.

10. **Emotional Freedom Technique** EFT or Tapping. No matter the type: Tapping,[119] Meridian Tapping, SET,[120] Faster EFT,[121] etc.—get tapping!

11. **Chiropractic** care.[122] There's typically much more to offer in addition to spinal adjustments.

12. **Stretching**[123] for full-body relaxation. Implement a simple stretching routine twice per day—morning and evening—for soothing results.

13. **Deep breathing.**[124] Choose deep belly breathing, diaphragmatic breathing, metabolic breathing, alternate nostril breathing, etc. and practice daily.

---

113   https://www.verywellmind.com/using-guided-imagery-for-stress-management-3144610
114   https://www.youtube.com/watch?v=BGbGpm7M12w
115   https://rebuildingwellness.com/self-care-must-fibro/
116   https://parade.com/702779/juliebawdendavis/10-benefits-of-restorative-yoga/
117   https://rebuildingwellness.com/moving-meditations-healing/
118   https://abc-counselling.org/2018/03/02/build-resilience-with-chinese-exercise/
119   https://www.thetappingsolution.com/what-is-eft-tapping/
120   https://www.eftdownunder.com/energy-techniques/what-is-simple-energy-techniques-set/
121   https://fastereft.com/
122   https://www.healthsourcechiro.com/healthy-living/21-benefits-of-chiropractic-adjustments/#gref
123   https://www.youtube.com/watch?v=jgly5NaKL7I
124   https://www.youtube.com/watch?v=F28MGLlpP90

14.   **Humor.**[125] Lose yourself in laughter, comedy, and light-hearted activities.

15.   **Smile.**[126] Do this even when you don't feel like it.

16.   **Sleep.**[127] Make sleep a priority and enjoy the healing, restorative benefits.

17.   **Read.** Browse books, magazines, articles, and anything that helps you to disconnect from the day—even if for a moment. Transport yourself to another place and time. Even better? Engage your mind in materials that elevate your understanding of God's plan for the healing world around you.

18.   **Pamper yourself.** Take bubble baths, watch the sunset, enjoy a manicure, self-massage, etc.

19.   **Hugs.**[128] This refers to either giving or getting healing hugs—all good!

20.   **Rewards.** Acknowledge both big and small accomplishments. Validation is a reward in itself. (TIP: *Please do not reward yourself with food.*) Positive rewards fuel motivation.

21.   **Negativity cleanse.** Commit to seven days of thinking only of what's helpful and what's going right. Consider Biblical support from Philippians 4:8.

22.   **Aromatherapy.**[129] Quality essential oils and natural scents interact directly with the limbic system (the emotional center of the brain) for powerful mood-boosting and whole-body healing benefits. Avoid artificial scents.

23.   **Music therapy.**[130] Find the tunes and tones that soothe, energize, and rejuvenates your soul.

---

125   https://www.youtube.com/watch?v=MdZAMSyn_As
126   http://www.crosswalk.com/family/parenting/5-reasons-to-smile-even-if-you-don-t-feel-like-it.html
127   https://www.youtube.com/watch?v=WpkfMuXJnWI
128   https://www.psychologytoday.com/us/blog/the-asymmetric-brain/201812/3-surprising-ways-hugging-benefits-your-well-being
129   https://draxe.com/limbic-system/
130   https://www.health.harvard.edu/mind-and-mood/how-music-can-help-you-heal

24. **Biofeedback** and **cognitive behavioral therapy**— **CBT.**[131] Don't forget the FIVE 180 Reset method found in Chapter 5.

25. Take a **technology fast.** Turn off cell phones, tablets, computers, TVs, etc. and enjoy the solitude for a specified period.

26. Put **power questions** to use. What would you do differently today if you knew you couldn't fail? What would you do today if you had twice as much courage as you do now? What actions would you take if you were healthy, vibrant, pain-free, etc.? Use these questions to prompt action.

27. **"Engineered" meditations.** Use recorded binaural beats, brainwave entrainment,[132] white noise,[133] Paraliminals,[134] Holosync,[135] MindMovies,[136] Positive Prime,[137] or other meditative CDs, Mp3s, etc. for relaxation, motivation, and health.

28. **Train Your Brain.**[138] A positive brain-training program from bestselling author Dana Wilde, host of *The Mind Aware Show.*

29. **Journaling.**[139] A written self-discovery, self-expression, creativity practice to relieve stress and bring you into the present moment. Some refer to journaling as an "ink it when you think it" process.

30. **Forgiveness.** Employ methods such as Byron Katie's The Work,[140] the Sedona Method,[141] Ho'oponopono,[142] etc.

31. **Exercise/fitness/body movement.**[143] Moving the body in healthy ways is great for detoxification, mood-boosting,

131   https://www.psychologytoday.com/us/basics/cognitive-behavioral-therapy
132   https://www.huffpost.com/entry/brain-wave-entrainment_n_4142898
133   https://simplynoise.com/
134   http://www.learningstrategies.com/Paraliminal/Home.asp
135   http://www.centerpointe.com/v2/
136   http://www.mindmovies.com/
137   https://app.positiveprime.com/login (Please use referral code **sue-1136**)
138   http://www.danawilde.com
139   https://rebuildingwellness.com/present-stress-relief/
140   http://thework.com/en/do-work
141   https://www.sedona.com/Home.asp
142   https://www.psychologytoday.com/us/blog/focus-forgiveness/201105/the-hawaiian-secret-forgiveness
143   https://www.prohealth.com/library/evergreen_pages/exercise-for-fibromyalgia

memory, attention span, cellular and vascular health, production of brain cell repair neurochemicals, energy, the population of beneficial bacteria in the gut, and much, much more.

32. **Posture.**[144] Change your mood and energy state by changing your compromised sitting or standing posture.

33. **Physiology shift.**[145] Shift your body position. Even ten minutes of body movement—especially something fun and engaging—changes your mood, thoughts, optimism, and mental clarity. Physical movement is perfect for times when feeling stuck or indecisive.

34. **Acupuncture.**[146] This therapeutic practice helps to restore blocked energy pathways in the body. As with massage, finding the "right" practitioner makes all the difference.

35. **Gardening.**[147] Beautify both your inner and outer world with nature's variety and bounty.

36. **Body mechanics.**[148] Learn proper spinal alignment and skeletal support for exercise, sitting, walking, working, balance, and healthy aging, etc.

37. **T-Tapp exercise.**[149] This amazing practice created by the wonderful Teresa Tapp features full-body, toning, anti-aging, non-impact, anti-inflammatory body movements.

38. **Outdoor adventures.** Plug into nature whether the beach, woods, an arboretum, park, or your own backyard. Get outdoors and take a deep breath. Take advantage of the health benefits of **Grounding** or Earthing.[150]

144   https://www.healthline.com/health/fitness-exercise/posture-benefits
145   https://www.health.harvard.edu/blog/how-simply-moving-benefits-your-mental-health-201603289350
146   http://blogs.discovermagazine.com/crux/2017/10/06/acupuncture-brain/#.XLIwxjBKjIU
147   https://articles.mercola.com/sites/articles/archive/2014/08/21/gardening-impacts-brain-health.aspx
148   https://www.stjoes.ca/patients-visitors/patient-education/a-e/PD%205844%20Resp%20Rehab%20-%20Back%20Pain%20and%20Posture.pdf
149   https://www.t-tapp.com/
150   https://draxe.com/earthing/

39. **Creative expression.** Enjoy painting, sketching, sculpting, or mixed media crafting—whatever feels creative and reflects your self-expression.

40. **Micro mindfulness.**[151] Use an app[152] or downloadable clock or timer to remind yourself hourly to pray, breathe, stretch, or whatever present moment behavior you desire.

41. **Handcrafting.** Practice crafts or activities that feature mindless motion such as knitting, crocheting, weaving, woodworking, etc.

42. **Coloring.** Use craft and activity books to color, paint, or draw. Might I suggest my book, *Chronic Coloring?*[153] It features pretty mandalas, positivity quotes, and healthy food/activity word games designed to engage the brain, stimulate the RAS, and elicit positive relaxation.

43. **Pet therapy.**[154] Enjoy the healing benefits of playing, stroking, and caring for your pet. Adopt or borrow someone else's for an intentional cuddle-fest.

44. **Get mesmerized.**[155] Relax by watching fish in a tank, flames in a fire pit or fireplace, or waves at the ocean, etc. Enjoy the soothing benefits of getting mentally lost.

45. **Sound therapy.** Enjoy therapeutic sounds such as singing bowls,[156] drums, ASMR[157] audios, guided meditations, guided imagery, and stress-relieving hypnosis recordings.

46. **Dance.**[158] Move and groove to your own healing rhythms or hula hoop.

151   https://heleo.com/conversation-the-powerful-benefits-of-micro-mindfulness/15708/
152   https://www.insighttimer.com/
153   https://rebuildingwellness.com/ChronicColoring
154   https://rebuildingwellness.com/teacher-have-fur/
155   https://tonic.vice.com/en_us/article/qvep4q/aquarium-therapy-good-for-health
156   https://rebuildingwellness.com/sound-therapy-singing-bowls-fibro/
157   https://well.blogs.nytimes.com/2014/07/28/rustle-tingle-relax-the-compelling-world-of-a-s-m-r/
158   https://www.psychologytoday.com/us/blog/the-athletes-way/201310/why-is-dancing-so-good-your-brain

47.   **Soothing sips.** Drink soothing tea or something delicious-
       ly healthy[159] and warm while cuddling the mug. Or perhaps
       something fresh and fruity.[160]

48.   **Socialize**[161] and **Connection.** Enjoy the company of old
       and new friends. Volunteer. Share. Humans are wired for
       connection and wilt without it.[162]

49.   **Reenact success.** List, acknowledge, and embrace your
       past achievements. Remember what you've overcome. Relive
       it in your mind like a movie and remind yourself of what you
       can do to achieve it again.

50.   **Gratitude/appreciation practices.**[163] Do these morn-
       ings and nights to start. Grow into creating time for them
       during the workday, too.

51.   **Productivity practices.** Journal or track your accomplish-
       ments daily. This shifts your focus to the positives of your
       achievements rather than to the negatives of what's not yet
       done.

52.   **Applied kinesiology**/muscle testing.[164] Use AK or muscle
       testing to learn more about what your body is telling you and
       what it needs.

53.   **Mantras, affirmations, and afformations**®. Revisit
       Chapter 7 for more information and application suggestions.

54.   **Aqua therapy.**[165] Experiment with therapeutic warm water
       swimming, floating, aerobic, and aqua therapy classes.

55.   **Sunshine.**[166] Make your own bio-available Vitamin D with
       healthy, safe, monitored sun exposure.

---

159   https://blog.paleohacks.com/hot-paleo-drinks/#
160   https://rebuildingwellness.com/healthy-summer-recipes/
161   https://www.prohealth.com/library/chronic-isolation-risk-for-fibro-part-1-42760
162   https://thriveglobal.com/stories/why-humans-need-connection/
163   http://ripplerevolution.com/write-a-gratitude-journal-30-day-experiment/
164   http://www.drweil.com/health-wellness/balanced-living/wellness-therapies/
applied-kinesiology/
165   https://rebuildingwellness.com/fibro-aqua-therapy/
166   https://www.mercola.com/calendar/2018/vitd.htm

56. **Release techniques.** Practice releasing negative emotions and beliefs with prayer, meditation, NLP, EFT,[167] the Release Technique,[168] the Silva Method,[169] etc. Connect with your heart, HeartMath,[170] for greater intuitive sense of connection.

57. **Gupta Programme.**[171] A brain-retraining program for Chronic Fatigue Syndrome, Fibromyalgia,[172] and chronic illness.

58. **DNRS—Dynamic Neural Retraining System.**[173] A brain-retraining program for limbic system dysfunction—applicable for many chronic illness health challenges including fibromyalgia, chronic fatigue syndrome, food sensitivities, multiple chemical sensitivity, and more.

59. **Essential oils.**[174] Therapeutic topical and inhalation applications for muscle pain, skin issues, breathing assistance, mood elevation, and much more.

60. **Go to the movies, a play, the opera, or read a book.** Take a "reality" break.

61. **Go to the symphony, ballet, or museum.** Broaden your horizons with culture and expanded learning.

62. **Go to a favorite sporting event or recreation center.** Cheer on your favorite teams and feel energized.

63. **Quit toxic habits.** Stop smoking, and/or the overuse of alcohol, medications, caffeine, fake foods, or any other addictive behavior that's negative and harmful to the body.

64. Utilize the **casual observer viewpoint.** Choose to view your circumstance as if you are a casual observer. This allows for compassion, acceptance, and objectivity *without judgment.*

167   https://rebuildingwellness.com/tapping-fibromyalgia/
168   https://www.releasetechnique.com/
169   https://www.silvamethod.com/use-this-technique-to-unchain-yourself/
170   https://www.heartmath.com/
171   http://www.guptaprogram.com/
172   https://rebuildingwellness.com/gupta-amygdala-fibromyalgia/
173   https://retrainingthebrain.com/
174   _https://www.prohealth.com/library/the-science-of-scents-moods-and-essential-oils-for-fibromyalgia-47813

65. Amp up **kitchen creativity.** Create mealtime recipes and routines that fuel, sustain, support, and nourish your healthy lifestyle plans.

66. **Hydration.**[175] Drink plenty of clean, pure, filtered water.

67. **Therapeutic massage.**[176] Find a therapist who is knowledgeable, capable, and a good listener. You know your body best. You get to set the preference for the pressure and intensity of your massage.

68. **Daydream.**[177] Allow spontaneous minutes during your day to let go of tension and anticipate something pleasurable or fun.

69. **Banish perfectionism.** Perfectionism is a thinly-veiled excuse to justify critical and negative self-talk.

70. **Soaks.**[178] Baths and showers (with or without Epsom salts and essential oils) provide a soothing kinesthetic opportunity to relax, unkink muscles, detoxify the body, and organize your thoughts.

71. Enlist support from an **NLP practitioner.**

72. Enlist support from an **EFT practitioner.**

73. Enlist support from a specialized **Clinical Therapeutic Hypnotherapist.**

74. Enlist support from a **mentor, health coach**, accountability partner, or a supportive friend.

75. Slip into **silliness.**[179] Laughing—including laughing at yourself—is therapeutic. Genuine belly laughs are particularly tension relieving.

---

175   https://rebuildingwellness.com/water-hydration-tip-sheet/
176   https://www.massagemag.com/5-benefits-massage-fibromyalgia-patients-36430/
177   https://www.smithsonianmag.com/science-nature/the-benefits-of-daydreaming-170189213/
178   https://pmaonline.com/posts/adult-primary-care/10-scientifically-proven-health-benefits-of-taking-a-bath/
179   https://www.prohealth.com/library/top-10-benefits-of-laughter-for-fibromyalgia-5538

76.   **Declutter.**[180] Whether spiffing up your home, office, bag, car, or just one drawer, decluttering has proven to have effective health benefits.

77.   **Dream.**[181] Set aside intentional time—such as before falling asleep—to dream about places you'd love to go, things you'd love to do, creative endeavors you'd love to begin. What do you *long for?* What desires pull at your heart? Be sure to stir up emotions of hope, joy, love, and anticipation.

78.   **Call a friend.**[182] Grab your partner in crime and laugh, gab, share, and support each other—all good for the health and healing of the body.

79.   **Reframe your fears**—also known as **Anxiety Reappraisal.**[183] Using strategic word swaps, change negative statements to constructive ones. For example, if you feel anxious, change your inner dialogue to neutralize the impact. Any time the word "nervous" pops into your head, change it to "excited." The body feels identical cues and sensations with both words, yet the meanings differ greatly. It makes all the difference. This 30 Positive Reframes article[184] has many reframes to try.

80.   **Go to a local market—a farmer's market** if possible. Spend time in the fresh produce section and marvel at the bright colors, the variety of scents, and the vast array of textures found in just-picked fruits, veggies, and greens. Of course, be sure to fill a basket, or two, and take them home to enjoy.

81.   **Future pace**[185] (rehearsing a future result). Imagine what you desire as if it's already happened. Step into the future—

---

180   https://www.psychologytoday.com/us/blog/in-practice/201802/6-benefits-uncluttered-space
181   https://www.huffpost.com/entry/the-power-of-writing-down_b_12002348
182   http://thinkhealth.priorityhealth.com/the-health-benefits-of-friendship/
183   https://www.theatlantic.com/health/archive/2016/03/can-three-words-turn-anxiety-into-success/474909/
184   https://www.theemotionmachine.com/positive-reframes/
185   https://www.youtube.com/watch?v=b8ZiF4Eaoaw

minutes, days, weeks, or even years from now—and vividly imagine that what you want is already true.

82. **Sanctuary surroundings.** Design a favorite sitting area, office, or bedroom as your private sanctuary. Be selective. Choose photos, art, scents, fabrics, furniture, and sounds that feed and soothe your soul. Make it your own.

83. **Assemble your own tribe.** Choose to share your life with like-minded, kind-hearted, and soul-supporting friends. Gather a small group of trusted friends who not only get who you are, but who encourage you to stretch yourself into who you want to become.

84. **Take a heuristic[186] approach** to life. Explore. Become wildly curious. Learn something new. Go somewhere new. Embrace and welcome the serendipity of an unplanned event.

85. Invite **pronoia**[187] into your life. Embrace the opposite of paranoia. See the beauty around you. Enjoy the goodness in all you see. Experience the world as a supportive and helpful place. Expect and see how others "conspire" to care for you and have your back. Live by the credo that circumstances happen *for* you rather than *to* you. You get to choose your perspective. Why choose anything short of wonderful?

■ Build-a-Better-Brain practice summary

Deliberately choose your surroundings.

Surround yourself with people, circumstances, media, and nourishments that support your desires. What are your consistent exposures?

---

186   https://www.verywellmind.com/what-is-a-heuristic-2795235
187   https://www.cnn.com/2016/06/24/health/words-for-emotions/index.html

> **"You become that to which
> you are most exposed."**
> —Denis Waitley

As children, we often don't get to choose our surroundings. But as adults, we do. Choose wisely. Become selective about what you see, read, hear, and taste. Sort your choices by the Change or Chains process discussed in Chapter 13. Will that book, TV show, or processed food-like product support your goals? Will they inch you closer to your desires? Or will they move you further away?

The most important surroundings to choose, of course, are your thoughts. *What you think the most* is what you'll become. Your thoughts will drive you toward your outcome. *We move in the direction of what we think about most.* So, choose your thoughts with care.

Remember that we're not talking about every single thought or action. Perfectionism is a sure-fire way to throw your motivation into reverse. Self-recriminations are wolves in sheep's clothing. Aim for progress—not perfection. And, as always, choose kind thoughts. Ones that support you and your desires. Choose thoughts that in the long run, help you to build a better brain.

■ One more essential workaround

The brain likes immediate rewards. Since the nonconscious mind doesn't track time in the same way that the conscious mind does, future benefits don't feel real. This is why future rewards aren't terribly effective when it comes to motivation.

It's difficult to feel motivated to make small changes now that will benefit you days, weeks, months, or even years down the road.

The future doesn't stir up visceral feelings for the nonconscious mind.

Therefore, visual tracking methods are more effective. Visibly seeing a chart or calendar with Xs, stars, or colored-in boxes can help your nonconscious mind to experience this daily micro-step progress. Choose a way to track or monitor your steps that feels supportive to you. And, just like everything else in this book, your positive focus is key. Tracking your progress is about focusing on how far you've come. When there are missteps, setbacks, or even derailments, tracking is simply a visual reminder to get you back in the saddle.

For example, if you've committed to a daily positivity practice and apply it five (or any number of) days out of seven, *celebrate the progress.* Other than casually observing the behavioral changes that may have triggered the misstep, there's NO benefit to analyzing or becoming critical of your perceived failure. Tracking allows you to see how far you've come, and the foibles are put into perspective.

"It's win or learn, not win or lose."
—Based on a quote from Nelson Mandela

Timing is everything

Want your tomorrow to be different from your today? Something's gotta change. If one or more of these practices piques your interest, take action. Don't shrug and say, "I'll try it next time I get a chance."

The nonconscious mind loves action, specificity, and simple direction. Choose a practice, a time to do it, and bring it to fruition pronto.

> *Your nonconscious mind is listening.*
> *It's just waiting to help you*
> *make your dreams a reality.*

Implement your favorite practices several times per day for a collective hour or so. No need to do it all at once. Your brain needs this repetitive focus to rewire and tame its overreactive tendency.

Think of taking action—right away—as confirmation for the mind. You may feel prodded in many directions, but the steps you take (on any one of them) affirms the feeling of action over inertia. Once you get moving, the nudges will continue.

Immediacy (taking action now) helps to define your path and make it clearer to follow. Consistency helps your brain to view it as familiar. Familiar is good.

■ Chapter 16 – Head Work

1. When you think back to your past struggles (whether to heal, change a behavior, or develop new habits), what can you now identify as your biggest hurdle? Was it negative self-talk?

Self-sabotage? Limiting beliefs? Identify your common health hurdles and decide on a different path.

2. Which of the Build-a-Better-Brain practices do you already do? Which ones were completely new to you? Which ones have you decided to implement? Go back and highlight those of interest.

3. Do you have an idea of what tracking method you'd like to put into place? Whether it's plain, fun, colorful, or whimsical, make sure it's simple to do and visually available every day.

As if the Build-a-Better-Brain practices aren't motivating enough, next up is a powerful list of their psychological and physical benefits. I'm willing to guess that at least 50% of these facts will really surprise you.

CHAPTER 17

A Cascade of Brain Benefits

H ow did you do with the Build-a-Better-Brain practice of your choice?

To activate this new behavior, I've compiled a few wins you'll enjoy when you turn these practices into regular habits. I've assembled a list of over 60 benefits to make it inescapably obvious.

Think of these practices as "mental hygiene."[188] They have the power to improve your emotional, mental, and physical wellbeing in ways that at this point, may be unfamiliar.

Here are the benefits you can experience from applying positivity practices.

188   https://www.psychologytoday.com/blog/feeling-it/201309/20-scientific-reasons-start-meditating-today

The Benefits of Build-a-Better-Brain practices[189, 190, 191, 192]

Usage of these techniques—
- Increases a sense of spiritual connectedness—a sense of belonging
- Increases the ability to feel, experience, and embrace a sense of love
- Increases energy and vitality
- Increases mental focus
- Increases a sense of positivity and happiness
- Increases a sense of calm, relaxation, centered-ness
- Increases the ability to make decisions and come to conclusions
- Increases feelings of pain relief and wellbeing
- Increases work and life satisfaction
- Increases perception and ability to see the big picture
- Increases a sense of wisdom and inner knowledge
- Increases blood flow and stabilizes/reduces heart rate
- Increases and widens perspective and ability to see beyond the moment
- Increases a sense of compassion and understanding for your-self and others
- Increases a general sense of confidence and assurance
- Increases levels of creativity, self-expression, and internal freedom
- Increases the ability to be introspective
- Increases brain size (gray matter) and function—especially emotional regulation
- Increases enjoyment level of music, art, and creative experiences
- Increases the positive neuroplasticity ability of the brain

---

189   http://ineedmotivation.com/100-benefits-of-meditation/
190   https://www.psychologytoday.com/blog/feeling-it/201309/20-scientific-reasons-start-meditating-today
191   http://mentalhealthdaily.com/2015/03/26/scientific-benefits-of-meditation-list/
192   http://www.huffingtonpost.com/2013/04/08/mindfulness-meditation-benefits-health_n_3016045.html

- Improves problem-solving skills
- Improves memory
- Improves the ability to manage weight concerns including weight loss
- Increases the ability to handle multiple interruptions and activities
- Increases the brain's ability to "turn down the volume" on stress and pain
- Improves vagal tone
- Improves healthy and efficient digestion
- Improves the health and vitality of the immune system
- Improves and stabilizes the metabolism
- Improves sleep and the ability to achieve restorative sleep
- Improves wound healing
- Improves athletic performance
- Improves performance and productivity toward desired goals
- Improves fertility, PMS, and other feminine, stress-related concerns
- Improves hormone levels and promotes hormonal balance
- Improves feelings of stability and the ability to prioritize
- Improves the motivation to exercise and move your body in healthy ways
- Improves the ability to tolerate (without reacting to) the drama of others
- Improves the ability to let go of negative beliefs
- Improves the symptoms of asthma and respitory challenges
- Improves the symptoms of environmental allergies
- Improves the symptoms of food sensitivities/intolerances, IBS, etc.
- Improves headaches and migraines
- Improves and protects your telomeres
- Improves and protects against mental illness
- Improves feelings of self-control and confidence in your healthy choices

- Improves a sense of intuition and inner guidance
- Improves symptoms of depression and sadness
- Improves productivity
- Improves listening skills
- Improves cardiovascular function
- Improves self-awareness
- Improves the ability to take exams and possibly improves grades overall
- Improves the ability to embrace acceptance of your circumstances
- Improves decisiveness and the ability to make confident decisions
- Improves the ability to focus and pay attention
- Improves fluid intelligence and neurodegeneration[193]
- Improves the ability to forgive (especially yourself) for past perceived wrongs
- Improves distribution of willpower for your desired goals
- Improves the ability to develop and stick to healthy habits
- Improves physical brain health in areas responsible for paying attention
- Reduces levels of generalized anxiety
- Reduces a sense of pettiness and frustration
- Reduces repetitive negative thoughts
- Reduces the intensity of fears and phobias
- Reduces and stabilizes blood pressure
- Reduces racing thoughts
- Reduces inflammation at the cellular level
- Reduces the need or desire for addictive behaviors or addictive substances
- Reduces feelings of stress
- Reduces feelings of loneliness and isolation
- Reduces or slows down the progression of disease manifestation

---

193   http://mentalhealthdaily.com/2015/03/26/scientific-benefits-of-meditation-list/

Wow! Who wouldn't want to experience as many of these amazing health benefits as possible? The astonishing favorable results from these practices have surprised and flustered even the most skeptical clinicians.

When Lissa Rankin, M.D., a traditionally trained physician, struggled to understand her research into proven studies of spontaneous remission (cases of healing from critical diseases), she was perplexed. Her findings made no sense to her medical school trained brain. She finally ended up asking herself this question, "Can the mind really heal the body?"

She was as surprised as anyone to find the answer to that is *yes*. She discovered cases of reduced inflammation, heart disease reversal, and spontaneous remission of skin disorders, autoimmune disease, cancer, and more. Her book *Mind over Medicine* was groundbreaking in its perspective of taking the clinical science of medicine and applying it to the airy-fairy world of mindset.

You may or may not need this "proof" to move forward in your healing journey. But as someone who loves research, I continue to find books such as hers a valuable part of my studies.

Dr. Rankin's reports on spontaneous healings revealed astonishing and unexpected findings. Seemingly unrelated circumstances from the participants such as quitting a soul-crushing job, leaving an unhealthy relationship, or embarking on a dream career or a trip of a lifetime preceded their recoveries. It didn't make sense... at first.

Then she drew this parallel.

By making these critical and life-altering changes, those who healed had dramatically lowered their stress levels AND increased their sense of self-satisfaction. They felt hopeful and optimistic about their futures.

What soul-affirming practices can help you to feel hopeful and optimistic about your future?

Applied locomotion

There's a crucial difference between learning and knowing. You can cram in statistics and facts to pass an exam, but your data recall will suffer. Knowing and understanding something comes through application. Putting what you've learned into action allows you to create a practical belief in the subject. It's the engine that moves you down the tracks.

Understanding new concepts takes practice and application. It's a solo venture. In the coaching world, this phrase is common—*you can help your clients learn, but you can't understand for them.*

Understanding takes personal investment. It's an outside-to-inside experience. The process comes through reading, seeing, studying, and even doing. Deliberate and intentional practice evolves into knowledge and understanding.

It may be slow going, but it's a process that's totally worth it.

I can vouch for that. I may not be the fastest person to adopt new ideas, but when I do, I dig in and don't come up for air until it makes sense to me.

For over 17 years, I've shared information on how I recovered from fibromyalgia and chronic illness. In hindsight, my path wasn't all that complicated. I mainly followed these four steps:

■ Sue's path to chronic illness recovery

1. I willingly opened myself to new ideas.
2. I willingly applied them to my life and tried them on for size.
3. I willingly and consistently made adaptations to what I learned and expanded into what came next.
4. I willingly continue to become a new and improved version of myself as I walk this path and make fresh discoveries.

What are you willing to do or who are you willing to become?

Notice that step #4 isn't a finite stopping point. It's not a finish line to cross where you wipe your brow and ask "where's my trophy?" The steps here are cyclical. I'm always beginning something new and ending something that's become familiar.

The steps are simple… but not simplistic.

The process from chronic illness to chronic wellness is neither quick nor clear-cut.

And, for that I'm glad.

In fact, I'm super glad. The time I've spent in the "adaptation" phase of learning has taught me the most. Persistence provided me with opportunities to make changes and find supportive resources. From there, I just leaned on my faith and put one foot in front of the other. Over time, I've developed an inner trust of what feels right. I didn't just change how I think; I changed who I am.

As I went through my recovery, I connected with that inner voice that had been silent. I developed an unexpected reliance on my own abilities. The healing benefits of the Build-a-Better-Brain practices shared in this chapter are waiting for you. The practices are something to embrace for now and trust that they'll bear fruit later.

I hope you have a hunger for change and a desire for transformation.

Consider these powerful truths as you decide:

1. Our results in life reflect the thoughts we think the most.
2. We can release and even obliterate unhelpful thoughts when viewed through the lens of the casual objective observer.
3. Passionately focusing on thoughts that are instructional, supportive, and positive, can shift our life's course from adrift to well-charted.

Where do you want to go?

Your life isn't created based on what you want. It's created based on what you believe you can have. Do you recognize the difference?

Change your beliefs. Change your life.

Great change doesn't have to come from something completely new (although it may). Change can come from something heard before but never applied. Is there anything in this book that rings a bell and you now see it differently?

I'm guessing so.

Go back and read, re-read, and re-highlight parts of this book for future study. Create a daily healing recipe like the one below for yourself.

Daily healing recipe

Ingredients:

ONE part **Willingness** to discover something new

ONE part **Acceptance** (without analysis) for where you are now

TWO or more parts **Build-a-Better-Brain practices**

ONE part **Curiosity** (observe without judgment)

ONE part each of **Patience**, **Kindness**, and **Self-Compassion** to keep going

Directions:

After establishing a daily practice, notice how your thoughts change, then notice how your feelings change. Finally, notice how your body changes in response. Continue to mix these ingredients, working out the lumps where necessary. Enjoy!

As the body soaks up the healing process, don't forget about the brain. Follow the eight great tips listed below for optimal brain-health results.

Eight great brain-healthy tips

The following tips provide a handy overview on the feeding and care of your brain.

So far, I've shared encouragements for nourishing the body with the highest quality foods and supplements possible (that fit within your budget and circumstances). In addition to nutrition, here are brain-specific practices you can do to keep yours in peak condition. As a bonus, keep in mind that through their vital interconnections, what's good for the brain is also good for the heart, gut, and the whole peripheral nervous system.

1. **Healthy soul nourishment.** Choose soul-nourishing books, movies, TV, podcasts, radio, magazines, newspapers, games, friends, and activities, etc.

2. **Healthy thoughts.** Put your Build-a-Better-Brain practices to work!

3. **Healthy movement.** A healthy body supports a healthy brain and vice versa. Make it a daily practice to move your body in healthy ways.

4. **Healthy, real nourishment.** Drink plenty of clean, filtered water. Choose a wide variety of living, natural, whole, nutrient-dense, and fiber-rich foods.* We are each unique. Experiment with and discover *your* optimal balance of macronutrients: healthy fats, clean proteins, and carbs (mainly from veggies).

5. **Healthy environmental nourishment.** Surround yourself with clean, pure air, water, and beauty/body/cleaning products. Do your best to limit your exposures to environmental toxins from herbicides, pesticides, fungicides, solvents, artificial scents, toxin-filled body care and health and beauty products, chemicals found in both prescribed and over the counter medications, dental amalgams, artificial sweeteners, artificial food flavorings, nicotine, and caffeine.

6. **Healthy support.** It bears repeating—we typically cannot see our own stuff. We all need encouragement and guidance from outside sources. And, feeling connected to others is vital. Reach out and get the support you need.

7. **Healthy sleep**. Deep, restorative sleep is necessary for the brain to rest, rebuild, and repair. Implement a healthy sleep hygiene routine and make it a priority.

8. **Healthy curiosity**. Investigate and seek out things that pique your interest. Try something new. Step out of your comfort zone (even just a little bit) to stretch your imagination and promote your sense of creativity.

*Additional tips on item #4. A healthy digestive system is the alpha and omega of good health. Gut bacteria balance (a healthy microbiome) is created by consuming a wide variety of nutrient-dense, fiber-rich foods. Fiber (from real, not fake foods) is a whole-body healing miracle. Fiber "feeds" and builds-up good bacteria rather than causing the overpopulation of harmful yeasts, candida,[194] and mycotoxins.[195] Fiber helps to restore vital gut balance.

Addressing candida overgrowth, a common concern for those in the chronic illness community begins as a two-prong dietary approach. Drink plenty of water. Add fiber-rich natural foods such as leafy greens and vegetables. Add healthy fats such as coconut, olive, and avocado oils. Consume clean, grass-fed meats, organic eggs, and wild-caught fish. Flavor-boosting foods such as oregano, basil, cloves, ginger, and garlic can also prove effective.

While on a candida elimination diet, remove sugary processed foods as well as foods that turn rapidly into sugar such as most fruits, grains, alcohol, beans, potatoes, and dairy.

---

194   https://knowthecause.com/getting-started/
195   https://knowthecause.com/candida-diet-is-it-the-same-as-the-phase-one-diet/

The gut and the brain have a unique connection and information transmission system. Every nutrient we consume and emotion we feel passes through the gut or at least starts there. The gut isn't called the second brain by Dr. Mark Hyman[196] and other brain experts for nothing.

It stands to reason that any opposing factors to the above can limit the optimal performance of your brain. So do your brain a favor. Take notice of where you may need a boost. Apply a liberal dose of them all to your daily regimen. Focus on the ones you may lack.

Make it a habit protocol

String these key concepts together to help make your new habits stick. They can lift you over the hump of struggle and into the ease of automaticity.

You've got the tools; just apply and rely on your sense of guidance.

1. Decide what habit to begin. Make it specific and simple. Don't worry about making it too small or that it takes too little time.* You can always add to it or make it more complex later once it's automatic.

2. Chain or stack the new habit either before or after something you already do daily. (Revisit Chapter 10.)

3. Make it early in the day. Go easy on yourself. Implement this habit first thing while your willpower reservoir is fresh. (Revisit the subject of decision fatigue in Chapters 12 and 15.)

4. Make it non-negotiable and repeat regularly.

---

196   https://drhyman.com/blog/2014/10/10/tend-inner-garden-gut-flora-may-making-sick/

5. Reward yourself and honor your progress. Don't skimp on acknowledging your effort. The investment of your time is more important than the results you believe, or don't believe, you see. **Perceptions of our progress are unreliable**. It takes time to see results. Stick with it!

Make it a small step. Walk in place for five minutes. Drink one glass of water. Do three minutes of deep breathing, meditation, or tapping. Eat a large salad once a day. Experiment with one new veggie per week. Declutter one drawer or shelf. Soak in an Epsom bath once per week. You get the idea.

For additional help with your follow-through, apply the easy steps and prompts provided in my *Get Back into Whack Workbook*.

■ Chapter 17 – Head Work

1. Review the Benefits of the Build-a-Better-Brain list. Highlight those you'd like to achieve most. Notice how the practices you've chosen in Chapter 16 align with these highlighted benefits. Create or revisit your Build-a-Better-Brain practice plan and keep these new benefits in mind.

2. After reviewing the four steps I was willing to take to recover from fibromyalgia, do you notice any that relate to you? Do any of the steps create feelings of resistance? Zero in on any that may pose more of a challenge (possibly steps two and/ or three). What actions will you take to overcome or work through these challenges?

3. Review the Daily Healing Recipe offered in this chapter. Write down the key ingredients on an index card or sticky note and place it where you'll see it daily. Apply these "ingredients" liberally to your overall health plan.

＊

This chapter is all about the "now." It should leave you with the feeling of standing on the starter's block waiting for the race to begin. What feels like a natural first step for you? Honor that nudge and take note. Or, if you're left feeling unsure and full of hesitation, that's okay too.

Coming up next, discover strategies to shift the uncomfortable feelings that can potentially throttle progress. You'll also find a final summary overview of a few essential thoughts.

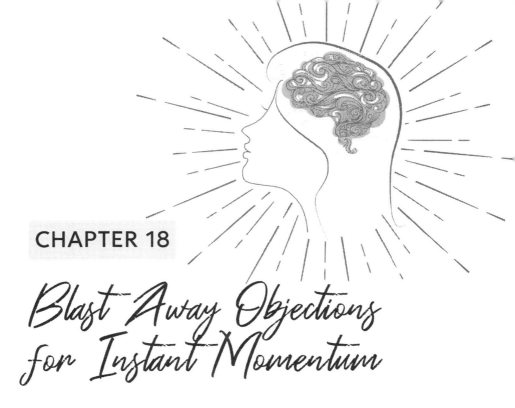

Blast Away Objections for Instant Momentum

When it comes to change, I've made a lot of suggestions so far. As a student of human behavior, I can also hear your potential objections. You probably feel them if not hear them yourself.

That's how we're wired. At this point, it's helpful to identify resistance in advance of the journey. Think of this section as an "X marks the spot" map revealing hidden objection landmines.

I object!

Your mind is an objection-making machine. It believes you're safer by staying put. Change, therefore, is perceived as dangerous or threatening.

Would you like to stay exactly where you are and not make any changes at all? Here's how to NOT get results from this book. Agree with the following seven objections, and you can be sure of one thing... nothing will change.

1. ***I've heard this all before.***

There's a grain of truth to this. You may have heard much of this before. But take a moment to consider the principle actions outlined in this book. Have you implemented them? Some, all, or none? Do you have the results you desire? Take a quick assessment of your health and satisfaction with life. Is there any room for improvement? If you answer yes, then consider that some of the tips in this book can be applied or reapplied for further progress.

Benefits don't arrive from knowledge alone. *It's not about knowing what to do; it's about doing what you know.*

Don't dismiss particular exercises suggested in this book without application. Give them at least a minimum 30-day trial run.

2. ***My problems are complicated, unique, and unlike anyone else's.***

In the coaching world, this is known as the "my problems are special" objection. Please don't take offense. This is how the mind works, and we've all felt this way before. The nonconscious mind wants us to believe that our circumstances or problems are different, so that suggested solutions don't apply and we don't have to take action. We're then off the hook. We don't have to make any changes.

This great injustice limits all concerned.

Believing your issues are special blinds you from potential solutions. The practices in this book are designed to provide foundational healing. That's why they work. They're basic, fundamental, root-level approaches—which can apply to anyone.

3. ***These strategies are too simple to get the complicated results I want.***

If you asked a CEO of a Fortune 500 company to break down his or her daily success ritual into a few vital steps, it could look like:

1. Create a morning routine of stretching, meditation, juicing or a superfood breakfast, and a brisk walk
2. Combine tasks when possible (i.e., listening to positivity podcasts while reviewing data charts, etc.)
3. Maximize efforts by engaging in strategic management activities while limiting non-productive ones such as long meetings

Are these simple strategies? Sure. But the outcomes achieved are anything but. These basics provide the executive with focused direction and mental clarity. They also provide the foundation for sustained energy to get through the day, knocking off one to-do after another from their list.

Any large task when broken down into bits helps make things look doable. If the steps in this book look simple to you, that's awesome. I hope so. Simplicity feeds motivation when it feels that the path is clear.

4. ***These strategies are too complicated to get the results I want.***

Just as with objection #3, we feel a sense of frustration from whatever confuses us the most. Things may appear too complicated *or* too simple. The main concept to understand is that somewhere in our gut (our inner guidance), we do not feel that "just right" sense of assurance.

It's a good thing that a confident gut feeling isn't necessary for success. At least, not at the start.

Confidence is typically absent from the first several stages of the process. Taking action anyway (despite "not feeling it") is a learned skill. It's one you'll benefit from for the rest of your life.

5. *I read so-and-so's book, and it said the same thing.*

Great! I'm glad you've read similar books on brain health, positivity, and healing. I'm glad that you recognize similar themes. I read dozens (maybe hundreds) of books on multiple topics that interest me. Each author has a different angle or take on the subject and delivers it from a diverse perspective. I read them and collectively synthesize my understanding and conclusions.

We all need to read, hear, or see information in ways that resonate best with us. Reviewing multiple sources to improve our understanding is valuable. Don't fall into the trap of looking for that "one" perfect book, method, or resource. While it's fine to have favorites, feeling that each one is "not it" is a sure-fire way to stay stuck. As always, I want you to take action NOW.

6. *I liked X and Y about this book, but Z was a total turn off. So, therefore, it's all bunk.*

I've had clients tell me, "I love Tapping, but relaxation methods make me antsy, so I won't get anything out of your workshop." Or "I love meditations, but affirmations don't work, so don't waste my time telling me about them."

This makes me want to sing "One Bad Apple" from my well-worn 1975 Jackson 5 album. It's not that any method is "bad," per se. But throwing out every option because of one thing slams the door to success. It's okay to have opinions on various recovery methods. My prayer for you is that you stay open to whatever method(s) work best for you. And, how will you know unless you're open to experimentation?

And speaking of prayer, this objection goes for your take on religion too. If some of my comments don't align with your specific spiritual philosophy, feel free to edit and insert your own. It's your journey.

Stay open-minded and try something new. Look for resources that support your own beliefs. Step forward into the unknown. There are dozens of methods from which to choose. Some you'll love, others maybe not. Lean toward what feels right and trust your gut. What's not helpful is to slam the door to all of them.

One of the best learning skills I've developed is the process of sifting. From books, videos, lectures, documentaries, and workshops, I find the key takeaways that resonate with me. Along the way, I minimize or discard what doesn't sit well with me.

Rather than judging it, I simply don't take it in.

For example, I don't happen to be a woo-woo airy-fairy person. I like concrete data. But I've read books by authors who march to the woo-woo beat and slant toward the airy-fairy side of things. I don't base my decisions on their slant. I can glean their intent and re-word it in my head to suit my needs. I can also reject ideas that don't align with my beliefs. I can sift for what resonates most. You can too.

7. ***My mom's friend's neighbor's boss said that healing from (fill in the blank) is impossible. It's not worth even trying.***

Free advice from others is worth every penny you pay for it.

That's a tongue-in-cheek retort, but you know what I mean. When given unsolicited advice, just smile and nod. If you want to know more, ask questions. If you don't, walk away.

Consider this first. Is that acquaintance or the one they're referring to someone who has experienced the topic personally? Have they personally found ways to heal? Or does this person often share negative or fear-based opinions? Is there a personal agenda behind the negative news?

You get to determine the veracity of others' remarks. You get to measure their worth and choose (sift) whether or not to allow it in.

8. ***I'll figure this out myself using my own logic.***

While this may not seem like an objection, it is. Remember Chapter 1, where we discussed the differences between the conscious and nonconscious mind? The conscious mind is logical and practical. It's where we try to fix things and make sense of the world. It's a pattern-making and pattern-recognizing part of the mind. What's important here is that the logical part of our mind can ONLY relate to the past. Meaning it can only compare patterns, behaviors, and experiences to those that have already happened. So, objections that come to mind such as "I can't do what it takes" or "I'll fail and won't follow through" are only based on the past. Therefore, if you have not been successful YET at something, the logical mind has no way of making that part of the equation.

It's human behavior to want to figure things out. We want to "fix" something in ourselves that we perceive is broken. The problem with this approach is summed up by this famous quote.

> **"We cannot solve our problems with the same thinking that created them."**
> —Albert Einstein

Doesn't it seem rational that if you could "logic" your way out of a problem, you would have done so already? It makes sense then to instead look toward the future.

Become uncomfortable with what you don't know instead of mired in what you believe you already know. Try something new. Dip a toe (or dive) into the world of the future—a place of encouragement and faith where your body has what it needs to heal.

The practices in this book may be uncomfortable at first, but just like any other new protocol, it takes time to see results. Focusing your attention on this "future place of healing" is where it begins. Test-drive it through prayer, meditation, or whatever practice makes you want to get in, turn the key, and drive.

Here's another favorite quote.

> **"Attention is a skill just like golf or tennis."**
> —Dr. Joe Dispenza

Give yourself the leeway to hone that skill. If your mind drifts back into familiar old habits, that's okay. Keep practicing this new skill. Give it the patience and attention it needs to become familiar. When it becomes a habit, visible changes arrive. Our thoughts and beliefs program our cells.

Now that we've addressed objections, it's time to look at obstacles. The following strategies can help to streamline your healthy habit formation plans.

Ten blast-away-the-obstacles strategies

1. **Decision:** Make a clear commitment to yourself that this small habit is one you PLAN to make. Flex the muscle of your mind and put it to work for you.

2. **Distraction Guidelines:** Set clear boundaries around the timing of the habit you wish to create. This could mean no internet surfing, game playing, or TV watching, etc. until your 15-minute positivity practice is done. Notice this is an internal practice. It's a guideline you set to achieve success.

3. **Environment Guidelines:** Make sure your surroundings and environment support your new habit-to-be. Do you plan to eat more veggies yet have none on hand? Get out of your own way. Take the simple steps needed to support your goals. Arrange your home, work, car, or any place you spend time accordingly.

4. **Planned Derailment:** Every habit creation plan has bumps in the road. You may get sick, take a trip, have company, endure bad weather, or experience an unfortunate injury. Stuff happens. Plan ahead and just move forward. Get back

into the routine as soon as humanly possible. Don't dwell on the derailment. Don't give it energy. Bumps in the road don't stop success. *Choosing to stop* moving forward does.

5. **The Pit of Despair:** See item #4. Choosing to see a bump in the road as failure is disastrous. A bump is not a failure. (They're all bumps, by the way.) Failure thinking spirals downward into emotional quicksand. If you view forgetting to plan dinner as a failure, you may find yourself scarfing down a couple of sleeves of frozen Girl Scout cookies. Forgetting something is no big deal. It's human. How we view forgetting something makes all the difference. Don't add insult to injury. Instead, view each incident as a minor blip on the radar and get back on track.

    Also, don't RSVP to your own pity party invitation. Sit with your emotions for just a moment as the casual observer. No judgment. Emotions are fluid sensations. Soon enough, they'll move on. The feelings will pass (I promise).

6. **Mirror Test:** Do you expect to see results right away? Have you ever eaten one meal that includes a side of green beans and then tried to slip on your jeans from high school? What about working out at the gym once and then signing up for a marathon?

    I'm using hyperbole to point out the implications. Unhealthy expectations can sink your boat. Skewed expectations cause snowballing thoughts such as, "I'm just wasting my time. This is too hard. I can't afford it. This is hooey…"

    Recalibrate your expectations and shut down the negative chatter. Forge ahead. With patience and kindness, take a deep breath when you have a negative thought. Tell yourself. "Thanks for the memo. For now, I'll just put a pin in it."

> *Progress often looks like nothing at all. Incremental steps seem insignificant. Fall in love with the idea of small, repeated actions rather than splashy displays.*

We can't all drag a red wagon full of fat across a giant TV stage to show how far we've come. That's what Oprah did in 1988 to demonstrate her weight loss journey. Isn't it interesting how much we too want to SEE our progress? It's only natural. Visual displays of success feel good. While we may want them, the warning here is that they can't be our only measure of success. Feeling good along the journey is just as important (or more so) than feeling great at the destination.

TIP: *If you're not already aware, you need to know that the destination is always a moving target. By the time you "arrive," you'll have new insights and experiences under your belt. You'll have new notions of where to go and what's next for you. When you know this to be true, it makes sense to place a greater focus on the journey.*

7. **I've Failed in the Past and Don't Finish Things:** From what I've read, every person who has climbed Mount Everest had previous circumstances where they climbed and either through practice or failure, did not reach the peak. No exceptions. Then, at some point, they did reach the peak.

The same goes for you. Each former attempt at habit formation was simply your method of practice. Practicing allows you to align your goals with success. Success is inevitable (not to mention just around the corner) as long as you continue to practice. Keep your eye on the peak!

TIP: *Here's a behavioral pattern fact. We're more likely to stick with and finish anything that we invest in. Whether that means our time, money, energy, or any other resource, investing can be a powerful motivator for follow-through.*

8. **I Just Don't Feel Like It:** Don't allow backward thinking to trap you. Feelings dictate your actions. If your actions don't mesh with what you desire, it's time to change what you're feeling. Review Chapter 15 for more inspiration.

9. **Someone/Something is in My Way:** It's hard to focus on goals when we're trying to see through an obstacle. What do you believe is blocking your success? Once identified, the next step has nothing to do with "proving" whether or not it's true. If you believe it's true, it is. The next step is to consider alternatives. Can you choose to open the door of possibility enough to seek other options? Can you look for ways to move over, under, around, or even through this obstacle? The answer to this question is a simple yes or no. With a yes answer and some contemplation, your next (often tiny) step becomes evident.

10. **I Don't Have (Time, Support, Equipment, Supplies, Money, Access, or Other Resources) That I Need to Succeed:** There are two key factors to this belief. The first is that answers lie somewhere outside of your reach. The second is that you don't have access to them. Your body feels the sting of lack.

To counteract this sting, list your assets. What do you have access to? Do you drive, are you able to use a computer, do you have at least some support? Do you eat regularly? Embrace the blessings that are often taken for granted. List the skills and tools you possess. Focus on your unique brilliance and on what you have to offer. From that perspective of abundance, plan your next step.

■ Healthy habits as a scapegoat

Don't make an enemy of the good. Once you install a new healthy habit, don't make it the scapegoat for your life changes. For example, if your new habit is to replace junk foods with healthier fare, don't make it a negative process. Phrases such as "I can't go to that fast food place because I'm trying to be good," or "I'm not allowed to have that anymore" will sabotage your success from the get-go. Your nonconscious mind will object to the change and make the process harder than it has to be.

> ### *Vilifying your new healthy habit*
> ### *defeats your purpose.*

Sacrifice and martyrdom might be compulsory characteristics for a saint, but they're disastrous for the average Jane or John Doe. They're also disastrous for habit formation. Eating healthier, moving your body, implementing relaxation practices, etc., aren't the problems— they're the solutions. It's imperative to get this straight.

Your logical mind may say, "Yeah, I know this," but your nonconscious mind may harbor resistance if your mental images don't match. Thinking of your goal as deprivation, for example, clashes with your goal to eat healthier. The mental images are incongruent. Instead, visualize images that represent happiness, joy, love, peace, comfort, and especially fun in tandem with your new goals. When your mind makes the connection that it's a pleasant thing, you've simplified the process.

A simple two-word fix?

Choose to speak from a place of empowerment. It's easy. Replace the phrase, "I can't" with "I don't." There's a world of difference between saying, "I can't smoke" and "I don't smoke." Your nonconscious mind catches the difference. The word "can't" tells your body (and mind) that you're at the mercy of some outside force. Something outside of your control. It leads to feelings of victimization. The words "I don't" come from a place of personal power and choice. This identity shift is powerful. It changes the focus to who you are rather than what you're doing. Feel the difference between "I don't eat gluten" and "I can't have those pancakes." The "I can't" example is rife with inner struggle.

It's storytime

Feeling like flotsam adrift in stormy seas is awful. Do you often feel tossed around by the storms of life and at the mercy of others?

Understanding and accepting your current experience has the power to shift you into a type of peaceful state that isn't achieved in any other way. Acceptance gives you the authority to make changes in how you feel and react to life. It gives you agency over all you do. It's the difference between being the victor or victim in your own life.

You decide.

It takes time (not to mention patience and self-compassion) to gain this perspective. When I first read about it from author Byron Katie,

I had a lot of knee-jerk defensive reactions. How could I let go of my beliefs of being wronged? Or that things happened to me in the past that were outside of my control?

It took time and a collective influence from other trainings including NLP and the Sedona Method to finally arrive at a better understanding. I discovered that it wasn't about blame as much as it was about feeling out of control. I can't control what transpires outside of me, but I can manage and have influence over my own thoughts, emotions, and the attachments I create.

We're master storytellers after all. We just need to figure out how to tell better stories.

When it comes to stories of the past, recognize that you're likely using an unfair—and unjust—view of things. It isn't reasonable to measure something you did in the past through the lens of who you are today. You've grown. You're a different person. You now have more knowledge, experience, understanding, and awareness.

Remind yourself that whatever actions you took (or didn't take) were based on who you were at the time. Give yourself a break. Stop holding yourself responsible and allow yourself to view it with detached objectivity.

While you're at it, do that for others too.

Your family and friends are doing the best they can with the knowledge and skills they possess. Influenced by their own experiences, those who seem to be destructive (to themselves or others) are limping through life trying to get by. Not everyone has great insight, which is a skill that needs nurturing.

Refining insight is a solo task. You can only work on your own and give others the grace to work on theirs. Yes, some need more grace than others.

Healing chronic illness overview

When my book, *FibroWHYalgia*, was released, I received dozens of kind notes and emails from faithful readers. Here's the gist of what I heard most. "I now feel inspired to change. I know that I need to change. I just don't know how to change."

One person even said, "I loved *FibroWHYalgia*, but I need a *FibroHOWalgia!*"

This book is a result of that request. I've filled these pages with a plethora of healing options. To better understand the chronic illness body, I've written the following outline, in short, bulleted snippets. It helps to illustrate the dysfunction of chronic illness so that the remedies make more sense.

■ The overreactions of chronic illness body

- **The chronic illness body is overreactive to external exposures.**

Right? You don't need me to tell you that. Whether you have fibromyalgia, an autoimmune condition, or any chronic health challenge, your body is hypersensitive to some, if not many things. In *Fibro-WHYalgia*, I aptly referred to fibromyalgia as "Systems Gone Berserk Syndrome."

It's hard to guess what overreactions will happen from one day to the next, but most of us are overreactive to one or more of the following: lights, sounds, smells, temperature changes, the moods of others, and touch.

We're hyper-sensitive to everything that surrounds us.

- **The chronic illness body is overreactive to internal exposures.**

We're also sensitive to everything that we put *in* us. We're affected by the foods, drinks, medications, immunizations, supplements, and even the lotions we use, and health and beauty products we "wear" on our skin, hair, mouth, and nails.

I might feel as if there's a knife going through my forehead if I catch a whiff of a cigarette or an air-freshener from a passing car. In this, I'm not unusual. (Synthetic scents are often referred to as the new second-hand smoke.[197]) Many of you have shared similar stories of a body gone wonky. But when it comes to what we eat, the lines blur. Some cling to the belief that food, and especially the chemicals found in fake foods, don't matter. Or that the toxic heavy metals from body products, dental amalgams, immunizations, and environmental exposures don't have an impact.

> *Doesn't it stand to reason that if we're overreactive to what surrounds us externally, we're also overreactive to what we're subjected to internally?*

---

197   https://www.huffingtonpost.ca/lisa-borden/natural-fragrances_b_14086978.html

- **The chronic illness body has an overreactive brain in general and an overreactive stress response in particular.**

At the systemic level, our bodies (including the brain) are stuck in an overreactive cycle. Our autonomic nervous system (ANS) is over-stimulated by our thought patterns, which places wear and tear on our adrenal system. Whether you refer to it as Sympathetic Dominance (the chronic hormonal stress response), a central nervous system issue, or an ANS problem, our bodies are in trouble.

We live out a cycle of perpetual dysfunction. Overworked adrenals tell the thyroid to slow down. Slowed thyroid function affects the detoxification abilities of the liver. Poor liver detoxification contributes to poor digestive health, which then sends out more stress signals to the body. The cycle of dysfunction starts all over again. This is a bidirectional process meaning the problems flow in both directions.

While this is an oversimplification, I hope you can see the cyclical impact of this overactive and overreactive ANS response. Our body-regulating hormones and systems run amok.

The chronic illness body lives every day with one foot on the gas and the other on the brake. Our bodies become accustomed to overreacting to everything we experience, including our anxious thoughts. The unfortunate thing is that our thoughts don't have to be all that anxious to kick it off. Even small worries can trigger an overreactive response.

> *The chronic illness body is riddled with exposures that perpetuate the stress response cycle.*

Hindsight is an amazing tool. I can now see how I healed my body and recovered from fibromyalgia. But I couldn't see it while I was in it. I've mentioned the Restoration Trio before and here's how it applied to me.

1. I first changed what I ate. I eliminated fake foods and added in real foods. *I healed my leaky gut and stopped the toxic dump of processed foods, drinks, and medications into my body. I eliminated added sugars. In doing so, I tamped down my body's overreaction to these foods and eliminated the gut dysbiosis (candida and mycotoxin overgrowth, etc.) that plagued me.*

2. I next changed how I moved. I started fitness and body movement programs. *Physical movement is a powerful way to help the body eliminate toxins while simultaneously balancing hormones and restoring a sense of mental and emotional clarity and optimism.*

3. Last—and most importantly—I changed my thoughts. I became aware of *and* changed my unhealthy and unproductive thought patterns. I shifted my focus to the life I wanted to lead rather than the one where I felt I had no choice. *I now recognize this to be the most crucial step of all. By changing my thoughts and implementing stress management techniques, I reset my ANS response. Over time, I reduced my ANS overreaction.* **The process described here can be referred to as ANS or limbic retraining**.

> ***Want to change anything in your life? Change your patterns. Begin by changing your thoughts.***

This happens to be the order in which my healing took place. I currently approach this journey with clients by meeting them where they are. Some need more support with nutrition, while others need stress management the most. We work through the process in a simultaneous fashion rather than one step at a time.

NOTE: Even though my body is still overreactive compared to someone who does not have a fibromyalgia or autoimmune-related challenge, it's much better than in the past. My body is less reactive. Recovery and lowering the ANS response is an ongoing process. Limbic retraining takes intention, practice, and consistency. *A daily practice must be in place* (see options in Chapter 16). If you put these aspects together, you too can change your body's over-reactive response.

> ***"The pain is not in your head,***
> ***but the solution is not in your body."***
> —Nicole J. Sachs, LCSW

■ Chapter 18 – Head Work

1. Which objections or obstacles listed in this chapter resonate with or surprise you the most? Did you feel ownership of it right off the bat or did you have to sit with it a while? Sometimes objections are clouded by other beliefs, and they may feel only partially true. Sometimes obstacles feel insurmountable. Do a quick internal survey. Notice and acknowledge their presence. Tell yourself you'll address them later if needed. For now, suspend objections that thwart your forward progress and address the obstacles accordingly.

2. Write down "I don't…" on a sticky note or index card. Keep this phrase handy as you plan healthy changes. Create your non-negotiable behaviors. Practice reframing your thoughts

(i.e., *I don't sit down to watch TV before going on a walk, I don't buy snack or junk foods that only tempt me to eat poorly, I don't stay up after 10:00 pm as I need my wind-down time, I don't eat after dinner, etc.*).

3. Review the steps of the Healing Chronic Illness Overview. Which step needs the most attention to create your recovery story? Start there and craft your own plan. For true healing, reverse the brain patterns that keep you sick. Implement Build-A-Better-Brain healing practices multiple times per day. Do your best to see that you're spending at least an hour collectively each day on these practices. These are the building blocks of our recovery. Whether it's six blocks of ten minutes, four blocks of fifteen minutes, or two blocks of thirty minutes each, stack them throughout your day to rebuild a better brain. *Reclaim your physical and emotional health!*

SUMMARY

We've covered a wide variety of topics in this book.

I've shared proven strategies known to help you shift your mind, body, and health from a negative place to one that's more positive and conducive to healing.

And I can hear you say—"Let's get real. What about the daily drama of *my* life?"

Life's a struggle, right?

When it comes to making changes, it's supposed to be… a struggle that is.

I'm sure you've heard the story of a young child eager to see his first butterfly appear from a chrysalis. With excited impatience, he helped pry open the delicate structure. Unaware of the insect's need to struggle to become strong his "help" did irreparable damage—the butterfly never emerged.

You need that struggle too. You need to flex unused muscles. You need to stretch and try new things, applying them even when immediate success doesn't appear on the horizon.

> ### *Full-body healing takes a new approach.*
> ### *One that cares for both the body and mind.*

Let's tackle your options right now. From the choices listed below, is the definition of your reality either A or B? (Or perhaps some of both.)

A. In this world, people are mainly in it for themselves. They're not supportive of my needs and certainly not there for me as often as I wish. I've been held back and let down by others. I've even let myself down.

B. I know exactly what's gonna happen. I'll put this book down and move on with my life, and nothing's gonna change. I might get somewhat inspired, but I know something will happen to squash even that glimmer of hope.

Do you recognize the difference between these?

In scenario A, the definition of reality is a reflection of the past. In scenario B, the definition of reality is a projection of a potential future. Both list reasons to reject the option for hope.

Notice that neither one applies to the reality of NOW.

Your true reality is IN this very moment. Right now. Take this opportunity to accept what's happened in the past (when it comes to your behavior), and move forward anyway. In the present moment, you have the opportunity to forge the future you plan to create—not the one you're afraid will be created for you.

You're at the "two pain" precipice. You're either living in the pain of staying where you are (and feeling in your gut there's something else much better out there for you). Or you're feeling the pain of taking action and making a change. Doing something different can be scary. But always remember this….

You're in charge. You get to choose.

Here's your "in the moment" reality. At this moment in time, you're safe. You probably get enough to eat regularly. You likely have access to shelter from blistering heat, rain, snow, wind, and freezing temperatures.

Remind yourself of these things. Tell yourself that you're safe. (If you weren't, you wouldn't be reading this right now.) Acknowledge, be grateful and thankful for this moment of safety.

This is a pivot point for you. All that's in front of you is one small step. My hope is that you take it right now. From this action, I pray you find a spiritual connection and meaning in life that takes you further than you've ever before imagined.

> **Be the architect of your own brain (and life). Not just a transient tenant.**

* * *

RESOURCES

Sue's Books, Blog, and Articles:

Get Back into Whack Workbook: 30-Day Quick Start Guide, and Beyond

FibroWHYalgia: Why Rebuilding the 10 Root Causes of Chronic Illness Restores Chronic Wellness (a #1 Amazon chronic illness bestseller)

Chronic Coloring: Stress-Relieving Coloring Pages and Activities to Encourage Healing from Chronic Illness and Inspire Rebuilding Wellness

Rebuilding Wellness Blog: www.RebuildingWellness.com/Blog (featuring over 500 articles!)

Find dozens of archived fibromyalgia health articles that I've written for **ProHealth.com**. Search a topic of interest + fibromyalgia + Ingebretson + ProHealth.

Sue's SoCal Local Favorites:

The Bookman (used bookstore and online book sales), https://orange.ebookman.com/

Glen Depke, Traditional Naturopath, http://depkewellness.com/

Timothy Noble, DC, http://www.anaheimhillschiropractic.com/

Bill Janeshak, DC, http://yorbalindafamilychiropractic.com/

Mother's Markets, https://www.mothersmarket.com/

Next Advanced Medicine, Candace Hall, DC, https://nextadvancedmedicine.com/

Villa Park Medical, Aniko Lengyel, PharmD, CNS, http://www.naturaldoc.net/

Tapping Resources:

Tapping Q&A, Gene Monterastelli, https://tappingqanda.com/

Gene's Set-up Phrase Generator, https://tappingqanda.com/2011/07/creative-and-alternate-set-up-statements-generator-for-tapping/

Gene's Script Generator, https://tappingqanda.com/2012/06/eft-script-generator/

The Tapping Solution, Nick Ortner/Jessica Ortner, https://www.thetappingsolution.com/

EFT Universe, Dawson Church, Ph.D., https://www.eftuniverse.com/

Faster EFT, Robert Smith, https://fastereft.com/

EFT Down Under, Steve Wells, https://www.eftdownunder.com/

Carol Look, https://www.carollook.com/welcome-to-eft-tapping/

Brittany Watkins, https://www.brittanywatkins.com/

Brad Yates, https://tapwithbrad.mykajabi.com/

Nutrition Resources:

How to get started with a chronic illness-friendly, low-inflammatory foods diet:

https://rebuildingwellness.com/fibro-diet-1-start/

https://rebuildingwellness.com/fibro-diet-2-newbie/

https://rebuildingwellness.com/fibro-diet-3-name/

Fitness, Posture, and Body Movement Resources:

T-Tapp Workout, https://www.t-tapp.com/

Yoga—Shoosh Lettick Crotzer, http://yogawithshoosh.com/

Pilates, Yoga, and Posture—Lora Pavilack and Nikki Alstedter, https://pilatesstudiocity.com/

Walking Videos—Leslie Sansone, https://walkathome.com/ (DVDs for every fitness level—can be found at many large retailers)

NLP Training Resources:

I've personally purchased and taken classes, courses, and certifications from all of these companies.

Transform Destiny, Michael Stevenson, https://www.transform-destiny.com/

Rapid Empowerment, Jay Williams, http://www.RapidEmpowerment.com/

Christian NLP, Mike Davis, http://www.renewingyourmind.com/ Articles/Christian_Use_of_Change.htm

Brain Retraining, Limbic System Training, Vagal Nerve Retraining, Amygdala Retraining, Chronic Pain Retraining Resources:

Dynamic Neural Retraining System, DNRS, Annie Hopper, https://retrainingthebrain.com/

The Gupta Program, Ashok Gupta, https://www.guptaprogram.com/

ANS Rewire, Dan Neuffer, https://ansrewire.com/

EFT, Emotional Freedom Technique or Tapping (see Tapping resources above)

Pain Care | VR™, A drug-free, digital wellness program to train your body and mind's response to pain using virtual reality. https://www.paincarevr.com/

Vagal Stimulation (via natural means), https://www.ncbi.nlm.nih.gov/pmc/articles/PMC6189422/

Somatic Approaches (shaking off trauma), https://traumahealing.org/overwhelmed-physical-sensations-soothe/

The Cure for Chronic Pain, Nicole J. Sachs, LCSW, https://www.thecureforchronicpain.com/

Neurosculpting Institute, Lisa Wimberger, https://www.neurosculptinginstitute.com/

HeartMath Institute, https://www.heartmath.com/

APPS:

ThinkUp, Positive Affirmations, https://thinkup.me/

Pain Pathways, https://www.pathways.health

Cures A-Z, https://thinkup.me/

Do Something Different, https://dsd.me/

The Tapping Solution, https://www.thetappingsolutionapp.com/

Tapping Q & A, https://apps.apple.com/us/app/tapping-q-a/id1021347200

Gupta Program, Meaning of Life, https://themeaningoflife.tv/

Calm, https://www.calm.com/

Insight Timer, https://insighttimer.com/

Supplement Resources:

Metagenics, Pharmaceutical-grade nutrients: https://rwellness.metagenics.com/ (Rebuilding Wellness Metagenics store)

Or click on the Metagenics icon on the right sidebar of my blog page: https://www.rebuildingwellness.com/blog

ProHealth, https://www.prohealth.com/

Mercola, https://articles.mercola.com/vitamins-supplements.aspx

Visualization Resources:

The Gabriel Method, Jon Gabriel, https://www.thegabriel-method.com/

Gaiam, https://www.gaiam.com/blogs/discover/meditation-and-visualization

Chopra Center, https://chopra.com/

Health Websites & Resources:

ProHealth for Fibromyalgia

Health news, articles, studies, abstracts

https://www.prohealth.com/

Joe Mercola, MD

Large database of searchable articles

https://www.mercola.com/

Mark Hyman, MD

https://drhyman.com/

https://brokenbrain.com/

Andrea Nakayama (Gut Health and Microbiome)

https://fxnutrition.com/

Fibromyalgia Resources:

End Fatigue with Dr. T, Jacob Teitelbaum, MD, https://secure.endfatigue.com/

Cal State Fullerton Fibromyalgia and Chronic Pain Center, http://fmcp.fullerton.edu/

Fibromyalgia Coalition International, Yvonne Keeney, http://www.fibrocoalition.org/

Chronic Pain, Fatigue, and Support Group, Kaye Witte, https://www.meetup.com/Chronic-Pain-Fatigue-and-Fibromyalgia-Support-Group/members/8092607/

International Fibromyalgia Support Network, Melissa Swanson, https://supportfibromyalgia.org/

Counting My Spoons, Julie Ryan, https://countingmyspoons.com/

William Rawls, MD, https://rawlsmd.com/

Biologix Center for Optimum Health, Jernigan/Hart, https://biologixcenter.com/

Nichole Sachs, LCSW, https://www.thecureforchronicpain.com/

Chris Kresser, M.S., L.Ac., https://chriskresser.com/reverse-chronic-illness/

Bible Study Resources:

YouVersion App, https://www.youversion.com/the-bible-app/

E-Dibs, Pastor Paul Stark, http://www.edibs.life/

Book Recommendations / Self-Help Reading:

Jacob Teitelbaum, MD

From Fatigued to Fantastic, A Clinically Proven Program to Regain Vibrant Health and Overcome Chronic Fatigue and Fibromyalgia New, third edition

The Fatigue and Fibromyalgia Solution: The Essential Guide to Overcoming Chronic Fatigue and Fibromyalgia, Made Easy!

The Complete Guide to Beating Sugar Addiction

Dawson Church, Ph.D.

Mind to Matter: The Astonishing Science of How Your Brain Creates Material Reality

The Genie in Your Genes: Epigenetic Medicine and the New Biology of Intention

The EFT Manual, 4th Edition

Josh Axe, DC, DNM, CNS

Keto Diet, Your 30-Day Plan to Lose Weight, Balance Hormones, Boost Brain Health, and Reverse Disease

Essential Oils: Ancient Medicine for a Modern World

Eat Dirt, Why Leaky Gut May Be the Root Cause of Your Health Problems and 5 Surprising Steps to Cure It

William Rawls, MD

Suffered Long Enough, A physician's journey of overcoming Fibromyalgia, Chronic Fatigue, & Lyme

Unlocking Lyme, Myths, Truths, and Practical Solutions for Chronic Lyme Disease

Peter A. Levine, Ph.D.

Waking the Tiger: Healing Trauma

Jonny Bowden, Ph.D.

Smart Fat, Eat More Fat. Lose More Weight. Get Healthy Now

150 Healthiest Foods on Earth

Doug Kaufmann

The Fungus Link (Books 1-3)

Cooking Your Way to Good Health

The Fungus Link to Weight Loss

Kristen Willeumier, Ph.D.

Rewind Your Brain

Charles Duhigg, Ph.D.

Power of Habit, Why We Do What We Do in Life and Business

Kathryn Hanson

Brain over Binge: Why I Was Bulimic, Why Conventional Therapy Didn't Work, and How I Recovered for Good

Glenn Livingston, Ph.D.

Never Binge Again: Reprogram Yourself to Think Like a Permanently Thin Person. Stop Overeating and Binge Eating and Stick to the Food Plan of Your Choice!

Brian Wansink, Ph.D.

Mindless Eating, Why We Eat More Than We Think

Susan Peirce Thompson, Ph.D.

Bright Line Eating, The Science of Living Happy, Thin & Free

Caroline Leaf, Ph.D.

Switch on Your Brain The Key to Peak Happiness, Thinking, and Health

Switch on Your Brain Workbook

Twyla Tharpe

Creative Habit, Learn It and Use It for Life

James Clear

Atomic Habits: An Easy & Proven Way to Build Good Habits & Break Bad Ones

Sara Gottfried, MD

Brain Body Diet: 40 Days to a Lean, Calm, Energized, and Happy Self

The Hormone Cure: Reclaim Balance, Sleep and Sex Drive; Lose Weight; Feel Focused, Vital, and Energized Naturally with the Gottfried Protocol

Deanna M. Minich, Ph.D.

The Rainbow Diet: A Holistic Approach to Radiant Health Through Foods and Supplements

The Complete Handbook of Quantum Healing: An A to Z Self-Healing Guide for Over 100 Common Ailments

Glen Depke, Traditional Naturopath

Fat, Fatigued and Frustrated? How to Reverse the Clock and Feel Young Again

Gene Monterastelli

Comprehensive Anger Management (Sue's note: About so much more than anger)

Gretchen Rubin

Better Than Before, Mastering the Habits of Our Everyday Lives

James Clear

Atomic Habits: An Easy and Proven Way to Build Good Habits and Break Bad Ones

Nick Ortner

The Tapping Solution: A Revolutionary System for Stress-Free Living

The Tapping Solution for Manifesting Your Greatest Self: 21 Days to Releasing Self-Doubt, Cultivating Inner Peace, and Creating a Life You Love

The Tapping Solution for Pain Relief: Step-by-Step Guide to Reducing and Eliminating Chronic Pain

Jessica Ortner

The Tapping Solution to Create Lasting Change: A Guide to Get Unstuck and Find Your Flow

The Tapping Solution for Weight Loss & Body Confidence: A Woman's Guide to Stressing Less, Weighing Less, and Loving More

Mark Hyman, MD

Food: What the Heck Should I Eat?

The UltraMind Solution: Fix Your Broken Brain by Healing Your Body First

The Blood Sugar Solution: The UltraHealthy Program for Losing Weight, Preventing Disease, and Feeling Great Now!

Dana Wilde

Train Your Brain: How to Build a Million Dollar Business in Record Time

Joe Dispenza, DC

Breaking the Habit of Being Yourself: How to Lose Your Mind and Create a New One

You Are the Placebo: Making Your Mind Matter

Shawn Achor

Happiness Advantage: How a Positive Brain Fuels Success in Work and Life

Big Potential: How Transforming the Pursuit of Success Raises Our Achievement, Happiness, and Well-Being

Norman Doidge, MD

The Brain the Changes Itself, Stories of Personal Triumph from the Frontiers of Brain Science

Stephen W. Porges

The Polyvagal Theory, Neurophysiological Foundations of Emotions, Attachment, Communication, and Self-regulation

John E. Sarno, MD

Healing Back Pain, The Mind-Body Connection

Susan Peirce Thompson, Ph.D.

Bright Line Eating, The Science of Living Happy, Thin, & Free

Dan Neuffer

CFS Unravelled: Get Well By Treating The Cause Not Just The Symptoms Of CFS, Fibromyalgia, POTS And Related Syndromes

Shoosh Lettick Crotzer

Yoga for Fibromyalgia, Move, Breathe, and Relax to Improve Your Quality of Life

Lora Pavilack and Nikki Alstedter

Pain-Free Posture Handbook, 40 Dynamic Easy Exercises to Look and Feel Your Best

Leslie Sansone

Walk Away the Pounds: The Breakthrough 6-Week Program That Helps You Burn Fat, Tone Muscle, and Feel Great Without Dieting

Teresa Tapp

Fit and Fabulous in 15 Minutes, Lose 2 Sizes in 4 Weeks with the T-Tapp Workout

APPENDIX

Chapter 5 Reference–

5 Factors that Connect Fibromyalgia to a Negative Focus (excerpt from my original article, *The Negativity Connection**)

1. **Pain**

Let's start with the obvious. If we're in pain, we're more likely to be in a negative frame of mind. Pain can blunt our ability to think clearly and definitely impacts our ability to think positively.

It's the "no end in sight" nature of chronic pain that can profoundly sabotage our thoughts. And, if our thoughts are negative, it's far more likely that our words, comments, and actions will be less-than-optimistic if not downright negative.

Because pain plays a role—to varying degrees—for most of us with fibromyalgia, this factor is primary and exists in tandem with any of the following.

2.   **Defense**

Many people with fibromyalgia feel that they need to "defend" themselves against a world that often misunderstands their condition. This need to defend can spread to anything related to their health challenge(s).

The very act of defending their choices and beliefs feels good and/or necessary. It feels as if they're standing up for themselves and validating not only their experiences—but *who they are.*

Feeling unheard adds a layer of insistence and frustration to this factor. The more they feel ignored or misunderstood, the more likely they'll act out in negative ways.

Everyone wants to be heard.

3.   **Group dynamics**

Along the same lines, there's an interesting dynamic that occurs when groups of people with similar health challenges congregate.

Have you ever participated in a fibromyalgia support group?

For most people, this experience tends to be polarized to either a negative or positive experience. It's natural to want to share your symptoms and circumstances with others. It feels good to hear that others feel as we do. It provides us with a much-needed sense of belonging.

Sometimes, however, this tendency can lean toward one-upmanship. I've heard conversations at fibromyalgia support groups that transpire like this:

Attendee 1– *"I can't turn my head today because I just had an injection of cortisone in my neck."*

Attendee 2– *"Oh, just one? I had three injections the other day! I got them in my neck, my shoulder, and my hip!"*

Sound familiar?

Even if you don't relate to the details, you probably relate to the concept. It's interesting to observe the group dynamic in action. The tone of the group can spiral downward into a free fall of negativity pretty quickly without a strong group leader. And, likewise, a strong leader can keep the comments and conversation flowing in a helpful and productive manner.

When this group dynamic takes place online, you may observe factor #4.

4. **Online Disinhibition Effect** (1)

Have you heard of this? This term refers to the behavior of commenting in a negative manner on online forums simply because of the "arm's length" distant feel of an online experience. It's different than sitting next to someone and saying the same thing. The Online Disinhibition Effect comes into play when the person leaving a comment feels that their identity is unknown or at least, not obvious.

Deindividuation (2) is also part of the equation. The anonymity factor insulates those who behave negatively, giving them a feeling of security. This insular effect sometimes leads to the tendency to use harsh, critical, or even intentionally derogatory language.

Dr. James Olson, a social psychology professor of Western University in London states, *"Deindividuation makes people less likely to follow norms... and to conform to an expected way of behavior."* He continues, *"Therefore, they're more willing to express opinions that might be politically incorrect, aggressive, or more insulting than they would to someone in person."* (3)

You've probably seen the effects of this on blogs and online forums. The conversations can get fairly heated, with no real benefits or solutions provided.

Now, we're on to factor #5, which is quite interesting. It shows us how and why negativity can actually serve us in a healthy way.

5.   **Survival wiring**

This topic is positively intriguing. Literally. I enjoy the study of how the mind works and where our tendencies lead us. I enjoy it all the more when it sheds light on how our behaviors can change for the better.

Keep in mind that our thoughts always precede action.

> ***Therefore, if our thoughts are negative, our actions will stem from that frame of mind.***

I happened to receive an email today that has the subject line, "Is your brain diseased?" Of course, the answer to that is no, but while my brain isn't diseased, it *is* predisposed. It's predisposed toward negativity... and yours is too.

Surprised?

It's a survival thing. It's an evolutionary thing.

When it comes to the survival of the human race, we must be acutely aware of our safety and our surroundings. Are there threats? Does danger loom ahead? It's only natural for our focus to be centered on this heightened awareness.

If we could compare our levels of focus, it's clear that we're *more* aware of the potential for danger than for the potential for something pleasant. Pleasant experiences aren't usually a matter of life or death.

> ### The tendencies to look for and react to threats are hard-wired into our brains. (4)

The way this plays out in our everyday behavior is that we naturally think of negative things. We ruminate over what we haven't done, what we should have said, what we wish we could have (but don't), etc.

It's common for every human being to have this natural tendency. But, it's amplified for those of us with chronic health challenges. Our pain and our experiences have shown us that perceived threats can transmute into real threats. We may have felt that others have let us down. We may feel that we've let others down.

While we all have negative thoughts, it's the *persistence* of negative thoughts that can turn the tables toward worsened health.

This excerpt from an article is my original work and first appeared at ProHealth.com. It is reprinted with kind permission and may be viewed here: https://www.prohealth.com/library/the-fibromyalgia-negativity-connection-37393

References:

1.   http://www.wired.co.uk/news/archive/2013-05/30/online-aggression

2.   http://www.chathamdailynews.ca/2015/01/25/online-anonymity-form-of-deindividuation

3.   http://www.chathamdailynews.ca/2015/01/25/online-anonymity-form-of-deindividuation

4.   http://www.centreforconfidence.co.uk/pp/overview.php?p=c2lkPTEmdGlkPTAmaWQ9NDU

Chapter 8 Reference–

List of signs of inflammation mentioned in Chapter 8. (Excerpt of my original article, *Do You Have these Fibromyalgia Symptoms of Systemic Dysfunction?**)

77 Symptoms of Adrenal Dysfunction
(in no particular order)

1. Unrestorative sleep (feeling as if you hadn't slept, even if you did)
2. Fatigue
3. Intolerant to stress
4. Food cravings (sweets and/or salty)
5. Shifts in weight
6. Inability to lose weight (if overweight)
7. Blood pressure imbalance (either too high or too low)
8. Cognitive dysfunction (fibrofog)
9. Reduced ability to cope
10. Feelings of constant overwhelm
11. Frequent infections (colds, flu, etc.)
12. Reduced sex drive
13. Increased PMS symptoms
14. Inability to either fall or stay asleep
15. Lack of stamina and/or endurance
16. Lack of get up and go
17. Energy bursts—all or nothing (rarely all/mostly nothing)
18. Feeling anxious or short-fused (as in, "You're on my last nerve!")
19. Autoimmune disorders
20. Increased allergies and/or asthma
21. Issues with memory / recall

22.   Lightheaded when standing from a seating or reclined position
23.   Dark circles under the eyes
24.   Skin issues (any of these—dry skin, rashes, hives, psoriasis, etc.)
25.   Frequent mouth sores
26.   Endometriosis
27.   Fibrous breast tissue
28.   Panic attacks
29.   Adrenaline rushes
30.   Poor metabolism (especially of simple carbohydrates)
31.   Hair loss or thinning
32.   Sensitivity to wireless connections, electric magnetic fields, etc.
33.   Food sensitivities
34.   Facial tics
35.   OCD—obsessive compulsive disorder
36.   Chemical sensitivities (i.e., to paint, cleaners, detergents, scented items, etc.)
37.   Joint pain
38.   Muscle pain
39.   Frequent urination and / or thirst
40.   Depression / sadness
41.   Fatigued in the late afternoon (possible burst of energy in the evening)
42.   Dependence on coffee, tea, energy drinks (caffeine or stimulants)
43.   Increased abdominal fat
44.   Inability to regulate body temperature (feel too cold, too hot)
45.   Temperature intolerance (especially to heat)
46.   Exercise worsens symptoms (slow recovery after exercise)
47.   Early menopause
48.   Infertility
49.   Premature aging

50. Low back pain (other than from an injury)
51. Cold hands/feet
52. Diminished ability to focus
53. Heavy feeling in the hands, arms, or legs
54. IBS—irritable bowel syndrome
55. Tinnitus
56. Numbness in the extremities / poor circulation
57. Heart palpitations
58. Shortness of breath
59. Tenseness / inability to relax
60. Fibromyalgia (unchanged after basic protocols)
61. Chronic Fatigue Syndrome (unchanged after basic treatments)
62. Grave's disease
63. Hashimoto's disease
64. Exaggerated startle reflex
65. Breast cancers due to estrogen dominance
66. Dizziness
67. Hypoglycemia
68. Headaches
69. Swelling / inflammation
70. Hemorrhoids
71. Varicose veins
72. Hyperpigmentation (bronzing or brown patches on the skin)
73. Pale lips (little to no color)
74. Hyper-sensitivity to bright and/or flashing lights
75. Hyper-sensitivity to loud or intermittent/irritating sounds
76. Hyper-sensitivity to touch and pressure on the skin
77. Hyper-sensitivity to smells and odors (artificial/synthetic scents in particular)

This excerpt from an article is my original work and first appeared at ProHealth.com. It is reprinted with kind permission and may be viewed here: https://www.prohealth.com/

library/do-you-have-these-fibromyalgia-symptoms-of-systemic-dys-function-37277

References:

1. Lam, M. "75 Signs, Symptoms and Alerts of Adrenal Fatigue Syndrome." *DrLam.com*. Retrieved 9/11/15.

2. "What Are the Symptoms of Adrenal Fatigue?" The Adrenal Fatigue Solution. Retrieved 9/11/15.

3. Donovan, P. "18 Overlooked Symptoms of Adrenal Fatigue." Natural News. 12/02/08.

4. Sarah. "6 Little Known Signs of Adrenal Fatigue." The Healthy Home Economist. Retrieved 9/11/15.

5. "Do You Have These 17 Adrenal Fatigue Symptoms?" *Adrenal-FatigueRecovery.com*. Retrieved 9/11/15.

6. Lane, P. "Feeling Burnt Out? The Adrenal Fatigue Link." *Believe Midwifery Services.* 12/08/13.

ACKNOWLEDGMENTS

To my greatest teachers. There's nothing better than living and breathing examples. Some of you showed positive leadership, teaching me to adapt and providing me with opportunities to grow. Others demonstrated what not to do in the midst of chaos.

In all cases, I'm grateful for your influence and lessons.

LET'S GET CONNECTED!

....

 Follow my blog: https://www.rebuildingwellness.com/blog

 Facebook: https://www.facebook.com/pg/
FibroWHYalgia/

 Twitter: https://twitter.com/sueinge

 Pinterest: https://www.pinterest.com/sueinge/

 Instagram: https://www.instagram.com/sue.ingebretson/

 LinkedIn: https://www.linkedin.com/in/sueinge/

ABOUT THE AUTHOR

Sue Ingebretson is a much sought after symptom-relief expert in the fibromyalgia, chronic illness, and autoimmune communities. Known for getting to the root of health challenges, her methods deliver long-term results using a light-hearted approach without quick-fix remedies that only mask symptoms.

She's an author, speaker, certified nutritional therapist, clinical hypnotherapist, master NLP practitioner, and an integrative nutrition health coach. She has additional certifications which include EFT, Time Line Therapy,® and Success Coaching. She leads workshops and seminars and  writes for various in print and online publications.

Her #1 Amazon bestselling book, *FibroWHYalgia* details her personal healing journey. Her activity book, *Chronic Coloring*, features fun, informative, and creative stress management solutions. Her newest books, *Get Back into Whack* and *Get Back into Whack Workbook* detail the brain's role in healing chronic illness while laying out a plan to do so.

Sue has been featured in *FIRST for Women* magazine, TV, ABC radio, and podcasts. She's active on a wide variety of social media platforms, and her blog with 500+ posts can be found at www.Rebuilding-Wellness.com/blog.

About Rebuilding Wellness

Sue's life was out of control. She suffered from more symptoms than she could even list. She saw more than a dozen doctors who prescribed double that number of prescriptions.

She tried them all.

Finding no solutions, she took matters into her own hands and figured it out herself. Applying holistic healing and natural methods, she discovered what works best with the greatest economy and efficiency. It took time, tenacity, and a willingness to try new things to climb out of the pit from chronic illness to chronic wellness. But she's grateful for the journey.

Today, Sue encourages others to do the same—without the difficulties of going it alone. Seeded with light-hearted humor and support, she leads others (mostly women) through a step-by-step protocol designed to help them leave limiting symptoms behind and move toward a healthier and happier lifestyle. Want to learn more? Contact her here: http://rebuildingwellness.com/contact.

Printed in Great Britain
by Amazon